KING JOHN, HENRY III

AND ENGLAND'S LOST CIVIL WAR

*'If everyone else abandoned the king, do you know what I would do?
I would carry him on my shoulders, step by step, from island to island,
from country to country, and I would not fail him, not even if it meant
begging my bread.'*

William Marshal, 1st Earl of Pembroke, 29 October, 1216

*Voracious envy, that overthrows morality,
That sets fire to faults, tore away their solace.
Without an equal of a leader,
A spiteful people of an averted mindset got ahead of the glory of his
brightness.
England, bewail thy Marshal,
Bewail him with tears!
The reason is, why?
Because on thy behalf England bewailed to love!
The virtue of the army,
The protection of the fatherland,
Through the fraud of its own people
It tumbled down.
God have mercy on the one who is dying!*

The Annals of Waverley on the death of Richard Marshal,
3rd Earl of Pembroke, April 1234

KING JOHN, HENRY III

AND ENGLAND'S LOST CIVIL WAR

JOHN PAUL DAVIS

PEN & SWORD
HISTORY

AN IMPRINT OF PEN & SWORD BOOKS LTD.
YORKSHIRE - PHILADELPHIA

First published in Great Britain in 2021 by
PEN AND SWORD HISTORY
An imprint of
Pen & Sword Books Ltd
Yorkshire – Philadelphia

ISBN 978 1 52675 007 5

A CIP catalogue record for this book is available from the British Library.

Typeset in Times New Roman 11.5/14 by
SJmagic DESIGN SERVICES, India.
Printed and bound in the UK by CPI Group (UK) Ltd.

Pen & Sword Books Limited incorporates the imprints of Atlas, Archaeology,
Aviation, Discovery, Family History, Fiction, History, Maritime, Military, Military
Classics, Politics, Select, Transport, True Crime, Air World, Frontline Publishing,
Leo Cooper, Remember When, Seaforth Publishing, The Praetorian Press,
Wharncliffe Local History, Wharncliffe Transport, Wharncliffe True Crime and
White Owl.

For a complete list of Pen & Sword titles please contact
PEN & SWORD BOOKS LIMITED
47 Church Street, Barnsley, South Yorkshire, S70 2AS, England
E-mail: enquiries@pen-and-sword.co.uk
Website: www.pen-and-sword.co.uk

Or
PEN AND SWORD BOOKS
1950 Lawrence Rd, Havertown, PA 19083, USA
E-mail: Uspen-and-sword@casematepublishers.com
Website: www.penandswordbooks.com

Contents

Introduction

The village of Upavon in Wiltshire isn't particularly well known outside its local area. Mentioned in passing in the Domesday Book, this charming rural parish on the northern edge of the Salisbury Plain differs little from many of England's small rural settlements.

The original spelling – 'Oppavrene' – offers a clue to its whereabouts. The upper section of the River Avon has meandered through its green fields since the earliest of times, the constant erosion causing subtle changes to the local surroundings. By the thirteenth century, what had started life as a small Saxon hamlet sited close to an Iron Age hill fort was prospering. A market square was created to the west of the imposing Norman church that had replaced an earlier Saxon structure; to the south was built a manor house, from which the lord enjoyed views across the surrounding countryside. Discounting those who visited the market, it is doubtful the population reached 1,000. Eight centuries later, little has changed.

In 1229, the manor of Upavon was the property of one Peter de Maulay. Born in a village that carried his family name in the French region of Poitou, de Maulay had found both fame and infamy in England as an 'evil' counsellor of King John. During the minority of John's eldest son, Henry III, he remained a principal advisor, as well as a loyal ally of the controversial Bishop of Winchester, Peter des Roches – briefly John's justiciar before Magna Carta and also Henry's tutor. Loathed in certain quarters for his poor influence on the young king, as the 1220s came to an end, the king stripped de Maulay of the manor. On refusing to vacate it, a stern warning from the justiciar Hubert de Burgh that continued disobedience would see him relocated to a place where he would be able to see 'neither his hands nor his feet' ensured his compliance. In so doing, he joined the already ousted des Roches in political ignominy.

As a consequence of de Maulay's loss, the English-born justiciar oversaw the transfer of the manor by a royal grant to one Gilbert Basset, son of the prominent English baron Alan Basset, who had fought valiantly for the royalists in the First Barons' War (1215-17). Over the next three years, Gilbert distinguished himself on the baronial scene, his successful negotiation of a truce on the king's behalf with Llywelyn ap Iorwerth, Prince of Gwynedd, a particular highlight. Already of ancient baronial stock, his marriage to the niece of the late William Marshal, 1st Earl of Pembroke all but cemented his place in the upper echelons of the so-called 'popular' party. By building a life on such solid foundations, fortune and glory, it seemed, was already in the palm of his hand.

But this was the thirteenth century. And this was England. A time and a place when even in peacetime life in a typical village could be turned upside down in the wink of an eye. Such an occurrence awaited on 6 February 1233, when the good fortune that had blessed Gilbert four years earlier was dramatically reversed. After de Maulay came to the king's attention during the French campaign of 1230, Henry's government reopened the Upavon case and decided to return the manor to him.

On learning of the king's change of heart, the new earl of Pembroke, Richard Marshal, presented Gilbert's grievances before Henry personally. Furious that the king had denounced his royal grant, Marshal argued that by denying the legality of his own ruling, Henry was in danger of bringing about a constitutional crisis. In a further attempt to seize the initiative, he carefully framed his argument in a way that took it far beyond that of an ordinary domestic dispute. By pointing the finger of blame squarely at the reinstated des Roches, he demanded an end to the lawlessness of the king's close foreign advisors who had 'perverted the king's heart'.

As was so often the case in medieval England, not only was the accused party present to hear the charges, its leader also dared to take it upon himself to answer on the king's behalf. Des Roches's lengthy response on the matter still speaks volumes, not least his claim that: 'the king is surely allowed to summon as many foreigners as he chooses for the protection of his kingdom ... to reduce his haughty and rebellious subjects to their proper obedience'. If the bishop's perceived arrogance alone was not enough to incite the wrath of the king's fiercest critics, less than six months later matters reached a tipping point. When word reached Marshal and Basset that a council convened at Westminster was merely an orchestrated ruse to snare them into captivity, the pair stayed away. Accused of treason for their failure to attend, both they and their key followers were outlawed. Just as had been the case in 1215, hatred of the royal advisors and question marks over the king's ability to abide by his charters had brought England to the brink of war.

Exactly what transpired in England 1233–34 remains somewhat unclear. Researching my biography of Henry III, *The Gothic King* (2013), one thing that immediately became apparent to me is just how little of his reign has ever been in the public consciousness. As is so often the case researching historical matters, especially relating to a king who lived for sixty-five years, reigning fifty-six, one of the most significant problems is deciding how deep to dig. In the introduction of that book, I stated that it could have been ten times longer. On reflection, I could have added another zero to that.

Almost a decade on from when a chance countryside walk started me on that initial journey, what was clear to me then remains so now. That book would not be a one-off. Back in 2013, there was no full-length, chronologically arranged biography of Henry III currently in print. Prior to that time, only the endeavours of Sir Maurice Powicke, David Carpenter, William Hunt and Thomas Frederick Tout had even come close. *The Gothic King*, unquestionably, was a pioneer effort. Since that time, no less than four biographies of Henry III have followed, including Carpenter's recently released life work. All in their own way add to Henry's story. What has both amazed and inspired me in equal measure, particularly in the cases of Matthew Lewis and Darren Baker, is just how different our books are. This would be a remarkable feat under normal circumstances, though perhaps less so concerning a man who ruled for so long in a country perpetually afflicted by powerful forces both home and abroad.

Yet even in the light of recent efforts, there remain areas of Henry III's reign of which past historians and enthusiasts have barely even begun to scratch the surface. Henry III's brother, Richard, Earl of Cornwall is still crying out for an updated, full-length biography. The same is true of many of their younger siblings and children, especially the women. Henry's attempt to purchase the crown of Sicily for his youngest son, Edmund, is a tale in itself; not since the days of Henry Richards Luard and Abbot Francis Gasquet has detailed analysis centred on this. The same is true of Henry's relations with the papacy.

But of all the episodes of Henry III's long reign, one, in particular, has continued to intrigue me: that contemporarily known as 'The Marshal

War'. For many years, I've found myself asking the same questions: What exactly brought about this war? Just how significant was it? The fact that the chroniclers referred to it as a war is itself noteworthy. As it involved such prominent subjects of the king, some foreign some English, and took place primarily in England, should the Marshal War be considered a domestic conflict or part of something more significant?

Ask the average British citizen about civil wars in England and most will say similar things. The nation has experienced only one civil war: occurring mostly in the 1640s between Charles I's cavaliers and Oliver Cromwell's roundheads. Why this particular feud has been universally christened the 'English Civil War' has always baffled me. Not only did the 'English Civil War' consist of three major campaigns – 1642–46, 1648–49 and 1649–51, respectively – even at the time it was by no means the first of its type. It is commonly agreed that prior to the rise of Cromwell, England had endured no less than five domestic conflicts: the Nineteen-Year Winter between Stephen and Matilda, commonly known as the Anarchy (1135–54); the rebellion of Henry the Young King against his father Henry II (1173–74); the two Barons' Wars, (1215–17 and 1263–67), and the Wars of the Roses (1455–87).

Nor did civil wars in England stop with Cromwell. In 1685, passions were again ignited in the Monmouth Rebellion; a second, more protracted and more successful campaign against James II culminated in him losing his crown in the Glorious Revolution three years later. If this isn't enough, some historians will argue more examples should be added to the list. Further to Robert Curthose's rebellion of 1088 in response to brother William II's succeeding their father, William the Conqueror, the Roger Mortimer-led rebellion against Edward II and the controversial Hugh le Despenser in the early 1320s is also commonly cited.

Deciding what type of conflict constitutes a civil war begs an important question: if every major rebellion or coup can be considered a form of civil war, should the same be true of shorter campaigns or revolts? Violent insurrection by Wat Tyler, Jack Cade, Robert Aske and Robert Kett are just a handful of significant conflicts to have concerned the contemporary powers that be, albeit they all lacked the longevity of those previously mentioned. Henry IV famously dethroned his cousin Richard II in 1399, though this was achieved without the need of a battle. Does time of conflict, therefore, play a decisive role in what constitutes a war? Is the total number of dead also a factor? Alternatively, does a war require a minimum number of battles? Returning to the events of 1233–34, this leaves us with another intriguing possibility:

Was the Marshal War merely a minor skirmish whose contemporary labelling exaggerates its real importance or does English history have on its hands a civil war that has largely been forgotten?

Even now, looking back at this particular part of the thirteenth century, it is difficult to shake the feeling that all is not as it seems. If the study of Henry III has taught me just one thing, it is that viewing the events that shaped England during this period can almost be compared to looking through a kaleidoscope. Different patterns continuously emerge, often from seemingly nowhere. Some tend to repeat themselves, a sign some have argued that in Henry we had a king who didn't learn his lessons quickly. In some cases, such patterns help establish a bright and vibrant picture; in others, they fog the mind. In times of doubt, the safest approach is always to return to the original sources. Yet there are times, especially concerning the work of the chroniclers, that the monks themselves struggled to paint a coherent picture. If xenophobic bias or an overly vivid imagination doesn't call their authority into doubt, glaring inconsistencies or inaccuracies certainly do. Then, we are also forced to contend with the most considerable frustration of all. Just when we reach the crucial bits …

Silence.

On deciding to revisit this one specific area of Henry III's reign, my initial temptation was to concentrate on these two years alone. Fortunately, it didn't take me long to realise what a poor decision that would have been. To even begin to understand what took place in England during the 1230s requires not only an in-depth re-examination of his earlier reign, but also the circumstances that brought him to the throne. When looking through the kaleidoscope and focusing on one aspect, the inevitable result is to miss the bigger picture. No era or event exists entirely in a vacuum; particularly one concerning war.

With this in mind, the purpose of this book is three-fold. Firstly, to offer an overview of the history of England from the days of the Angevin Empire up to the beginning of Henry III's majority in 1227, thus presenting the events that led to the war in their proper context. The second is to explore the lives of two of Henry III's most influential magnates, William and Richard Marshal, first and third earls of Pembroke, respectively, who played such leading roles in the wars of

Henry's early reign. Finally, and perhaps most importantly, it is my hope to present the conflict of 1233–34 in a way that makes it more accessible to the population at large.

As is always my intention when writing works of nonfiction, on beginning this book, my principal aim was to present the facts without bias, leaving detailed discussion and evaluation to the final chapter. In the case of revisiting the reign of Henry III, my biggest problem is not so much favouritism of individual characters, but whether old feelings still hold. On learning of the Marshal War a decade ago, my initial impression was that this conflict was every bit as significant as those of 1215–17 and 1263–67. In a way, a pivotal turning point in England's history. Whether I will feel this way at the end of this endeavour, I hope that the voices of the notable participants will come across clearly.

Similar to when writing *The Gothic King*, there are few stereotypes or legends that need addressing. Dare I say it, this is as close as any researcher can get to a blank canvass. In many ways, this book should also be regarded as a pioneer effort. Besides the recordings of the chroniclers, the only major works done on the Marshal War are those of Björn Weiler's *Kingship, Rebellion and Political Culture* and Professor Nicholas Vincent's biography of Peter des Roches, an excellent book: one might say, a legacy. His broad discussions on the war are frankly invaluable. Without it, this book would have been very different.

In writing a full biography of Henry III, the greatest obstacle was how deep to dig. In this case, I recognise I have the opposite problem. One of the great benefits of the pipe rolls is that they allow the qualified historian to take in otherwise untapped resources and for these I am greatly indebted to individuals who have taken the time to put these into print or on the web. One of the greatest lessons I have learned is how they offer insight into personal quarrels. If one thing can influence politics, it is personal quarrels.

The Gothic King was about a man and his time. This book can perhaps be better described as being about a time that history itself appears to have forgotten. A time that was relatively brief but had profound, lasting effects. Not only did it shape the destiny of a king, but gave rise to a new national identity that would go on to develop England for centuries to come. Whether or not you agree with my conclusions, I leave entirely in your own capable hands.

I hope you find the story interesting.

Chapter 1

940–1204
The Devil's Brood

A howling gale tore through the streets of Newark on the evening of 18 October 1216. A mid-sized market town located some forty miles inland from the North Sea, it was rare for a storm to give rise to the levels of concern often felt by citizens of its coastal counterparts. Lying on both the Great North Road and the Fosse Way, the area was popular with travellers, especially cloth and wool merchants in town to sell their wares. The early twelfth-century bridge over the Trent had improved the trade links further, and by the reign of Henry II, the market had become well established. Though most of the buildings were of timber construction, even at the height of winter weather damage was often repairable.

This was not the first time the town had been forced to endure such a tempest.

Behind the sturdy stone walls of the nearby Norman castle, the abbot of Croxton had far more troubling issues to address. The south riverside fortress, though by no means immune to regular splashback, was far better prepared for nature's challenges than the earlier motte-and-bailey that had preceded it. The same lack of worry, however, could not be said of the crisis that had brought him there. Renowned for his medical expertise, it didn't take him long to realise that the patient he had been asked to treat was beyond hope of recovery. Rather than prolong the inevitable, he heard the dying man's confession and performed the last rites. The storm was over by sunrise.

Blighted by a combination of chronic fatigue, dysentery brought about from years of poor diet and a sudden fever, King John passed away in the early hours of 19 October after more than seventeen years on the throne. His final year had been a black one for England. Accusations of betrayal against his own family and an inability to keep his allies on side had contributed in no small part to humiliating defeat on the Continent. By 1214, the loss of much of his ancestral birthright had been compounded by domestic discord. Loathed in equal measure by natural adversary and should-be follower, John's life ended ignominiously amid a strange alliance of foreign invader and baronial rebel. Somewhat surprisingly perhaps, it ended through natural causes.[1]

If John's fall from grace was not extraordinary in itself, his path to the throne was every bit so. The fifth and youngest son of Henry II and Eleanor of Aquitaine, John's chances of wearing the crown had been slim. Having lived through the deaths of two of his older brothers, Henry the Young King and Geoffrey, Duke of Brittany, the former of whom had ruled briefly as joint king alongside his father before his ill-advised uprising preceded his premature downfall, on the older king's death the throne passed to his one surviving brother, Richard.

Famed in both history and literary romance for inheriting his father's fortitude, less so his restraint, the Lionheart subsequently ruled for ten years over an England he rarely saw as he concentrated instead on his life mission of bringing about a Christian Holy Land. In his absence, the inevitable cracks in government began to appear, and a kingdom that included Ireland, the duchies of Normandy and Aquitaine and the counties of Poitou and Anjou slowly began to fragment. While the 'Angevin' empire's erosion may have been reversible under a prolonged Ricardian kingship, a chance hit by a crossbow bolt in the neck as he inspected his troops at the siege of Chalus-Chabrol doomed him to an early death. Minus a legitimate heir, the dying king was left little choice than to offer his blessing to the brother who had connived to usurp him. With this, John, the last standing of Henry and Eleanor's infamous brood, was proclaimed heir to the throne of England and ruler of all of his father's territories.[2]

How the rulers of England had come to acquire such vast swathes of land is itself a story that has often been retold. Indicative of the name, the Angevin Empire had its ruling dynasty in Anjou, the so-called Garden of France whose regions included the Loire Valley and its capital at Angers. The lucky – or unlucky – beneficiary of this had been Henry II himself.[3] Son of the empress Matilda, daughter of Henry I, Henry was, on his father's side, also descended of the original counts of Anjou, who had dominated the county since the tenth century. In the eyes of Henry's contemporaries, this was of no little significance. Back in the reign of Edward the Confessor, the future saint prophecised that the green tree of England would once again flourish when the split parts of the trunk were rejoined, something that Henry's accession appeared to satisfy. As the grandson of Matilda of Scotland, the first wife of Henry I and *ipso facto* descended of the Saxon kings, Henry was the first descendant of Alfred the Great to occupy the throne of England since the Norman Conquest. Ever mindful of this, Henry made sure to promote the idea, a fact that helped ensure Edward's canonisation and translation to Westminster Abbey in 1163.[4]

It was the success of these original counts as previously unknown castellans that helped pave the way for such remarkable wealth. Renowned for the typical characteristics possessed of a leader, namely intellect, prowess in battle and devotion to the church, a far rarer knack for warcraft, diplomacy and a string of carefully arranged marriages had brought almost unprecedented success in France that even in Henry's own time remained a highly fragmented kingdom.[5]

Of the origins of the house, there are many stories. From the mists of obscurity, the first to rise is Ingelgar: a somewhat legendary soldier of fortune who made his name fighting his way through the Loire Valley. Building on these early victories was his son, Fulk the Red, who in 941 became count of Anjou: a title that in the tenth century came close to rivalling that of king of France. Over the coming 180 years, further successes gave rise to more fanciful legend. Preceding the antics of the influential eleventh-century warlord and later pilgrim, Fulk Nerra, who apparently achieved victory over the count of Brittany by preventing his army's retreat with the creation of a 'gale sweeping corn', few tales compare with that of Geoffrey Greygown (Count of Anjou 960–987), who reputedly single-handedly slew a giant.[6]

By 1128, the rule of the giant slayer's descendants reached new heights when the respected Fulk V was chosen to replace the childless Baldwin II as king of Jerusalem. In Fulk's absence, the rule of his son Geoffrey the Fair as count of Anjou saw the Garden of France flourish. It was Geoffrey who laid the foundations for future prosperity by conquering Normandy and laying claim to the throne of England through his impressive wife Matilda – the same Matilda who was a daughter of Henry I and Matilda of Scotland. Though Geoffrey would never wear the crown of England, partly due to Matilda's hatred of him, the honour would soon be bestowed upon their son, named in honour of his grandfather and crowned, Henry II.[7]

3

Both on the surface and beneath it, Henry had much in common with the original counts, especially his father. Handsome and tall, both father and son were strong of mind and body. Labelled 'the little fox' by his enemies, apparently in honour of both his red hair and a passage in the *Song of Solomon*, Henry inherited not only his father's determination but also an occasional wrathful streak. Of the latter, the little fox appears to have been particularly proud. In conversation with his court confessor, Henry is alleged to have remarked, 'And why not, when God himself is capable of such anger?' Charming and affable when the mood suited, both men were well educated in the arts of warcraft and politics. Shrewd administrators, they shared their ancestors' spirit of adventure and were often generous to the poor. As time would tell, Henry would also follow his father's example of being extra careful when it came to choosing a wife, accepting a woman a decade older than himself with a significant dower. It is equally vital that Henry bore his father's surname 'Plantagenet', sprung from Geoffrey's wearing a sprig of a broom in his hat.[8]

By 1144, Geoffrey's conquest of Normandy had almost been completed, ending nine years of conflict in the hope of cementing Matilda's claim to both there and England. As the daughter of Henry I, Matilda's claim was unbroken to William the Conqueror, who had been invested with the dukedom back in 1035. On Henry I's death in 1135, a number of the barons reneged on their oaths to Matilda and declared Stephen king on his arrival in England. For Geoffrey and Matilda, news of Stephen's rushed accession placed them on a path to war with the new king in both England and Normandy. Further to Angevin control of western England, Geoffrey's investiture as duke of Normandy as well as inheriting Anjou ensured approximately half the future Anglo-Norman dominions were already safely under his rule. When a bloodthirsty Henry faced Stephen at Wallingford in 1153, the pressure was on for the latter to submit. The following year, Henry's time finally came. Thus ended the nineteen-year-winter and began a dynasty that would be fraught with both intrigue and turmoil.[9]

As history would later recall, under Henry II's rule the ever-developing empire would reach its zenith. As a consequence of his marriage to Eleanor of Aquitaine in 1152, new dominions were added to the originals, most significantly the region after which she was named. Despite the plethora of biographies of Eleanor written over the centuries, what is known of her as a person is disappointingly limited and plagued

4

by legend.[10] Annulment of her marriage to Louis VII of France had been a contentious issue. Fifteen years together had delivered two daughters. In her earlier years, she had gained notable sway over the French king and was derided as a bad influence by future saint and leader of the Cistercian order, Bernard of Clairvaux. Evidence suggests that on her divorce from Louis, she set her sights on Henry early. His own set on her duchy, Henry was only too pleased to oblige, and their marriage followed two months later. The fact that Henry later imprisoned her for sixteen years is undoubtedly a testament to her capabilities and the threat she possessed, not least in terms of her intellect and influence over her children.[11]

From the early efforts of the self-made Ingelgar to Geoffrey of Anjou's conquest of Normandy, this unique combination of skills and circumstances had gained Henry an empire that stretched from the borders of Scotland in the north to the Pyrenees in the south. Never before in the history of England or France had the people known one overlord. In the eyes of the contemporary chronicler, such power could only have been born of sinister origins. If the musings of Gerald of Wales were to be believed, Plantagenet success had come as the unholy consequence of one of the early counts being seduced into marriage by the daughter of the devil, who later flew screaming out of a window on being forced to endure Holy Communion. In later times, Richard I took great satisfaction in such tales, stating: 'What wonder if we lack the natural affections of mankind – we come from the Devil, and must needs go back to the Devil.' Such legends would also leave their mark outside of the king's court. In the same chronicle, Gerard of Wales paid similar testament, taking inspiration from another Bernard of Clairvaux quote: 'From the Devil they came and to the Devil they will return.'[12]

Undoubtedly one of England's most competent monarchs, ruling over such dominions caused several problems, not least concerning his children's inheritance. On paper, the situation seemed simple. Come 1170, Henry had four living sons, his first-born son, William, IX Count of Poitiers, having died in 1156 at the age of 3. Consistent with the usual customs, his eldest surviving son, Prince Henry, would become king of England, duke of Normandy and count of Anjou – the three most important lands – with Eleanor's Aquitaine being granted to Richard. Geoffrey, the third child, would rule Brittany as Henry the Young's vassal, leaving John, the youngest of the bunch, lacking land. In a bid to appease his youngest son, Henry allocated him Chinon, Loudun and Mirebeau, a move that contributed in no small part to the younger Henry's rebellion of 1173–74.[13]

Such violent acts of rebellion by his own sons would have a profound effect on the mental health of the old king. It was recounted, again by Gerard of Wales, that one panel in his magnificent painted chamber in Winchester Castle had been kept deliberately blank before a painting was commissioned in his later years. True to the king's design, the image presented a fine eagle and its four young eaglets, one seated on the father's back while two tore at the flesh of its wings. All the while, the youngest sat patiently on the eagle's head. Viewed together, the scene represented a portentous thought in the king's increasingly paranoid mind that none of his sons could be trusted. Worse still, that his favourite would cause him the most pain.[14]

Henry's fears would soon become real, but not until after the heir to the throne, Henry the Young, lost his life to dysentery in 1183. On the king's death in 1189, the mantle fell upon Richard, who had also waged war against his father. Like Henry the Young, Richard had much of his father in him. A talented warrior and administrator in his own right, Henry had been reluctant to go to war for war's sake. Whereas both Henrys had died with their crusader vows unfulfilled, during Richard's reign the opposite would be true. For this, the empire suffered. The lands Henry had managed so carefully for more than three decades were, in the reign of his son, often seen as little more than a cash cow. Indeed, Richard famously claimed he would sell London if he could find a buyer.[15]

For the first time since the Norman Conquest, conflict with France would become a recurring theme. Richard's refusal to honour his long-time betrothal to the king of France's sister Alice reignited tensions on the Continent, which were compounded by his failure to father an heir with his chosen bride, Berengaria of Navarre. When Richard died, his reputation as a great warrior and crusader was already cemented. His failures were primarily limited to the Holy Land, his inability to recapture Jerusalem the major disappointment. At the time of John's accession, the Angevin Empire was still intact; thanks to Richard's charismatic personality and good relations with the Norman and Angevin nobles, loyalty to the Lionheart was far less in question than it had been in England. While Richard's absence can explain much of this, the ever-deepening entrenchment of Norman rule and interbreeding between Angle, Saxon, Jute and Norman alike would inevitably ensure that the different clusters of long-time native and the pre- and post-1066 settlers became gradually lost. Just as the term Norman had grown from Norsemen – Vikings who became Gallicised – by Henry II's reign Norman English had already given way to a softer Anglo-Norman. As time would tell, the ensuing schism would prove irreversible.

Replacing a king who had been absent for all but seven months of the last decade inevitably presented a unique set of challenges. Unfortunately for John, these would be compounded by new problems that tended to be self-inflicted. Spoiled by his father and intimidated by his mother and elder siblings, John's reputation as the runt of the litter was already well established. On Richard's death in April 1199, loyalty to John in Normandy was finely balanced, despite the recommendation of both Richard and his mother that the nobles should swear him fealty. In the ancestral home of Anjou, as well as the important and well-established territories of Maine and Touraine, the nobles had long memories, not least concerning John's earlier scheming against his father and brother. Ignoring Eleanor's pleas, the lords of Anjou declared their intention to follow the Angevin custom that the right of succession belonged not to the monarch's younger brother but instead to the eldest son of a deceased elder brother.[16]

Due to the deaths of both Henry the Young and Richard without legitimate issue, the only suitable candidates were John's nephew, Arthur, Duke of Brittany: the 12-year-old son of his brother, Geoffrey, and niece, Geoffrey's daughter, Eleanor of Brittany. Born 29 March 1187, Arthur was a posthumous child, Geoffrey having succumbed to either a jousting accident or acute chest pain in 1186. Richard's distrust of John had previously inspired him to declare Arthur heir to the throne before embarking on his crusade in 1189.[17]

Such concerns, alas, would prove well-founded. Conspiracy against Arthur by John preceded his accession. As Richard languished at Duke Leopold of Austria's pleasure after being captured on his return from the Holy Land, John's journey across the Channel to seal a pact with Philip to exclude Arthur from the reckoning swiftly followed. Sadly for John, this initiative failed to deliver as Philip was not ignorant of Arthur's potential. Aware that the prince had been acknowledged as rightful heir in Anjou, Le Mans and Tours, on Richard's death Philip summoned

Arthur to Paris, hoping to further his already considerable influence over him. It was partly these concerns that convinced Richard to confirm John as his successor. Keen to drive home his advance, John moved swiftly to capture Le Mans, before being invested duke of Normandy in Rouen on 25 April by the city's archbishop. After remaining in France for another month to take possession of Richard's treasures, John sailed home, landing at Shoreham in preparation for his coronation at Westminster on 27 May.[18]

Fittingly for a new king, the day of the coronation was Ascension Day: the feast of Christ's being raised into heaven. For John, the choice was of particular significance. In an age where the supernatural and spiritual were inexorably intertwined, what better sign could the people of England have possibly wished for than the coming of the new king on such a day, especially with the next century almost upon them. Since time immemorial, the people of Europe had been fascinated by the mysteries of the great beyond and prepared to put their faith in the immortal over deceitful mortals. Though the religious authorities banned almost every form of magic, that did not stop some from searching for answers in the darker arts. No less true was this of the primitive science of the stars. From apparitions of the recently departed to figures in the night sky, the Middle Ages were a time when any form of unexpected behaviour could be viewed as a sign from God.

The 1190s had been particularly notable for such omens. The chronicler William of Newburgh recorded in January 1193 that the sky appeared blood red for more than two hours, shining so brightly it seemed to be on fire. Similar was seen in February and November. The strange phenomenon – quite possibly aurora borealis – convinced many of the monks that there were buildings on fire. Three years later a double sun had been viewed as a sure sign that war with France was imminent, as indeed it proved to be. Whereas the famously sceptical Richard the Lionheart had dismissed reports of blood raining down from the heavens as he constructed one of his castles, for the people of England brought up on the stories of comets in the skies above Hastings or bubbling earth in the days before the murder of William Rufus, such events were often viewed with a sense of dread that God's displeasure was on show.[19]

The beginning of the new millennia brought about new portents. A three-hour eclipse of the moon was reported to have made it shine blood red and emit rays like fire on 3 January 1200. That same year, both the prominent chronicler of St Albans, Roger of Wendover, and the annalist of Burton recorded that five moons were seen in the skies above the province of York. While four of the five appeared at each point of the compass, a fifth, accompanied by several stars, began in the centre of the four before making a circuit of each one only to vanish altogether after about an hour.[20]

As the following years would illustrate, the concerns of the soothsayers would indeed prove well-founded. John's coronation successfully taken care of, any lingering threat to sound relations with the king of France was seemingly settled at the treaty of Le Goulet in May 1200.[21] Departing Shoreham on 19 June after a pilgrimage to the tomb of Thomas Becket, his ships well stocked with knights, foot soldiers and supplies, the king of France officially acknowledged John as duke of Normandy. For the privilege, John not only parted with 30,000 marks, but also agreed to submit to Philip as overlord of the French fiefs. The one exception was the duchy of Aquitaine, which John had inherited from his mother, who was still alive.[22]

For agreeing to part with so much, John was widely berated. Paying out £20,000 and yielding large swathes of the empire to fiefdom status to confirm what should, in theory, have already been his was unsurprisingly viewed as disastrous. To raise the cash, John imposed a tax of 3s on a carucate of land – an area tillable by eight oxen in a single season. As a consequence of the treaty, John also gave his blessing for the king's son, Prince Louis, to marry the Spanish princess, Blanche of Castile, daughter of John's sister, Eleanor, in addition to bestowing on him the lands of Auvergne and Berry, as well as many honours in Normandy and Gascony.[23]

Though John's concessions were generous in the extreme, the newfound peace soon hit troubled waters. The catalyst on this occasion, as was so often the way, involved the marriage bed. Now 33, John had been married for ten years. His wedding to Isabella, the granddaughter of the earl of Gloucester – an illegitimate son of Henry I – which had taken place shortly before Richard's coronation in 1189, was still to provide an heir. Whether this was for want of trying is unclear. Far more certain is that John wished to be rid of his wife, and the marriage was annulled within a year of his accession.[24]

Ending the union had been relatively easy, despite incurring the wrath of Pope Innocent III. The former archbishop of Canterbury, Baldwin, had previously declared the marriage void on the grounds of consanguinity; conversely, Pope Clement III had given official dispensation for the marriage, albeit expressly forbidding any sexual practices due to their being second cousins. After obtaining the help of, among others, the bishops of Lisieux, Bayeux and Avranches to gain an annulment, John took as his new queen another Isabella, daughter and heiress of the commune of Angoulême in Poitou. This marriage was also a contentious one. Uncomplicated in the familial sense, Isabella was already betrothed to the powerful earl of la Marche, Hugh de Lusignan.[25]

With the pope's blessing – and seemingly Philip's – the marriage took place in Poitou in August 1200, following which husband and wife returned to England for Isabella's coronation.[26] Such scenes of joy were sadly short-lived, as Hugh's discontent soon escalated into violent uprising in Poitou. Had John done the honourable thing and compensated Hugh for the loss of his fiancé, it is possible relations between the families – not to mention the two nations – would have been much smoother; however, by failing to do so, he sowed the seeds of disloyalty. On receiving news of Hugh's uprising, John summoned his barons to Portsmouth in preparation to crush the rebellion.[27]

The following year, John and Isabella crossed the sea for an audience with Philip. The terms of Le Goulet already settled, talks concerned other matters, including the endowment of Richard's widow, Berengaria.[28] Peace between the two nations again confirmed, John rocked the boat with a foolish attack on Hugh, leaving the earl of la Marche little choice but to take his grievances in a formal appeal to the French king. Despite John being Hugh's lord as count of Poitou, as feudal lord, Philip held sway over John in Poitou. When called upon by Philip to attend a hearing in Paris, John refused, stating it would be inappropriate for a duke of Normandy to attend court in Paris.[29] Motivated by John's ensuing feud with Lusignan and his refusal to appear before the nobles to explain his recent attack, the French lords sided against John and agreed confiscation of his French lands was just. As relations turned increasingly bitter, in April 1202, Philip knighted Arthur and announced the confiscation of John's territories in France in favour of the prince before undertaking preparations for Arthur to marry his daughter, Mary.[30]

What happened next would be of profound consequence to the history of both nations. Buoyed by the king of France's backing, Arthur took the war to John, conquering several castles during the following weeks. Despite delivering a successful counter-strike, John's troubles escalated when Arthur disappeared. Of the exact circumstances, history remains unsure. After capturing the important fortress at Mirebeau, where Arthur had foolishly been keeping Eleanor prisoner, John turned the tables on the young prince and kept him under lock and key. Since that time, rumour has abounded that John, or even Peter de Maulay, were personally responsible for the young man's death, quite possibly the culmination of a drunken rampage.[31]

That John initially made an order for the prince to be castrated and blinded, rendering him unsuitable for kingship, appears to be true. Of the three men ordered to carry out the dreadful deed, only one made the journey to the castle of Falaise, where Arthur was being held under the guardianship of John's chamberlain, Hubert de Burgh. Racked by guilt or having travelled there under false pretences, on entering Arthur's cell the would-be maimer informed the prince of the plot, at which point the young duke's wretched sobs gave way to a new stoutness of heart. Fortunately for all concerned, Hubert de Burgh had no intention of allowing such a violent act to take place. After lying to John that the sentence had been carried out and Arthur had since died of a broken heart, Hubert spread the news of it throughout the land. So great was the sadness that the mourning church bells rang out in his honour. Word was also spread that Arthur had been buried in the Cistercian monastery of St André-en-Gouffern.[32]

News of the prince's death was received particularly poorly in Arthur's dukedom of Brittany. When the Bretons took to the warpath, Hubert retracted the claim to appease them. According to the chronicler Roger of Wendover, John visited Arthur personally at Falaise, promising him many honours in exchange for leaving Philip's side, to which Arthur answered violently and demanded that John give up Richard's territories to him, including England, to which he was entitled as the son of Geoffrey. Troubled by the threats, John sent orders that the prince should be relocated to Rouen, after which nothing more is said. Later rumours claimed that Arthur's body was discovered by fishermen only to be subsequently hidden out of fear of reprisals. Less unclear are John's other acts after Mirebeau. His stock in the eyes of the French lords already near rock bottom, his reputation further deteriorated after he ordered the burning of the great city of Tours and le Mans.[33]

Throughout John's early reign, such tales set a disturbing trend. A particularly gripping example of what loyalty meant in the Anglo-Norman world at this time can be illustrated by the case of Count Robert of Sées and Alençon. One morning in January 1203, he breakfasted with John only to defect to Philip in the afternoon. In terms of his ability to maintain order on the Continent, such turns in fortune would prove catastrophic. Not only was John alienating essential allies, but in the case of count Robert, he also lost easy access into Maine. Consequently, after taking Mirebeau, John had been successful in capturing Hugh and Geoffrey de Lusignan and some 252 of the 'worthiest knights', only to lose the hero of the operation William des Roches through needless antagonism. A reputation for being domineering and bloodthirsty was often accepted as typical for a medieval ruler but, as Richard III would learn more than two centuries later, the population at large did not have the stomach for antagonistic child-murderers.[34]

Over the coming decade, maintaining control of the Angevin Empire, at least set out in the terms previously agreed at Le Goulet, proved impossible. By 1203, as England battled large-scale flooding, large parts of Normandy and Aquitaine surrendered into enemy hands. Within a year, the French king had subdued all of Normandy, Anjou, Brittany, Maine and the Province of Tours. For John, the loss of Normandy was the hardest to bear. Though Anjou was beloved as the ancestral homeland, in financial terms the lands of the north were worth quite possibly as much as the rest of the French fiefs put together.[35]

Yet in the eyes of the population at large, recent events took on a different type of significance. In losing the duchy, it was regarded that a prophecy of Merlin had been fulfilled, that in this year: 'the sword shall be divided from the sceptre'. With Normandy lost, so ended a chain that went back to the Norman invasion of 1066. As future years would show, 1204 would mark a watershed in England's history.[36]

Chapter 2

1204–1213
In God We Trust

Maundy Thursday 1204 was a particularly strange one in the city of Damascus. Throughout Europe, stories abounded that a bizarre miracle had occurred in the prison of the city's castle, which, at the time, was frequented predominantly by Christian soldiers as well as others of the religious life. At the heart of the tale was one particular soldier who removed from a box a phial that had been filled with oil dropped from an image of the Virgin Mary on display in the convent of Our Lady of Saydnaya: a city in the mountains some seventeen miles to the north. Confused to find the oil appeared to have become 'fleshy' and divided in two within the bottle, the soldier's attempts to remove the substance with a knife caused blood to flow freely.

Unbeknown to witnesses at the time, the miracle of the oil was not the only one associated with the image at the convent. Founded by a nun of Damascus sometime between the sixth and late-eighth century, the convent had welcomed, among its guests, a travelling monk on his way to Jerusalem. Asked by the nun to bring back a likeness of the Virgin Mary that she could put on display in the convent's oratory, the monk initially forgot to do so before the voice of an angel persuaded him to return to the city, following which the image saved his life numerous times. On returning to the convent and praying in the oratory, any second thoughts he had about keeping the icon for himself went away when the door mysteriously disappeared while he was inside, only to reappear once the image was set on the altar. In the years that followed, many miracles were reported, including one of a sultan recovering his sight.[1]

No such miracles would aid John in his bid to recover Normandy. Successful at least in obtaining subsidies to help combat the cost of the war, a willingness by the French barons to yield to Philip's rule proved swift. The one benefit for John of losing Normandy was that the Norman lords, in swearing loyalty to Philip, subsequently forfeit their lands in England. Enriched by the vast swathes of estates, John wasted little time in granting them as favours to his followers.[2]

As the next ten years would show, the loss of Normandy and Anjou would by no means put an end to the conflict between John and Philip. English recovery of the Channel Islands in 1205, after being lost a year earlier, offered John an ideal base for an invasion of Poitou and by the end of the year the port city of La Rochelle and nearby commune of Niort had both been relieved. No longer in such desperate need of funds and support, the situation in both had become far calmer than at any time since John's accession. This was a stark contrast to life back in England that suffered severe famine on the back of a hard winter that caused the Thames to freeze.[3]

On relieving Poitiers, the capital of Poitou, John marched his troops south into his mother's homeland of Aquitaine. With Bordeaux still in English hands, having held out bravely against King Alfonso of Castile, John quickly brought peace to the loyal city before completing a conquest of Gascony. After daring to march north into Anjou, he held court in Angers for a week before taking his charges as far as the border of Maine. At this point, Philip threatened to head south, forcing John to retreat. Though recent progress had come to an end, the mission had been a great success, consolidating both Poitou and Gascony by the end of 1206. After agreeing a two-year truce with Philip, John set sail for home and was greeted at Portsmouth harbour by the cheers of thousands of loyal subjects.[4]

Seventeen years could be considered a long time in medieval Europe – not least when it came to cementing a legacy. Had John's failures and evils been limited to the Continent in those first five years, his own would have almost certainly been far kinder. An able administrator with an energetic, if not restless, bearing, accompanied by the usual Plantagenet bloodlust, he lacked his father's faculty for warcraft. The same was true of international diplomacy, the consequences of which would prove especially important in his attempts to retain control of the ancestral possessions and maintain harmony across the sea.

While the perpetually imminent threat of French invasion was always likely to prove a struggle, sadly for John, political intrigue south of the Channel was only one of his problems. A somewhat dubious adherent of Christianity at the best of times, his willingness to profit from the revenues left by vacant bishoprics and other sees ensured his squabbles were not limited to those of secular status. Of particular abhorrence had been his treatment of the Cistercians, extortions of whom began when several abbots of that order visited the province of York back in 1200. Even prior to the first Cistercian house in England, the chronicler William of Malmesbury had written lovingly of the 'white monks' as possessing 'the surest road to Heaven'. Before the start of John's reign, the order had been exempt from all taxes. The sudden decision to reverse this inevitably caused problems: not least when a command by John to the sheriffs to punish the monks led to a mediation from the archbishop of Canterbury. Compromise from Hubert Walter that the order would pay John 1,000 marks on condition that John confirmed the liberties bestowed upon them by Richard I was rejected by the king. Throughout 1200, relations with the monks of every chapter threatened to deteriorate irrevocably. Only when John agreed to found a Cistercian chapter – at Beaulieu in the New Forest – did relations finally begin to improve.[5]

Throughout the decade that followed, similarly strained relations with the papacy ensured that threats to his right to rule would continue to hang over him like the sword of Damocles. To make matters worse, when the highly competent archbishop of Canterbury, Hubert Walter, passed away in 1205, John quashed the election of his successor, the sub-prior, leading to an ongoing feud with the monks of Christ Church.[6] Matters came to a head in 1207 when John refused to consecrate Pope Innocent III's preferred candidate, Cardinal Stephen Langton, out of anger that consecration of John's own preferred choice, the bishop of Norwich, had been denied. In retaliation, John expelled the Canterbury monks on 15 July, leading to them taking their case directly to Rome. Despite Langton's consecration by Innocent at Viterbo in June, John refused to follow the advice of the papal ambassadors and allow Langton to take up his see, threatening instead that Langton would be hanged if he dared set foot in England.[7]

A blood-red eclipse of the moon on 2 February 1208 was again perceived as an ominous warning. Coming around the time of the deaths of the bishops of Chester and Durham, it had also coincided with the feast of the Purification of Mary, coming five weeks after John had kept Christmas at Winchester.[8] Throughout the festive period, rather than give in to the spirit of the season, John's heart hardened. Arrogant in his views that the pope's authority was restricted to spiritual matters as opposed to temporal, John's unwillingness to compromise evoked Innocent's wrath. As winter gave way to spring, Rome's substantial judgment was declared. Commencing immediately after Passion Sunday on 24 March, England was officially placed under papal interdict.[9]

Although often regarded as an extreme form of punishment, interdict was by no means unheard of. In 1199, France had been placed under interdict, prompting many of the bishops to go to Rome.[10] Nevertheless, for the people of England at the time, the consequences of recent developments should not be understated. Since the restrictions came into being, stories abounded of corpses going unburied, some coffins hanging from trees until the interdict was lifted.[11]

True to his usual form, John used the new restrictions as opportunities to seize the property of the monks and clergy.[12] So obscene had his behaviour become that he renewed hostilities against the Cistercians, expelled the few who had remained at Canterbury – namely the blind and invalid – and confined the queen to close quarters inside the walls of Corfe Castle. By the summer, all of the bishops except for Peter des Roches, the bishop of Winchester, had gone into exile, some taking up residence at the Monastery of St Bertin in St-Omer; others headed for Scotland, Ireland or Rome. When John brought hostilities against the monks of Waverley, forcing the abbot to flee, des Roches is recorded as having offered them grain as a mark of charity.[13]

Significant as the interdict had been to England, of far greater importance was what awaited. Refusal to settle his feuds with the monks in 1208 saw excommunication follow in 1209.[14] Though John was successful in marching north with a large force to Scotland – which resulted in the Scottish king, William the Lion, releasing two of his daughters and his son to offer homage for the lands he held in the king of England's name – as an excommunicated monarch, John now found himself under the imminent threat of the long-mooted French invasion.[15]

Living at a time when – to quote a sixteenth-century Vatican historian – 'the thunders of the Vatican could shake the thrones of princes', the signs were looking bad for John. A further eclipse of the moon on 18 October 1211 was seen to have been of equally gloomy circumstance, not least for the abbot of St Edmunds and constable of Chester, both of whom passed away that day. Far more disturbing were stories that the forest of Cannock had been rocked by the terrible sight of several deer that, upon being plagued by stomach upsets, committed mass suicide in the waters of the Severn. Recorded among the deer by the Barnwell annalist was the bizarre appearance of a fawn with two heads and eight feet. Only in more recent times has the possibility of Siamese twins in the deer kingdom become witnessed; assuming, of course, that the story didn't originate simply from the sight of two fawns standing together![16]

Eclipses of the moon and the strange behaviour of local animals were not the only odd phenomena to be seen in England at that time. A bright rainbow was witnessed lighting up the skies above the village of Chalgrave in Bedfordshire in April 1212, the usual hues on this occasion denoting the colour of blood.[17] No less concerning was a shower of blood witnessed on 10 July at Caen in Normandy, occurring more or less simultaneously with that of three crosses doing battle in the sky above Falaise – the same fateful location from where Prince Arthur had been imprisoned. Of the possible contenders for the superstitious to choose from, 1212 would offer no shortage. As France reeled from the catastrophic failure of the so-called Children's Crusade – a seemingly spontaneous movement among the youths of the nation that culminated in large scale capture by slave traders and sale to the Egyptians – less than a month passed before John sent his knights into Poitou. After assembling his army at Canterbury and leaving England, the fleet wreaked havoc along the French coast, annihilating several French ships in the mouth of the Seine as well as laying waste to the towns of Fécamp and Dieppe.[18]

If blood-red rainbows were not an omen for burning towns and ships on the Continent, back home, John would have his own flames to put out. Four hundred and fifty-four years before the Great Fire of 1666 that would famously see the destruction of St Paul's, on 10 July the people of London watched on in horror as inferno rampaged through the borough of Southwark, destroying its church, Our Lady of the Canons. The cause of this is unclear, but it appears to have been the result of a rowdy drinking contest or 'scotale'. Sadly for all concerned, as numbers gathered on London Bridge – at that time, the only crossing in the city – apparently to help extinguish the flames, the northern end of the bridge also caught fire, trapping hundreds. Deepening the tragedy, when several ships came to rescue them, a further mishap ensued as the voluminous crowds swarmed the vessels, causing them to sink. The exact death toll has never been known though previous estimates have stated it could have reached 3,000. A contemporary who witnessed the flames concluded the happening was a divine intervention, in keeping with the great flood or the rapture of Sodom and Gomorrah.[19]

North of London, the king had other problems with which to contend. On 16 August 1212, while stationed at Nottingham, John learned of an unspecified baronial threat: either of an armed uprising, a plot to murder him or desert him on his simultaneous campaign in Wales.[20] Back in 1210, John had sent a large army into Wales under the leadership of William Marshal, his nephew, John Marshal and Ranulf de Blondeville, the earl of Chester, culminating in widespread damage. In so doing, it was reported by the chronicler, Gervase of Canterbury, that another Merlin prophecy had thus been fulfilled: 'The sixth shall pull down the walls of Ireland ... his beginning shall succumb to his own unstable nature.' If William the Conqueror was the first, logically John was indeed the sixth: having been granted Ireland by his father in 1185. In 1211, another expedition to Wales came unstuck initially when his charges ran low on provisions before later reclaiming the ascendancy. For a brief time, one could argue John had become the first king of England to hold sovereignty over the whole of England, Wales, Ireland and even Scotland.[21]

Trouble in Wales brewed again in 1212 when Innocent III absolved the Welsh princes from the peace of the previous year and relaxed the interdict. No sooner had John raised his forces to combat this than news reached him of a potential coup. The men behind this apparent conspiracy were both prominent among the baronage. The first was Eustace de Vesci, Lord of Alnwick. The other was the influential Lord of Little Dunmow, Robert Fitzwalter, whose property included the London fortress Baynard's Castle – one of two of Fitzwalter's castles John subsequently had dismantled. Once already Fitzwalter had incurred John's wrath after his apparent cowardice in surrendering the castle at Le Vaudreuil in Normandy in 1203 without a fight, allowing Philip to drive a stake through the heart of the duchy.[22]

Of Fitzwalter's motives, it is difficult to separate fact from legend. True enough, the intrepid future crusader had grievances concerning his claims to Hertford Castle. The story that appears in the *Dunmow Chronicle*, however, that John had attempted to seduce his daughter – named in the chronicle as Maud – only to murder her by use of a poisoned egg while forced to endure solitary confinement in the Tower of London is less likely to be factual. Intriguingly, the tale bears more than a passing similarity to the sixteenth-century play by Anthony Munday about Robin Hood, whose later legend has done more than anything to develop John's reputation. Better evidence concerns Eustace, whose wife had been the subject of similar abuses. That John had earlier seduced the wives of his barons is sadly well documented.[23]

Concerned that his safety was in jeopardy, John ceased his assault on Wales and spent part of the summer locked up in Nottingham Castle.[24] His position stabilised, John marched north in an attempt to bring the rebels to submission, prompting Fitzwalter and de Vesci to flee to France and Scotland. Rumour also abounded that year of John's murder at Marlborough, as well as the raping of his wife and decapitation of the young heir to the throne, Prince Henry. Undoubtedly inspired by such threats, he also had the young Prince Henry relocated and put under extra protection at an undisclosed location.[25]

Another eclipse, this time on 11 November 1212, was noted to have closely coincided with the deaths of three significant clerics. The first was John Cumin, Archbishop of Dublin, whose passing a fortnight earlier had culminated in the city passing into English hands. Preceding him earlier that summer was Mauger, Bishop of Worcester, who died in exile in Pontigny. Most significant of the three was the king's illegitimate half-brother Geoffrey Plantagenet, Archbishop of York, who also ended his days abroad, deprived of his see as a consequence of his opposition to John's taxation policy in 1207 and ongoing papal restrictions.[26]

With no sign of a compromise with the exiled clergy, in March 1213 Innocent wrote to John, rebuking him for his continuous crimes against the church. Conditions of reconciliation were also brought up in a separate letter. Concerned by the imminent threat of a French invasion and Innocent's decision to liberate his English subjects of any conditions John had previously placed upon them, on 13 May John did what no one had expected and forfeited England as a fiefdom of the papacy. Two days later, within the walls of the Templar church just outside Dover, he officially resigned England to the papacy's care, performing homage in witness of large swathes of the baronage.[27]

There to obtain John's submission on the papacy's behalf was Innocent's trusted Roman-born subdeacon, Pandulf Verraccio. Pandulf was already known in England, having visited in 1211: one of two papal envoys or nuncios – the other was named in the annals of Wigorn as Durand or Durandos – to have attempted to achieve peace between all parties. Finding himself in a bitter argument with the king, Pandulf is alleged to have carried out a papal sentence of excommunication in the presence of John and his court. It was also Pandulf in January 1213 who had presented Philip II with Innocent's letter charging him with the deprivation of John, i.e. an invasion of England. On receiving John's submission, not to mention John's overdue agreement to the terms that led to his excommunication, Pandulf travelled to Paris in a bid to prevent the French invasion.[28]

Of the real significance of John's surrender to the papacy, many arguments have been put forward, especially concerning its long-term ramifications. In the short term, by making what on paper was a significant gesture yet, in reality, had little bearing on his right to rule, John had at least been successful in saving his realm. True, it had burdened England with a future tithe of 1,000 marks per year, extended the power of the papal visitors and developed his reputation in the eyes of the barons as 'Softsword'; yet by bending the knee, he had obtained not only unconditional absolution and the return of the bishops but also convoluted Philip's power over John concerning the French fiefs – something which made a French invasion far more complicated.[29]

On 20 July, eleven days after landing in Dover, the arrival of the archbishop of Canterbury, Stephen Langton, in Winchester, as well as the bishops of London, Ely, Lincoln and Hereford saw Langton formally absolve a tearful John from excommunication. With this, a bitter feud that could so easily have been avoided was ended with a kiss of peace. So great was the transformation in the papacy's attitude that in October, Innocent wrote on John's behalf to William of Scotland and the most important officials in Ireland in the hope of ensuring the loyalty of both nations. Unsurprisingly, influence was also used to fill the other sees and canonical vacancies to which John had earlier refused ascent. The interdict was formally ended in June 1214, when compensation for the missing years was finally agreed with the church.[30]

Unfortunately for both king and pontiff, apart from obtaining the loyalty of the clergy, such things helped little concerning the barons. John's divisive personality and questionable practices had by 1214 alienated almost all the lords of the north, leading to their refusal to launch a long-awaited military expedition to reclaim the family estates in France. Though the chance success of the English fleet, led by William Longespée, the earl of Salisbury, had resulted in the annihilation of several French vessels at Damme in late May 1213, conscription of the Lusignans at the cost of giving away Saintonge and the Isle of Oléron would be as good as it got. Victory at Damme may have prevented any chance of a French invasion, yet the presence of Prince Louis in Anjou halted progress the other way.[31]

Swiftly followed the sucker punch. Following such a positive start, a coalition of English and foreign troops aimed at driving the Capetians out of Normandy, Maine and Anjou directed by John and his nephew, Holy Roman Emperor, Otho IV – himself excommunicated by Innocent in 1210 – ran into problems.[32] When John's forces launched against Philip's at the same time as Otho's at Bouvines on 27 July, a lack of strategy and coordination culminated in a meek surrender, despite the coalition outnumbering Philip's forces by approximately 9,000 to 7,000. While Otho's loss of the imperial standard would serve as a prelude to the decline of his empire, for John, the capture and imprisonment of the hero of Damme, William Longespée, was merely the tip of the iceberg.[33]

Learning of the catastrophe in mid-August, the king was devastated. Under pressure from both home and abroad, John had little choice but to agree to a five-year truce.[34] As the following twelve months would show, the defeat of the joined forces unequivocally put an end to any chance of reclaiming the lost lands of his father. For the youngest of the Devil's Brood, the road to hell now had a clear direction.

A water-meadow in Surrey called Runnymede.

Chapter 3

1214–1215
From Runnymede to the Wash

In the eyes of many of the barons, humiliation overseas was the final straw. Living in an age when victory or defeat in wartime was viewed as much a sign of God's blessing as signs in the sky, John's latest catastrophe seemed proof that the legend of the Devil's Brood was right after all. By no means distraught at the loss of the territories themselves – in reality, the ancestral lands were often viewed as a distraction by those of English birth – by now the greater danger in the minds of the magnates was whether John's son and heir would have any kingdom left to inherit.[1]

Disillusioned by his antics on the Continent, the king's policy at home also came under closer scrutiny. Before the year was out, a number of the barons met at St Edmunds, resolving to take up arms unless John agreed to specific terms. By the time they met on 6 January 1215 at a conference in London, discontent had spread. So seriously did the king take recent developments, an order was put out for the royal castellans to alert his castles in case of an uprising. This did not prevent him from evoking the fury of the barons further still by refusing to end his demand for a scutage – a tax issued on an area of land able to support a knight, also known as a knight's fee – for the recent disastrous expedition in Poitou.[2]

In previous years, such feelings had often brought with them an additional complication that all monarchs dreaded: usurpation. Fortunately for John, in contrast to the uprisings by his brothers against his father, his children were far too young to engage in any such endeavour. In the absence of an obvious candidate to lead a rebellion, the barons had another strategy to pursue: reform. Included in those terms was the insistence that John agreed to abide by a charter of liberties.

Although somewhat radical, such things were by no means unheard of in England. Besides those issued by Henry I and Stephen on their accessions, in practice more as PR stunts than any real promise of relinquished command, John had also granted a charter of liberties to the city of London on 17 June 1199 as well as confirming something similar for the Isle of Oléron by his mother in July. In October 1201, a charter of liberties was issued for the stannaries of Devon and Cornwall, while in March 1208 the king covered similar ground in confirming the burgesses of Yarmouth their ancient rights and liberties. There was also precedence for a king to grant a charter at the end of a war.[3]

This was also not the first time the subject had come up in John's reign. As recently as November 1214, he had tried to obtain Langton's support with a clerical charter concerning elections to abbeys and bishoprics. Rather than give in, Langton attempted to take a neutral stance and placed himself as something of a mediator between John and his leading critics. In reality, the archbishop's position was less in line with John. In fact, according to Roger of Wendover, less than two months after returning to England in 1213 Langton made the interesting claim that he had rediscovered Henry I's coronation charter of 1100, leading to a meeting in St Albans in August to discuss the matter. Whether or not such an event happened has been hotly debated. Sadly Wendover was the only chronicler to mention this, which makes trust in his reliability of particular importance.[4]

After John kept another Christmas at Winchester, the January assembly in London presented their version of the reforms, as well as swearing an oath to stand together for the 'liberty of the Church and Realm'. Faced with the demand he must confirm Henry I's charter, plus other select reforms, or face potential uprising, John played for time, stating that terms would be discussed at an assembly near Northampton on 26 April. His subsequent actions confirm John had no desire to comply with the barons' demands. Rather than embark on prolonged discussion, he instead made the very public decision to take up the cross and distribute the white crusader symbol among his supporters. Confident the papacy would never reciprocate the rebels' reforms, John watched on as in March 1215 Innocent positioned himself as mediator between the two parties. In May, John complained to Innocent, with some success, that he was unable to fulfil his crusader pledge due to the recent events.[5]

Such tactics, alas, failed to break the rebels' spirits. So concerned had the king become of likely uprising, he augmented his forces with mercenaries from the Continent. When the disgruntled barons of the north arrived for the assembly on 26 April, apparently with peaceful intentions albeit ready for war if necessary, John stayed away, fearing capture. Over the coming days, the rebels declined the opportunity to meet him at Oxford where Langton had called a provincial synod. Moving east, they gathered forces at Stamford in Lincolnshire and defied John formally on 5 May. Wary of a possible ambush, the rebel army, led by the influential rogue Robert Fitzwalter, began risings in Devonshire and Northamptonshire. After taking Lincoln, on 17 May, only ten days after John had attempted to appease the citizens of London with a new charter that included the right to elect a mayor, the capital opened its gates for the barons.[6]

What happened next would prove critical not only in terms of John's reign, but also what type of kingdom his successors would inherit. Fearing military annihilation, John agreed to what would later be dubbed Magna Carta. Following on from discussions that commenced around 10 June, a conference on 15 June saw history made at Runnymede. By agreeing to this original 63-clause charter – the numbering system was devised in the eighteenth century – John agreed to operate within the boundaries set by others, meaning that for the first time since the Norman Conquest the monarch ruled over an England whose constitution contained significant curbs on royal authority.[7]

Although the initial business was confirmed on 19 June, implementation, inevitably, proved slow.[8] By the middle of the following month, the only progress had concerned the xenophobic clause 50, most specifically John's removal of four foreign advisors the charter mentioned by name. That same month, negotiations were reopened at Oxford, as a consequence of which the king surrendered the Tower of London to Langton as part of the mediation process. A charter of liberties was also presented that month to the city of Dublin.[9]

Unbeknown to the barons, John had privately been preparing for this. Put off by the harshest of demands, namely that a committee of twenty-five barons – established as a consequence of clause 52 of the charter – would effectively take over command of the kingdom, John's public acceptance of the new reforms was immediately followed by his attempts to obtain the pope's help to repress them. As the barons prepared for a celebratory tournament, a sleepless night at Windsor Castle ended with the king setting sail to the Isle of Wight from where he opened up a correspondence with the Vatican. Arguing with some persuasion that the rebels were effectively putting a papal vassal under secular rule, Innocent denounced the charter as 'shameful' but also 'illegal and unjust'. Making something of a mockery of the barons' liberal values, a letter by Innocent on 24/25 August recorded the repentance of John for his past misdeeds, while criticizing the rebels for preventing him from carrying out his recent crusader vow. In doing so, the pope officially absolved John from his oath and urged the barons to renounce the charter.[10]

Within a month of the papal decree, and in response to messages from John concerning aid against the barons who had risen against him, Innocent wrote, somewhat ineffectively, to Langton concerning excommunication of the rebels.[11] A further letter to the bishop of Winchester and key members of the clergy ordering the excommunication of all disturbers of the peace, and the placing of their lands and possessions under interdict was largely implemented. The same was true of the pope's warning that any bishop who failed to publish the document should meet a similar fate. Ironically, in November this would lead to Peter des Roches and Pandulf adding Langton's name to the list of those suspended in retribution for his refusal to surrender Rochester Castle and for granting safe passage for baronial representatives to the court of Philip II. According to the Barnwell annalist, the sentence was carried out on board a ship as Langton prepared to sail for the Lateran Council. Just as before, such threats made little difference to the barons.[12]

Encouraged by these developments, John marched on London. In the first clash of what historians would later refer to as the First Barons' War, the rival forces saw action at Rochester, historically a royalist stronghold before the recent brief government of the twenty-five on the back of Magna Carta. The seven-week siege that followed was memorable for its intensity, the barons holding out bravely until depleted resources saw John take the city on 30 November. As fate would have it, John's tunnel vision allowed Llywelyn ap Iorwerth free rein in Wales, taking seven castles in just three weeks.[13]

Christmas at Nottingham was followed by John's peaceful acquisition of Belvoir Castle, around which time guardianship of the royal castles was established. Of particular note, William de Forz, Earl of Aumale was granted possession of Rockingham, Sanney and Bytham; Falkes de Breauté was given Oxford, Bedford, Northampton and Cambridge; Ralph le Tyris was granted Berkhamsted; Hertford was entrusted to Walter de Godardville. With the safety of the royal castles on a far more secure footing, John's other priority concerned the destruction of enemy property. Throughout the war, the barons had pursued a tactic often used in the Anarchy of Stephen and Matilda of putting up 'adulterine' castles: usually motte and bailey type structures without royal approval.[14]

With the war proceeding on so many fronts, for John, the new reality was one of divide and conquer. Or in some instances, be conquered. Forced to split his troops between London and the north, he led his forces towards Hadrian's Wall, taking out his frustrations on any passing town and village that had sided with the barons. North of the border, the king of Scotland had also sought the support of the twenty-five barons noted in clause 52 of the great charter in enforcing his country's claim for Westmorland, Cumberland and Northumberland as part of the late queen of Scotland's dowry. The devout, peace-loving William of Scotland had died the previous December, and had been succeeded by his third child and eldest son, Alexander II.[15] A bright, precocious lad, Alexander had been just 16 at his coronation in 1214; almost two years earlier, John had knighted him in London.[16] Now on opposite sides, Alexander found himself on the receiving end of the king's taunts, namely, 'We will rouse the red fox from his lair,' a reference to the young man's red hair. In early 1216, John invaded Scotland, achieving little beyond conquering Berwick before bringing his train of wreckage to East Anglia. By April, the only major success had been the taking of Colchester.[17]

News of the ongoing carnage had not been missed in Rome. Kept updated by letters between the papal court and Pandulf, Innocent ordered further excommunication of the rebels in December. In keeping with his previous threats, besides testing the nerve of the clergy, the latest demands made little difference to the barons. Successful at least in quietening the influential John de Lacy, 2nd Earl of Lincoln – himself one of the original twenty-five – Innocent attempted to bring about further order by appointing fellow papal diplomat Guala Bicchieri, also the cardinal of St Martin's, as legate of England.[18] Guala was not the first legate to have been assigned to England. His appointment ended the tenure of legate Nicholas of Tusculum, whose arrival following John's submission at Dover had proved somewhat ineffective on account of his lenience towards royal policy and close friendship with des Roches.[19]

On receiving word of his promotion from Innocent, Guala was immediately dispatched to France. Of particular concern were reports that the rebels had approached the French king in the hope of obtaining financial and military aid; prior to this, John had had similar thoughts. On greeting Guala with the expected cordiality, Philip soon confirmed the legate's fears. Of equal concern, the threat of excommunication still meant as little to the king of France as it had to the barons. Three years earlier, after John's submission at Dover, Philip had been keen to continue with his planned invasion. In the legate's presence, the French monarch argued that England was no faithful vassal of Rome and raised questions over whether any king could submit his kingdom without the magnates' approval. Further to accusation that John's past treachery against Richard the Lionheart rendered him unsuitable for kingship, rumour resurfaced of John's role in Arthur's disappearance.[20]

Of double misfortune for John, the promise of the throne proved too tempting for the dauphin of France, Prince Louis, to pass over. Heeding the rebel yell, as early as December, the advanced guard of a French invasion force had joined Fitzwalter's barons in London. Despite his growing popularity among the rebel barons, Louis's claim to the throne of England was weak. The only surviving son of Philip II and his first wife, Isabella of Hainault, he had no claim in terms of his right of blood succession. He was, however, married to Blanche of Castile, whose mother was Eleanor of England, the sixth child, and second daughter, of Henry II and Eleanor of Aquitaine, therefore John's sister.[21]

Unperturbed by the efforts of Guala, as well as a similar embassy to France attempted that spring by William Marshal and des Roches, to delay his plans to press home his dubious right to the English crown, Louis sailed north across the Channel. Putting the Cinque Ports on high alert, John worked hard to block Louis's path, but failed to prevent his arrival with a reasonable force at Sandwich in Kent on 22 May.[22]

Torn between facing his enemy on the route to London or concentrating on his defences, John pulled back to Winchester. Accompanied by des Roches, there he entertained Guala for the first time, allowing Louis to take Rochester before heading for London. There, he obtained the loyalty of John's half-brother, the earl of Salisbury – the same William Longespée who had brought John such good fortune at Damme. It has been alleged that the king seduced his wife after William was captured in the aftermath of Bouvines, which may have swayed the earl's thinking. Louis also achieved the submission of Hugh de Neville, another whose wife John had seduced. Thanks to a combination of affinity with the barons and the groundwork of the Marshal of France, the Londoners welcomed the potential claimant with open arms. On 2 June, Robert Fitzwalter personally oversaw the citizens swear the French prince fealty.[23]

With Langton suspended, the task of carrying out Louis's sentence of excommunication fell to Peter des Roches. This the bishop of Winchester did on 29 May, the day after Guala's arrival. The chance of Louis being crowned by an English prelate, at least for the time being out of the question, the bishop's actions had far less effect on the rebel prince's mission.[24]

Sensing God was on his side, Louis sought to drive home his advantage. He left London on 5 June and quickly conquered the castles at Reigate and Guildford as well as the keep of des Roches's Farnham. Siege was also laid to Odiham; however, thanks to the magnificence of its keeper Engelard de Cicogné it held out until 9 July. Learning the enemy was heading for Winchester, John, although his battle standard of a dragon had been raised, moved on to the West Country, settling at his favourite residence, Corfe Castle off the south Dorset Coast. Whether the heir to the throne, Prince Henry, was with him at this point is unclear. Better evidence concerns John's second son, Richard, born in 1209. The queen, meanwhile, was stationed further west in Exeter.[25]

In John's absence, control of Winchester was entrusted to Savori de Mauléon. On Louis's approach, Savori's attempts to burn the suburbs to slow their pursuit saw the rising of the citizens to admit the new overlords. Finding no sign of the king, Louis took control of the city peacefully on learning of John's willingness to surrender it. The castle was handed over on 25 June, as was des Roches's Wolvesey.[26]

With Hampshire now under rebel control, Louis offered command of the county to the count de Nevers, Hervé IV of Donzy, who sought to take Windsor, under the guardianship of de Cicogné since the fall of Odiham.[27] As was so often the way, the surrender led to many defections, including ending the brief submission of de Lacy and five other barons. By August, most of the east of England had fallen into rebel hands, along with the Cinque Ports excluding Dover. Hearing of the fall of Winchester, Alexander II of Scotland ventured south to pay homage to Louis, who agreed in return to honour the concession of Northumberland, Westmorland and Cumberland.[28]

Parallel to Louis's success in the south, the baronial alliance proceeded north with significant effect. In Yorkshire, John's past gains were being steadily undone. In Cumbria, Carlisle surrendered to the Scottish king in

August. Following the lead of their southern counterparts, the northerners pledged fealty to Louis in September. Furious at recent developments, John sought a counter strike, reinforcing the garrison at Lincoln on the way, which was currently under siege. Once more, he took petty revenge on areas that had earlier opposed him.[29]

It was here, fate prevailed, and fifty years of poor diet and hedonistic living finally caught up with him. On 9 October, John suffered a severe bout of dysentery and was still to fully recover on reaching Swineshead Abbey a few days later. Worse fortune preceded his arrival. Taking a shortcut to Lincolnshire across the Wash at low tide, catastrophe struck. If the evocative descriptions of Roger of Wendover are to be believed, while Louis encountered ongoing frustrations in his siege of Dover Castle, John had been committing terrible ravages in Suffolk and Norfolk, with a large force. After being well received in the town of Lynn, he encountered problems heading north. In crossing the River Wellester, he lost all of his carts, wagons and baggage horses, as well as large amounts of money, vessels, and what Wendover described as 'everything which he had a particular regard for'. Speculation has long claimed at least some of the crown jewels were also lost.

Precisely what occurred that fateful day has long been a matter of discussion. Claims by Wendover that 'the land opened in the middle of the water and caused whirlpools which sucked in everything, as well as men and horses, so that no one escaped to tell the king of the misfortune', would appear to stretch a point. Far more credible is his later claim that John narrowly escaped with his army and made his way to Swineshead only to be 'seized with violent fever and became ill'. Equally believable is his diagnosis of John's condition, that 'his sickness was increased by his pernicious gluttony, for that night he surfeited himself with peaches and drinking new cider, which greatly increased and aggravated the fever in him', which fits well with his known personality and the recordings of other chroniclers. Striking a chord are the words of Ralph of Coggeshall who tells, 'he lost on these travels, at the Wellstream, his portable chapel with his relics, and some of his packhorses with many household supplies. And many members of his entourage were submerged in the waters of the sea and sucked into the quicksand because they had set out foolishly and in haste before the tide had receded.'[30]

Regardless of the exact circumstances, a significant portion of his baggage train, accumulated from the spoils of ransacked castles recovered from the barons, does appear to have been lost beneath the waves. Whether Wendover was correct that the setback was detrimental to John's health, one can only speculate. The same is true of the legend that he was poisoned. On 14 October the king wrote to the new pope, Honorius III, sound in the knowledge death was nigh. Placing the future of the kingdom, including that of his children, into papal hands, he left Swineshead for Sleaford and was in great pain by the time he reached Newark. He died on the night of the 18th and was formally pronounced dead on the morning of the 19th.[31]

So passed one of the most controversial figures who would ever sit on the throne of England. It was written by the anonymous Barnwell annalist that John was a 'great prince, but seldom a happy one. Like Marius, he experienced the ups and downs of fortune. He was munificent and liberal to outsiders but a plunderer of his own people, trusting strangers rather than his subjects, wherefore he was eventually deserted by his own men and, in the end, little mourned.'[32]

Other accounts mirrored the chronicler's views. A footnote in Wendover comments,

> he caused many disturbances and entered on many useless labours in the world, and at length departed this life in great agony of mind, possessed of no territory, yea not even being his own master. It is, however, to be confidently hoped that some good works, which he performed in this life, may plead in his favour at the tribunal of Jesus Christ; for he founded a monastery of the Cistercian order at Beaulieu, and, when dying, gave to the monastery of Croxton land worth ten pounds.[33]

While Wendover offered hope, an inscription penned in Latin for his epitaph offered a more portentous view:

> *Hoc in sarcophago sepelitur regis imago,*
> *Qui moriens multum sedavit in orbe tumultum.*
> *Hunc mala post mortem timor est ne fata sequantur.*
> *Qui legis hæc, metuens dum cernis te moriturum,*
> *Discute quid rerum pariat tibi meta dierum.*

An English version is subject to interpretation. One possible translation is:

> This tomb carries the likeness of a king,
> Whose death has quietened much of the world's chaos.
> It is to be feared that an ill fate awaits him after death.
> You who are reading this, fearing your own death when you
>   look upon it,
> Examine the lesson brought forth to you.

Looking back a few years later, the annalist of Waverley offered a finely balanced view of the beginning of the war. Correct the chronicler was that many of the issues that John was forced to deal with throughout his reign – matters which led to the war – required a certain degree of finger-pointing at Henry II and Richard, he was equally right that many of the barons had possessed personal grievances against John. 'For some', to quote the annalist directly, 'he had disinherited without judgement of their peers; some he had condemned to a cruel death; of others he had violated their wives and daughters; and so instead of law there was tyrannical will.'[34]

Other accounts would be far less forgiving. Undoubtedly the most damning indictment Wendover also recorded. Not the product of the chronicler's hand but instead the sharing of a renown profanity, whose author was in no doubt of the king's fate: 'With John's foul deeds, England's whole realm is stinking, / As doth hell, too, wherein he now is sinking.'[35]

In such ways, it seems Bernard of Clairvaux's prophecy of the Plantagenets may have been right after all: 'From the Devil they came and to the Devil they will return.'[36]

Chapter 4

1146–1216
The 'Greatest Knight'

Whether condemned to hell or not, a combination of his reeling from such significant losses as he attempted a safe passage across the tidal estuary from Norfolk into Lincolnshire and his subsequent gluttony ensured John's dysentery-blighted condition rapidly worsened. He had survived the war, but not time. With his demise, we are presented a peculiar irony. Both in life and travel, it rarely pays to take short cuts.

At the time of John's death, more than half of the country had forsaken him, including the city of London who had already proclaimed Louis as their king. To the north and west, Scotland and Wales had him surrounded; on the Continent, he had lost Normandy, Brittany, Maine and Touraine. Besides Ireland, only Gascony, parts of Poitou and Anjou now remained of the family estates – a fraction of what Henry II and Eleanor of Aquitaine had together amassed. If the rebels' march continued unchecked, it was only a matter of time before the whole of England and what remained of the empire was lost entirely.

Never had the future looked bleaker for the Plantagenet dynasty.

Emotionally scarred by a crippling political crisis and surrounded by an ever-strengthening enemy, John's last will lacked the eloquence and garrulousness of many royal equivalents. Evidence no doubt of his failing limbs, if not failing mind, it also offers an insight into the urgency with which decisions were dictated. Besides the usual formalities of affirming the eldest son – in this case, Prince Henry – as the heir to the throne and demanding the allegiance of the kingdom be pledged to him, letters were also written and marked with his own seal to be delivered to the sheriffs and castellans to make this known. The future of the realm settled, at least on paper, on hearing his confession, the abbot of Croxton underwent one final formality. Before the new king was crowned, the old one would need to be buried.[1]

John's long time intention had been to be interred at Beaulieu Abbey. He had founded the Cistercian abbey there no later than 1204 and, despite his well-known feuds with the order, appears to have been highly fond of the place. Getting there, however, was problematic. Since the surrender of Winchester, the Louis-led baronial coalition controlled most of the south. Cut off from all of his English counsellors and surrounded only by foreign mercenaries, John instead made provision for his body to be moved from Newark to Worcester Cathedral.[2]

The choice was a sensible one. Though the city had briefly embraced the rebel cause before being captured by Ranulf, Earl of Chester and the Norman loyalist Falkes de Breauté, Worcester had many connections with John. In 1158, his father had attended a crown-wearing event there, culminating in Henry placing the crown on the cathedral altar, declaring his wish not to be crowned again.[3] A more significant reason still was the legend of its former bishop, St Wulfstan, who John held in high regard. As Richard the Lionheart had known only too well, few things were capable of capturing people's hearts and minds than legendary figures. From the stories of the apostles and later martyrs to the Arthurian romances, the previous century had seen the cult of saints reach new heights. It is perhaps not without significance that John had been king at the time the eleventh-century cleric was canonised.[4]

Born around 1008, Wulfstan served as bishop of Worcester from 1062 – thus making him the final pre-conquest bishop in England – until his death in 1095. A hagiography of Wulfstan – biography of a saint – was composed in English shortly afterwards by his former chancellor, following which a Latin version was penned by the chronicler William of Malmesbury. In 1201, two years before his canonisation, the annals of Waverley wrote glowingly of Wulfstan's miracles, the most significant of which was his apparent divine intervention in the curing of the daughter of Harold Godwinson.[5] In 1212, an apparent miracle of St Wulstan had inspired the building of a priory church in Ireland. While in the eyes of the annalist of Burton, the legend concerning Wulfstan belonged more to the famously religious Edward the Confessor, whereas John had been more like William the Conqueror – painted by the chronicler under the conqueror's less flattering name, William the Bastard – John's deathbed decisions were both penitent and remorseful. With his dying breaths, the king made known to those present, 'to God and St Wolstan I commend my body and soul'.[6]

With this, in motion the wheels were set. Partly as a consequence of John's portliness, the abbot of Croxton had his body opened and his insides removed, after which they were salted and interred under the abbot's gaze at his abbey. Of the king himself, what remained was dressed in royal robes and brought to Worcester Cathedral so that he be interred between the tombs of St Wulfstan and another local cleric St Oswald, the tenth-century archbishop of York. Of the ceremony, little is known, only that he was 'honourably buried in the cathedral church by the bishop of that place'. Most likely the service was a relatively quiet and sombre affair as opposed to a grand ceremony of state. Rather than desert the royalist cause, those who had remained close to John took it upon themselves to carry out this final request, as well as call upon the loyal barons to meet them in Worcester. After completing what could have been a treacherous journey, all gathered together as the king was lowered into his resting place in the Norman choir. In addition to the bishop of Worcester overseeing the ceremony, it seems likely the legate also played some role in the proceedings.[7]

Three months before John's death, Pope Innocent had also succumbed to the rigours of mortality. Elected either late 1197 or early 1198 and consecrated in January, Innocent had gone on to become one of the most influential popes in history. A figure capable of achieving seemingly unquestionable spiritual and temporal supremacy over the kings of Europe, his widespread reforms would go on to have a notable effect on Western canon law, most notably the Fourth Lateran Council of 1215. It was a direct consequence of John's fear of Innocent, not least that the pope's influence could encourage a French invasion, that saw his submission in May 1213. Ironically, as history would later recall, although it had proven a success in putting an end to any threat of Philip ruling England, it was this decision as much as anything that damaged John's political credibility the most.[8]

Taking Innocent's place on the throne of Peter was one Cencio Savelli, known henceforth as Honorius III. Among his first acts, the new pope wrote to Guala on 25 July 1216 to confirm that he should stay on as legate. That there was any short-term expectation in his highlighting of the importance of a Christian holy land, and John's being required to contribute, is unlikely. Honorius did, however, use the ongoing war as an opportunity to fill the vacant see at Hereford: another for which John had earlier refused the ascent of the elected candidate. Better news at the time had come with commands to the archbishop of Bordeaux, the most vital city in Gascony, to provide support against the rebels, not that it did him much good in the end.[9]

With the old king laid to rest, decisions now needed to be made regarding the accession of the new. Of some encouragement to the royals, as John lay dying, letters had made their way to Newark courtesy of the messengers of some forty rebel barons, indicating a desire to make peace. As fate would have it, John's worsening fever put paid to any possibility of dealing with such matters personally. Yet his death would not end the possibility of bringing the prodigal sons back onside. Indeed, in certain quarters, the tyrant's death was seen as a boon to the royalist cause.[10]

Far more clear at this point, due to the new king's tender age and geographical distance from John's key supporters, governance of the kingdom could not lie in the hands of the new monarch alone. Only too aware of this, the legate called a meeting on which many other essential matters would rest. Alongside Guala, of those present, one in particular was revered for his distinction and qualities of leadership. Subject of the renowned biography, *L'Historie de Guillaume le Marechal* that would impress and excite European audiences less than a decade later and celebrated by many contemporaries as the greatest of the magnates, in a career spanning more than fifty years this man had achieved the unique accolade of having served four different kings.

He was the influential earl of Pembroke, William Marshal.

Born in 1147, William was the fourth son of a minor lord named John Marshal. The family name is itself indicative of his ancestry: deriving from the office of marshal of the royal household. Exactly which of William's ancestors had been hereditary royal master marshal to the king is now unclear, only that it appears to date back to no later than the reign of Henry I, (1100–35).[11]

On the accession of Stephen of Blois on Henry I's death, John had supported Stephen, only to change sides in 1139 on the rise of Matilda – wife of Geoffrey of Anjou. This act of disloyalty did not go unnoticed by Stephen. Nor would the repercussions be without consequence to the young William's future. On laying siege to John Marshal's Newbury Castle in 1152, Stephen took the 5-year-old William as a hostage to ensure John honoured his vow to surrender it. Using his son's captivity as an opportunity to strengthen the garrison, when the king threatened to execute the innocent child if the surrender didn't occur, John responded by gesturing to his genitals and bragged that he could father more children. Fortunately for the young captive, Stephen seemed to take something of a shine to him and decided not to follow through on his earlier warning.[12]

Typical of the period, little else is known of William's childhood. A minor son of a minor nobleman, unlikely to inherit anything of value, he set off to France in his teenage years in a bid 'to win an honourable reputation'. By 1160, aged around 13, he began training as a knight at the household of William de Tancarville in Normandy and was knighted in 1166. Less than a year later occurred something many previous commentators have deemed a moment of providence. William participated in his first tournament.[13]

Tournaments were often viewed with considerable scepticism in the twelfth century. Splendid exhibitions of strength, talent and courage at their best, they also served as sources of uprising or spontaneous avenues for dissent at their worst. At heart, they were the stage of the mock battle: the place where an upcoming knight learned the art of warfare. Thanks in large part to the historical novel and the movie theatre, one often imagines scenes of mortal combat taking place before a baying crowd. Yet in reality, the competitors were required to do battle with blunt weapons. Similarly, the famous picture of such gatherings taking place inside a crowded amphitheatre was relatively rare; instead, the competition was often spread out across the countryside, usually for miles at a time. For the young swashbuckler with nothing to lose and everything to gain, the chance to take on a gallant knight and take them hostage was an ideal way to make his fortune; just as the opposite could be true of the wealthy knight. Equally important, it was in such arenas the successful competitor could catch the eye of a potential lord or master. As history would show, this would be particularly true of the previously unknown William Marshal.[14]

After enjoying a successful start on the tournament scene, Marshal returned to England around 1167, a couple of years following his father's death, and sought out his uncle, Earl Patrick of Salisbury. In late 1167, Marshal was recorded among Patrick's number when the earl accompanied Henry II to Aquitaine. A year later, having now arrived, William was noted as a guard of Eleanor of Aquitaine's royal cortege. Sadly for all concerned, problems arose when unruly Lusignans attacked the group, killing his uncle. Faring only marginally better, Marshal suffered a spear through his thigh before being strapped to an ass and forced to endure several weeks in captivity. Fortunately, Marshal's bravery made something of a mark on Eleanor, who paid his ransom and formally took him into her service.[15]

By 1170, the impressive young knight was well on his way to stardom. Highly regarded in the queen's eyes, he held a prominent position in Eleanor's party when she returned to England that summer for Henry the Young's coronation as joint king. A combination of his newfound fame, his prowess as a marshal, wit and honesty inspired Henry II to appoint him tutor to the young king later that year. For the next three years, William enjoyed the higher echelons of courtly life, until the political landscape turned on its head when the young king launched his ill-fated rebellion in 1173. William's valour in tournaments undoubtedly made a profound impression on the young Henry. Despite remaining a close guide of the young king throughout the rebellion, it is less clear whether Marshal approved of it.[16]

Defeated, humbled and now virtually unemployed as a consequence of his master's failure, William returned to the life he knew best: the European tournament circuit. By 1179 there is evidence that he had been permitted to compete under his own banner, as illustrated when he participated in a great tournament at Lagny-sur-Mayne. All the while, the bond between William and the young king continued to grow as together they took on the Continent's competitors. If William's famous biography is accurate, as a competitor and jouster, he had few equals and throughout his career conquered over 500 knights in tournaments.[17]

In 1182, occurred his only scandal. Still unmarried, the ever devout Marshal was accused of having an affair with Henry the Young's queen, Margaret of France. Whether such accusations were genuine or mischievous slander remains unclear. The chroniclers of the time dismissed the charge. His apologists, too, have long pointed the finger at five of Henry's men for enviously plotting his downfall. Though Henry used the opportunity to push for a divorce, it seems likely the queen's barrenness was the more significant consideration behind his thinking.

Sadly for all concerned, the accusation, nevertheless, caused a strain on their relationship. At the final tournament they attended together, the pair's estrangement had become evident, leading to Marshal's voluntary exile. Reconciliation, alas, was achieved before the young king was struck down by dysentery in 1183. Whether moved by remorse or brotherly love, in honour of the dying man's wish, Marshal agreed to take on Henry's crusader vow. He was not seen again in France until the spring of 1186.[18]

How William performed in the Holy Land is surprisingly absent from *L'Historie de Guillaume le Marechal*. If clues can be gleaned from the history of the time, not to mention his previous record on the tournament scene and the fact that he was absent for more than two years, surviving without a serious injury, it seems likely he acquitted himself well. Low on funds on leaving the Holy Land, the returning knight presented himself before Henry II during the king's visit to Normandy. Once again impressed by his late son's favourite, Henry was happy to overlook William's role in the rebellion of twelve years earlier – or at the very least was satisfied by William's objections to the fool's errand – and reappointed him to the royal household. So much had Marshal's lot improved, as the king's health declined he was offered the hand of Isabel of Clare, the wealthy teenage daughter of Earl Richard Strongbow of Striguil. After taking up his sword for the ageing king, Marshal found further fame by unhorsing the rebellious Richard the Lionheart when father and son engaged in battle outside Le Mans in 1189. On Henry II's death, William participated in carrying the late king's body to Fontevraud Abbey.[19]

With the older king laid to rest, William's fate again rested in the hands of a would-be usurper. That William privately feared retribution for his recent embarrassing of the Lionheart at Le Mans seems likely, yet fortunately for all concerned, such fears were soon put to rest. On being summoned by Richard, the pair quickly came to terms, following which the new king confirmed William's betrothal to Isabel before sending him back to England to deliver a message to Eleanor. In July of that year, Marshal wed Isabel in London, marking the beginning of a successful union that would in time bear ten children, including five sons. On Richard's coronation, further evidence that past feuds were forgotten were to be found in the knowledge that Marshal was given the honour of carrying the royal sceptre. Later that year, Richard also confirmed large parts of Isabel's birthright.[20]

Throughout his reign, one pressing issue would continue to occupy Richard's mind: the Holy Land. Unlike in 1183, William appears to have had no desire to return to Jerusalem; if he had, the king had no desire to take him. Accepting his biography at face value, William was content from his earlier crusade, 'no matter what others may say'. When Richard embarked on his own mission, the regency of the realm was placed in the hands of the much-loathed bishop of Ely, William de Longchamp, with Queen Eleanor charged with administering the wider empire. To support them both, William was appointed a co-justiciar. He would serve as an associate justiciar throughout Richard's reign.[21]

Marshal seems to have enjoyed his new career. Not only was he actively involved in day-to-day government, but following the death of his father-in-law, he was also invested as lord of Striguil – modern-day Chepstow. Such promotions appear all the more startling when placed in the context of his humble beginnings. Having started with nothing, his tale is one of rags to riches, albeit also illustrative of the chaos that had engulfed England during that time. For the first time in his career, William was a wealthy man. Nor would it be long before that wealth grew considerably. Of particular significance, his claim to the de Clare estates, confirmed *ipso facto* as a result of his marriage, included Usk and Gloucester.[22]

It has been speculated that Richard's enriching of William had been part of a broader strategy to ensure the still lacking in land John remained in check. If that were the case, this would soon backfire. Reluctant to burn bridges with the prince, now styled Count of Mortain – another famous county of France – William acknowledged John as lord of Ireland and, come 1191, John had forced Longchamp into exile. Whether Marshal approved of John's actions is unclear. What is less uncertain is that a series of councils, called by Eleanor with William in attendance, were successful in persuading John against allying himself with the king of France and attempting an invasion in Richard's absence.[23]

When John did finally commence scheming following Richard's capture in 1193, Marshal displayed his usual loyalty to the crown. On the death of his older brother – named John in honour of his father – he formally inherited the title of royal master-marshal, an event that more or less coincided with Richard's return from Austria. In 1194 he joined Richard in setting sail for Normandy where he took up his sword for the Lionheart. Just as with Henry II and Henry the Young King, a close bond blossomed between the pair. A short time later, William was appointed envoy to the court of Baldwin IX of Flanders in a bid to win his support against Philip II. In 1197, he excelled himself in the assault on the castle of Milly-sur-Thérain. When Richard received his mortal wound in 1199, one of his final acts was to entrust William with control of Rouen.[24]

On learning of Richard's passing at Rouen Priory on 10 April 1199, Marshal wasted little time in rousing Hubert Walter, the archbishop of Canterbury, before requesting of his loyal comrade, John of Earley, to return to England to inform the justiciar, Geoffrey fitz Peter.[25] News of Richard's death was a dark day for England. By no means as beloved by his English subjects as those of Normandy, a vacant throne was rarely a good thing. In contrast to the later commentary of John that hell had become 'fouler' on his arrival, Richard's achievements, at least on the Continent, were mostly celebrated. As was remarked by Roger of Howden, who followed Richard on crusade and chronicled much of his life, 'men might conquer cities ... death took men'.[26]

For the fourth time in his already distinguished career, William now had a decision to make regarding to whom he would pledge his allegiance. Faced with a straight choice of backing John or Arthur, William decided on the former. The official reason was that Marshal favoured John due to Arthur having no connections to the Anglo-Norman barons; whether his motivation was also swayed by John's presence in Leinster or his loyalty to Eleanor, one can only speculate.[27] Regardless of his exact thinking, just as would be the case with the young Henry III in years to come, William's decision would not be without consequence. Having offered John fealty, Marshal and the archbishop were sent by John back to England to obtain likewise of the English nobles. The decision was a good one: under Marshal's influence, many other members of the nobility, including the similarly distinguished Ranulf, Earl of Chester, swiftly obliged. Almost unthinkable fifteen years earlier, the prince who had famously lacked land was granted a clear path to the throne.[28]

As soon as Richard was interred alongside his father in the abbey church of Fontevraud, preparations were made for John to return home. Having returned to Normandy, Marshal was present with John on 25 May 1199 to accompany the new king as he set sail from Dieppe. In honour of their recent work, Marshal and Geoffrey fitz Peter were invested with their previously promised earldoms – Pembroke and Essex, respectively – and the man responsible for crowning the king, Archbishop Hubert, made chancellor. Adding to the recent gift of Pembrokeshire, in 1200 William formally took control of the de Clare lands in Wales of which Henry II had earlier deprived his father in law. Around that time, he also claimed Cardigan and Cilgerran.[29]

Good early relations with John would be tested as familiar challenges soon ensued. Chief among them was John's decision to wed Lusignan's fiancé. Though John had been successful in freeing Queen Eleanor from Mirebeau, the consequence of which eventually culminated in Arthur's disappearance, a plan to combat the king of France's movements ended with humiliating retreat. With Normandy on the brink, Marshal was reputedly sent to parley with Philip; if he did, the objective was fruitless. On 3 December 1203, John and Marshal returned to England, five months before Eleanor died at the impressive age of 78.[30]

Any first meeting having already proved ineffective, John sent his trusted earl on a second diplomatic mission to Philip's court. For Marshal, peace discussions had an added complication. Like many of Norman heritage, the Marshal family owned estates on both sides of the Channel. As part of an individual package, terms were agreed for Marshal to retain his Normandy holdings in return for instant surrender, 500 silver marks and homage to be paid to Philip within a year. Although the conflict of interests was apparent, such agreements were by no means without precedent. Better yet, John appears to have given William his blessing for dual allegiance. When Marshal returned to France to carry out the previously agreed submission, things reached something of an impasse when Philip requested further acknowledgement of fealty: precisely that of liege-lord that side of the sea. Reluctantly agreeing, William was granted the retention of Longueville only to discover news of the terms had already reached a furious John.[31]

Further problems arose when John prepared his long-awaited assault on Poitou. Still widely regarded as the best knight in the land, John's directions included a command for William to follow him to Aquitaine, to which Marshal protested due to the conflict of interest over the Norman lands. Intriguingly, on being labelled a traitor, Marshal demanded he be offered the chance to defend himself in a trial by combat. Be it out of respect for the man or fear that the 'judgement of God' could never go against him, no one accepted the chance of standing as his opponent. A short time later, in a scene that must have brought back upsetting memories of his childhood, John requested that his eldest son, William Marshal the younger, now 15, enter his custody. Reluctantly complying, Marshal was gradually eased out of court and withdrew to Striguil.[32]

Such setbacks aside, since marrying Isabel, William's gathering of the Pembrokeshire estates had continued to bring him considerable benefits. Successful in driving the Welsh prince Maelgwn ap Rhys from the district of Emlyn in 1204 – following which the marriage of Llywelyn ap Iorwerth to John's illegitimate daughter Joan in 1205 convinced the other Welsh rulers to submit to John – of even more significant advantage to William was that Pembrokeshire also served as a stepping-stone to Ireland. In 1207, preparation to make such a voyage came unstuck following John's decision to backtrack. Marshal's decision to make the trip anyway would lose him the castles of Carmarthen, Cardigan, Gloucester, St Briavels as well as the Forest of Dean.[33]

At some point during the autumn, Marshal called an assembly at Kilkenny in which he attempted to press his pregnant wife's birthright to Leinster. When William returned to Wales and subsequently arrived at the royal palace of Woodstock in November, John unleashed what was soon revealed to be a devious trap. Aware of recent happenings in Ireland, John had entered illicit negotiations to buy William's men off with land grants of their own. When William's request to return to Leinster was denied, Marshal was forced to join the royal train, during which he endured the frosty treatment of the entire entourage in the knowledge his wife's birthright had been lost to the justiciar of Ireland, Meiler FitzHenry. Adding insult to injury, and in a shocking illustration of John's fouler qualities, in January 1208 the king mockingly told William that his wife's present location of Kilkenny was being besieged and that at least twenty people had been killed, including two of his key supporters.

Fortunately for William, what he heard was wholly untrue. Alliance with the forces of Hugh de Lacy ensured Kilkenny not only held out resolutely but that the justiciar and a number of his men had been successfully captured. Hearing the news no later than March, on being brought before John at an audience in Bristol, an overjoyed Marshal feigned ignorance. Once again, such an act of humility would be of profound importance. By the end of that month, reconciliation was at hand, leading to the Irish lands, including Offaly, being returned, albeit with diminished power. Far more despairingly, his second son, Richard, was left little option but to also enter royal care. On returning to Leinster, William was reunited with Isabel at Kilkenny, most likely with a new babe in arms. It is further testament to William's calmness and restraint that the possibility of retribution against the guilty parties gave way to peace talks. The worst hit was FitzHenry who agreed all lands would pass over to Marshal on his death as well as hostages provided. Consequently, his role as justiciar of Ireland was also terminated.[34]

Unlike his forebears, Ireland was of particular importance to John. Granted to him by his father in 1185, the island had provided him both patronage and revenue.[35] In 1210, the king was back on the Emerald Isle, accompanied by a significant force with the intention of re-establishing some degree of control following the forced exile of Marshal's contemporary, William de Braose. Exactly why John and de Braose fell out remains a mystery. The king's citing of unpaid debts may have been a contributing factor, but that alone fails to explain why John practically went to war with the previously loyal nobleman. Having seized his estates in Devon and Sussex, as well as sent an invasion force to his property in Wales, John was unable to prevent de Braose from making the crossing to Ireland. Nor did he stop him from allying himself with Llywelyn when back in Wales and fleeing in the guise of a beggar. Around this time, the ghost of Arthur again came back to haunt John in being faced with the knowledge de Braose's wife, Maud, had been adamant that John had been personally responsible for the prince's murder. What happened next would be highly relevant in terms of the following years. Popular among elements of the baronage, John's capture of Maud and her son in Scotland and his subsequent imprisonment of them at Windsor saw the tide further turn against him. On being moved to Corfe Castle, both disappear from history. Their lives seemingly lost in the darkness of the dungeons.[36]

Ever the diplomat, on the matter of de Braose, Marshal adopted a neutral stance. After showing John the typical nobleman's hospitality, in August 1210, William was summoned to Dublin and forced to account for his own earlier harbouring of de Braose. Charged with improper conduct, William again demanded his honour be defended in trial by combat, leading to another uncontested victory. To subdue John's temper, he was nevertheless obliged to submit Dunamase Castle as well as relinquish a number of his best knights to the crown.[37]

Demeaned for the umpteenth time, Marshal's unequivocal loyalty to John would seem nothing short of remarkable. This would appear all the more astounding when considering his own ability to instil loyalty in others and his practically unrivalled levels of competence would have made him a major force in the event of rebellion. Fortunately for John, such obedience would be indispensable in the intrigue that followed. With England placed under interdict and John himself excommunicated, the allegiance of John's followers was relinquished in the eyes of the papacy. As history later recalled, the idea of Capetian overthrow no longer seemed so far-fetched. After establishing an army for the intention of sailing to France in 1212, plans were put on hold following news of Welsh insurrection and rumour of the de Vesci/Fitzwalter conspiracy.

Probably aware that John privately suspected every magnate in the kingdom, including himself, of complicity, William again openly displayed his loyalty by convincing twenty-six Anglo-Irish barons to pledge similar allegiance. Writing to John, William not only confirmed the Emerald Isle remained in safe hands but recommended John make peace with the pope, to which John spoke of his 'eternal gratitude'. Despite the offer to return to England, John requested the earl remain in Ireland, which suited William as it remained free of interdict. Reference was also made to William the younger, who had excelled himself in John's care. That concerns for his children influenced William's actions must be highly probable. It was with great relief that by the following year, both William the younger and Richard had left the king's custody, the former finding a home under the stewardship of William's great ally John of Earley.[38]

William's conciliatory tone had once again struck a chord. Whether influenced by hopes of augmenting his position against the Welsh or a genuine reward for William's loyalty, John strengthened Marshal's hand with the return of some of his lost lands, including Cardigan. He was also granted Haverford as well as command of Carmarthen and the Gower Peninsula, with other honours bestowed upon his kin. As the threat of a French invasion deepened, Marshal was finally recalled from Ireland in April 1213, arriving with a sizeable force on the Kent coast. A month later, on 15 May, William was present when John submitted England to the papacy. Having already agreed to become a Templar on his death, it is quite possible that Marshal was keenly involved in the events that followed. Further to being present inside the Templar house to witness the signing of the charter, he also appointed a Templar as his almoner.

Improved fortune at sea saw the English strike the French navy at Damme, during which William remained on watch for Welsh insurrection. For John, the excellent outcome at Damme proved only to be temporary as defeat at Bouvines in September ensured the beginning of the end. The following year, William was at the heart of John's negotiations with his barons, culminating in events at Runnymede. During this time, Marshal is recorded as having worked closely with Langton: the pope's choice as archbishop but no friend of John.[39]

Incredible though it may appear, throughout the spats and backstabbing, just as he had been to Eleanor, Henry the Young King, Henry II and Richard, William remained arguably John's most reliable ally. Along with des Roches, the closest thing he had to a true friend. On the king's deathbed, John made it known his regret over his earlier treatment of Marshal and his apology for it, stating: 'He has always served me loyally; in his loyalty, above that of any other man, I put my trust.'[40]

Whether motivated by a dying man's guilt or concern for his young heir, John entrusted his son to the custody of the Earl Marshal. Hearing the news, William rode north from Gloucester and oversaw the king's burial at Worcester. Having already served four kings, the greatest knight now faced what was arguably his toughest challenge yet with a fifth.[41]

Chapter 5

1216
The Hollow Chaplet

28 October was a revered date in the medieval Christian calendar. The previous day marked the vigil of Saints Simon and Jude, better known as Simon the Zealot and Jude Thaddeus. Besides being listed in the New Testament as apostles, little is known of them. According to early legend they set out to preach the gospels in Mesopotamia and Persia, enduring martyrdom for their faith. Regarded by the Catholic Church as the son of Mary, the wife of Cleophas, mentioned in the gospels as having stood alongside the Virgin Mary at Christ's feet during the crucifixion, Jude was the brother of St James the Lesser, who is believed to have been a relative of Jesus. Aside from his association with Jude, far less is known of Simon; it is probably for this reason they are celebrated together. Following the usual pattern in the Christian calendar, the day after their vigil was designated their feast day.

In 1216, the 28th fell on a Friday. All across Europe, communities came together in celebration, festivities ranging from processions to the preparation of special dishes, prior to which prayers would be offered up to the saints in question. Work was forbidden on those days, just as it was on the Sabbath. Also illegal was the holding of fayres or judicial hearings. A battle on a feast day was considered a particularly bad omen. Some regions banned any form of travel. In the city of Gloucester, proceedings were mainly treated as usual, yet with one notable addition.

It was on this day a new king of England was crowned.[1]

Henry III was just 9 years old when he ascended to the throne. The first minor to rule since the Norman Conquest, he was the first child king of England after the Saxon Æthelred the Unready had been crowned king of the English in 968 at the age of 12. No other king has been crowned at Gloucester either before or after that date. An ancient royal borough, in past years the city had become renown for the tradition in which the Norman kings would visit once a year and process through the streets wearing the crown.[2]

On this occasion, the decision to travel there was one of necessity. Henry had come to the throne suddenly and at a time when the circumstances of war were still conspiring against the royalists. Strong reinforcements of French troops had reportedly landed in the east of England around mid-October. In the north, Alexander II of Scotland had consolidated his position in the three northern counties; in the south and east of Wales, Llywelyn remained on the rampage. Nineteen out of the twenty-seven greatest barons supported Louis; the same was true of ninety-seven baronies as opposed to thirty-six, who remained royal. Cities as far apart as Winchester, London, Lincoln and Carlisle were now in rebel hands; the same was true of all of the Cinque Ports apart from Dover. For two-thirds of the country, the dauphin of France was now their rightful king.[3]

Yet for all the rebels' successes, there was one crucial bridge Louis was yet to cross. Warm welcomes from the people of London, followed by his being proclaimed king by the errant Robert Fitzwalter, had failed to solve the problem of fixing an official coronation. Worse still, the prince's excommunication and the pope's continuous warnings against the English clergy had left Louis with no prelate willing to crown him.[4]

The same was not true of John's heir. Born 1 October 1207, Prince Henry was the first of John's offspring with Isabella. Indeed, the first of the late king's legitimate issue with either wife. The same had not been true of his illegitimate children. John's promiscuity outside of the marriage bed, at least during his first union, was well known. His affairs had resulted in five children, two of whom he fathered with married noblewomen. Within the marriage bed, on the other hand, pregnancy and issue had been far from instant. After failing to father a legitimate heir with Isabella of Gloucester, better luck followed seven years into the second marriage, at which time the king had passed 40.[5]

Why it took so long for John to father a legitimate son can be put down to a combination of factors. His fruitfulness outside of the marriage bed during Richard's reign is possibly indicative of a lack of interest in his half-second cousin and first wife; alternatively, the fault may have lain with Isabella of Gloucester's ability to conceive. Unquestionably, the younger Isabella was different in many ways to his first wife, not least her ability to arouse the king's attention. If the anecdotes of Roger of Wendover are correct, when the king of France's armies invaded Normandy in 1203, John stayed at Rouen with his young queen, acting as though he was under a hex. Similarly, the author of the French work, *Histoire des ducs de Normandie* described John's behaviour at the time as acting 'as though he did not care, and devoted himself to the pleasures of hunting, falconry and to the queen whom he greatly loved'.[6]

Exactly how old Isabella was at the time of the marriage is a point of contention. Estimations of her age suggest anywhere between 8 and 15, which almost certainly explains why Henry took so long to arrive. The same is true of Lusignan's lack of urgency in cementing their planned union. More disturbingly, and what undoubtedly ranks among the more terrible examples of John's more vulgar traits, their marriage on 24 August 1200 appears to have been immediately consummated.

Appropriately for a future great king, Henry was born at Winchester Castle: an impressive Norman structure that survived largely unscathed until the English Civil War. The city itself dates back to the Iron Age and following the Roman invasion it had grown into the fifth largest settlement in England, known at the time as Venta Belgarum. After the erection of its first cathedral in the seventh century, the expanding city had replaced Dorchester-on-Thames as the capital of Wessex, and by the reign of King Egbert was arguably the most important city in England.[7]

Famous in the modern day for its magnificent cathedral and attractive centre, even for the young prince memories of the past would have surrounded him on every corner. No less than four of the Saxon martyrs were buried inside St Swithun's, the stories of which had a profound influence on him. In his later years, the king is often characterised for his lifelong devotion to St Edward the Confessor, which in turn inspired his rebuilding of Westminster Abbey.

Of the city the young man knew, the locals had Alfred the Great to thank. Famed for his exploits in battle, Alfred had overseen the new street plans, which replaced the original Roman outline that had been damaged when the city was the victim of a Viking sacking in 860. We can be confident from the clues provided throughout his life that Winchester meant a lot to Henry. Baptised in the historic font that still occupies the gothic niches of the old cathedral, it was in his home city he received much of his education and where he enjoyed many Christmases. The great hall, the one part of the castle that survived the onslaught from

Cromwell's Roundheads, dates from 1222–35 and was personally added under Henry's guidance.[8]

As is sadly so often true of the medieval world, little is known of Henry's childhood. Much of the time in his formative years appear to have taken place away from court, often in the south of England. Strong ties with his mother were critical throughout the years of unrest, becoming even more so during the First Barons' War. In addition to his mother, his progress would have been monitored by a select few, notably the trusted eye of a wet nurse named 'Helen of Winchester' with whom he enjoyed a close bond. It is noted in the pipe rolls that Henry regularly gifted her firewood later in life. From 1212 onwards, this circle was widened to include the bishop of Winchester, Peter des Roches, who was tasked with providing the young prince with a formal education. Similar was true of Ralph of St Samson and Philip d'Aubigné concerning matters of the saddle and all things military.[9]

Based on the limited evidence available, relations between John and Henry were loving. Certainly, there is no indication of any ill-feeling on the prince's part. Contrary to that of Henry II, John did not live long enough to evoke any significant quarrel with any of his children, nor would his actions directly have inspired it. One of the chief reasons, of course, was their youth. In the years that followed the prince's birth, John went on to father him four full siblings: Richard, born 5 January 1209; Joan, born 22 July 1210; Isabella, born some time in 1214; and Eleanor after John's death in 1216. Like Henry, all four lived their early life in the south of England, shielded from the political turbulence. Awarding his children peaceful upbringings away from courtly life can perhaps be viewed as one of John's better decisions and undoubtedly something born of his own experience.[10]

As the eldest son of the late king and his queen, Henry would not be plagued by the same questions of legitimacy as had concerned his father and cousin Arthur. Further to the usual right of blood succession, John had granted official confirmation of Henry's right to rule back in 1209 when he demanded an oath of fealty be sworn to him at Marlborough.[11] In October 1212, John also had William Marshal swear a similar, more individual oath to the prince, a clear indication that rumours of conspiracy were starting to play on John's mind. Around that time, John is also noted to have placed Henry safely inside one of the royal castles to shield him from Llywelyn's rebellion. Despite the rising influence of Louis, it is evident that none present at Newark questioned John's renewal of this demand and all are recorded as having sworn Henry a renewed oath.[12]

Before he arrived at Gloucester, Henry had been kept for his protection at Devizes Castle, which had been placed under the control of the loyal justiciar, Hubert de Burgh. Unfortunately for the new king, Hubert was unavoidably absent attempting to defend Dover Castle from the ongoing siege. Exactly when Henry had been brought to Devizes is unclear. As John breathed his last at Newark, the queen and most of their children were in the south-west, most likely Corfe Castle.[13] Henry may have been present in Dorset before being taken alone to the West Country on hearing of the legate's intention to press ahead with the coronation. Traditionally a royal castle that, despite the justiciar's absence, was still in royalist hands, on William Marshal's orders Henry was collected from Devizes by Thomas of Samford, along with those who had cared for him. A few days later, on the vigil of Simon and Jude, Henry met Marshal on a plain outside Malmesbury, which was approximately midway between Devizes and Gloucester.[14]

Henry's performance here won him both great praise and affection. A magnificent young boy of clear potential and possessed of a stocky figure, a handsome face, golden hair and a kindly temperament, he was in little doubt of the gravity of the situation. Exhausted from the long trip, the young man was carried into Marshal's presence by his governor, Ralph de St Sanson, and, face to face for the first time, is recorded as having greeted Marshal with the eloquent opening, 'Welcome, sir. Truly, I entrust myself to God and to you, that for God's sake you may take care of me; and may the true God who takes care of all good things grant that you may so manage our business that your wardship of me may be prosperous.' To this, the loyal earl took the king's hand in his and swore that 'as I trust my soul to God, I will be in good fealty to you, and never forget you, so long as I have power to do anything'. It was remarked that none present could hold back the tears.[15]

The initial meeting concluded, questions turned to scheduling. On reaching Gloucester, debate among the lords as to whether commencement of proceedings should wait until the arrival of Ranulf, Earl of Chester – celebrated along with Marshal among the greatest of the nobles – was swiftly settled. Agreeing that delay could be of catastrophic consequence, all of the available bishops and barons gathered in St Peter's Abbey on the morning of the 28th in expectation of the incumbent king's arrival. Just as had been the case at Malmesbury, Henry was carried inside and taken before the main altar. Described by an eyewitness as a 'pretty little knight, clad in his little royal robes', the silk of which had been provided by the abbot, the young king appeared every bit a child of destiny.[16]

Besides the occasion being a tearful one, details once again are infuriatingly scarce. Similar to John's funeral, it is likely that the legate was involved in some capacity. The annals of Tewkesbury specified Guala as the person responsible for crowning the king, but this contradicts most other sources. The evidence available indicates that Guala took on a far more modest part.[17]

Other questions have been raised about the precise manner of the crowning. The original crown was undoubtedly absent, whether located somewhere in the rebel-dominated south or a victim of John's incident in the Wash is unknown. In the absence of the key pieces, the king appears to have been crowned with a plain hoop of gold, apparently provided by his mother. That Isabella had something specifically prepared, or at least improvised, would be consistent with her keenness to ensure her son's crowning take place without delay. In the absence of the archbishops of Canterbury and York, as well as the bishop of London – the three most senior prelates in England – Jocelin, Bishop of Bath, undertook the administration of the coronation oath. Under Jocelin's dictation, Henry recited the traditional lines that he would, all the days of his life, maintain the honour, peace and reverence due to God and his church as well as to render justice to his people, abolish bad laws and evil customs.[18]

Also involved at various points were Richard le Poure, the bishop of Chichester, Simon of Apulia, the bishop of Exeter, and Sylvester, Bishop of Worcester. The latter had almost certainly been responsible for overseeing John's funeral. The task of anointing the king and placing the makeshift crown on his head was given to the bishop of Winchester, Peter des Roches, who seems to have ranked alongside William Marshal and Hubert as one of John's key supporters. Of des Roches's activities in the recent war, details are again frustratingly obscure. No longer in possession of the great seal, yet still enthroned at St Swithun's, it is possible he kept mostly to his see, perhaps taking a more hands-on role in the young Henry's education. Far more likely, he joined John on his trail of carnage.

Regardless of his exact movements, it was from the Frenchman's fingers, with the assistance of the bishops of Exeter and Worcester, that the simple golden hoop was placed on the young king's head.[19] From this brief act, Henricus of Winchester was officially crowned king of England, as well as the wider territories that remained of his grandfather's kingdom. He was the third Henry of England, named in honour of his grandfather. Under Guala's eye, and quite possibly at Marshal's prompting, he also swore fealty to Rome as his father had done three years earlier on the outskirts of Dover, and agreed to keep up the annual payment of 1,000 marks. The previous evening, the earl of Pembroke had been given the honour of knighting the king; forty-three years earlier, he had done the same to Henry the Young King. Ironically, had the Young King outlived his father he would have ruled England as Henry III and John almost certainly would not have been king and Henry III never been born.[20]

The ceremony over, Henry was carried out of the abbey. Such was the importance of the occasion that many strove for the honour of lifting him, the majority losing out to Philip d'Aubigné. On retiring to his chamber, his robes of state were substituted for lighter ones, after which a brief rest preceded the royal banquet.[21]

Besides the large following of abbots, priors and commoners, the number at the high table appears to have been relatively small for such an occasion. Apart from Henry, his mother, Marshal, the legate and the bishops, the list of attendees consists only of William de Ferrers, Earl of Derby, Philip d'Aubigné, John Marshal – William's nephew – as well as the Devonshire-based William Brewer and the Poitevin warrior Savari de Mauléon. That the mood was of celebration is doubtful. Far more likely, the general topic of conversation concerned more urgent challenges the evening had in store.[22]

Bleak though the situation was, the king was not without allies. In William Marshal and Ranulf, Earl of Chester, Henry had the support of two of the strongest earls in Europe. Aiding them and those at the top table was Walter Lacy, the lord of Ludlow; John of Monmouth, a lord of the South Welsh Marches, along with the Mortimers, Braoses, Cantilupes, and Cliffords, all of whom were powerful Marcher lords. While the rebel strongholds transcended every point of the compass, the Midlands and parts of the west remained staunchly royalist, thanks mainly to the continued loyalty of William de Ferrers and, fellow earl,

Henry de Beaumont, Earl of Warwick. The royal castles at Oxford, Wallingford, Scarborough, Durham, Nottingham, Lincoln, Bedford, Kenilworth, Knaresborough, Buckingham, Northampton, Sleaford, and Newark all remained in safe hands. Cambridge had fallen, but the same was not true of Windsor, despite still being under siege. Peak – more commonly known as Peveril – Castle, whose castellan John had ordered in June to surrender the fortress to de Ferrers, was also still under royal control.[23]

Equally good news for Henry and his advisors was that the heart of the population at large was yet to be swayed towards the rebel cause. Bias towards Magna Carta, though in the modern day often nostalgically viewed as the cornerstone of democracy, was less noteworthy in terms of the rights of the man in the meadow. War and reform were rarely popular among the commoner. Far from benefiting from any form of long-awaited justice themselves, many saw their livelihoods destroyed by acts of wanton violence. Many were becoming disillusioned. Murmurs of dissent were increasing that in continuing the fight against an innocent boy, the barons were now aiding a French invasion as opposed to fighting for the liberties of the native.

On promises and propaganda of this kind the war had initially come about, and on such things, the remainder of it would be fought. The wind of change that now enabled once hated figures like Peter des Roches to fade silently into the background also allowed the other key figures of the Midlands to concentrate on their own locality. The same was true of the vital Cinque Port of Dover where Hubert de Burgh continued to hold out resiliently.[24]

Blessed by the guidance of his battle-scarred advisors and the sympathy of the population at large, the young king still had one even more valuable strategy to call upon. His father's submission of the realm as a fiefdom of the papacy, since made by Henry himself at his coronation, confirmed his status as a papal vassal. Prior to Louis's invasion, Innocent III had already declared any attempt to usurp John's throne illegal; a stance Honorius had unsurprisingly maintained in the autumn of 1216. On Henry's accession, Honorius moved quickly to explicitly declare the young boy innocent of his father's offences. The penalty for disobedience, clerical or secular, remained that of excommunication. Just as it had been under John, support from the prelates was firmly with the king.[25]

Even before John had passed away, there were also signs that support for the war was starting to wane. Baronial hatred towards John, having reached its zenith in the months after the pope annulled the great charter, had achieved little more than a throne in a vacuum and a trail of wreckage across the country. As usual in times of war, the administration had broken down; the same was true of the legal system. Motivated either by news of John's decline or suffering the effects of war exhaustion, the readiness of the forty rebel barons to renew fealty to the king was a cause for genuine optimism.[26]

Such blessings would not, however, end the war of their own accord. Wary of both Louis's reinforcements and the movements of Llywelyn close to the Marches, security was of crucial concern for the young king's advisors in terms of implementing a new strategy. In the coronation ceremony, except for the interruptions of the abbot of St Peter's, the royalists had achieved their objective.

Yet, merely hours after proceedings within the cathedral were at an end, disaster struck.[27]

Chapter 6

1216–1217
The Long Winter

Meetings of Henry's council had scarcely begun when news reached Gloucester that Marshal's royal castle at Goodrich, located only eighteen miles away, had been attacked the previous day by a Welsh force led by the rebel baron Reginald de Braose. Son of the late William de Braose, who had successfully escaped John's antagonisms only to die mourning his wife and son in exile in France in 1211, Reginald had spent much of the remainder of John's reign out of favour, culminating in his marriage to Llywelyn's daughter, Gwladus ferch Llywelyn, in 1215.[1] How great a surprise this attack was is open to debate. Though unexpected enough to have caught the preoccupied Marshal off guard, this was far from the first Welsh onslaught against the royals. Concerned that the proximity of the rampaging enemy posed a real danger to the royal camp, Marshal dispatched a party of knights, sergeants and crossbowmen to relieve the garrison.[2]

With the coronation over and the threat against Goodrich also taken care of, the most critical task before the royalist group was to establish effective reins of government. The carnage inflicted by the royal forces on the towns and villages that had shown any form of support to the barons had been of key contribution to the collapse of the administration and the legal system. A further problem had arisen through the justiciar being marooned at Dover Castle. Such things begged an important question. With a new king on the throne, who would occupy the key positions in the new administration?[3]

Support for Hubert to continue as justiciar was strong. Indeed, except for Peter des Roches, who appears to have held a grudge against Hubert because of his earlier displacement as a result of Magna Carta, so great was the affection for the English-born administrator that even in his absence there was no sign of any attempt being made to replace him.

55

Far more pressingly, a new vacancy would need filling. The first king since the Norman invasion to claim the throne as a minor, Henry required the support of a capable regent until he reached the age of majority. This begged another question: would the appointment be a short-term fix or one of greater longevity? Had Henry's accession occurred in peacetime, the legate might well have argued for the latter. However, in the prevailing climate, the most vocal support was for Marshal. Ever modest, Marshal dismissed Guala's warm words, arguing instead that the earl of Chester was a more worthy candidate as well as being far younger. With no clear decision in sight, discussions ended for the night.[4]

Chester's candidacy was not without support. As was remarked by the royalist baron Alan Basset at the time, aside from Marshal he was the only contender.[5] Born in 1170, Chester – full name, Ranulf des Blondeville – was the sixth incumbent of that line: the eldest son of the fifth earl, Hugh de Kevelioc. Like Marshal, he was one of the few remaining great figures of the so-called 'old school' of Anglo-Norman barons. As firm a supporter of the Angevin Empire as England had, his loyalty to John had been less explicit in the early days but had come with the expectation of substantial reward. On inheriting the earldom of Chester as a minor, Ranulf had gone on to excel himself fighting for John's cause in the French lands, leading to his being granted the hand of Geoffrey Plantagenet's widow, Constance of Brittany. Although the marriage had proved unsuccessful, at one stage leading to Ranulf abducting her, it had brought him the earldom of Richmond and cemented his place among the chief magnates of the time.[6]

Less than a day later, Ranulf, along with many other key officials, arrived in Gloucester to pledge allegiance to the young king. Dismissing the claims of his apologists that the coronation should have been put back twenty-four hours, on entering the great hall and greeting the lords, Ranulf was quick to voice his support for the legate and back both the coronation and Marshal's merits to become regent. Here followed what must surely be considered one of history's most frivolous exercises in diplomacy. Undoubtedly aware of what the result would be, Marshal again dismissed his qualifications and pushed the case for Chester to be named regent. To this, Ranulf returned the pleasantries, vowing to serve him as best he could.

With the decision no longer in doubt, Guala took Marshal, Ranulf, des Roches and some of the other lords into an adjacent room and formally requested William accept the mantle. Consistent with his behaviour since arriving in England, Guala made no effort to obtain the regency for himself. Nor did he attempt to interfere in proceedings apart from publicly offering his support. Publicly reluctant, an emotional Marshal finally agreed on the condition that, 'If at this price I am absolved of my sins, this office suits me, and I will take it, though it weighs heavily upon me.'

With this, the man who had begun in life by narrowly avoiding execution at the hands of Stephen of Blois reached the pinnacle of an exceptional career. Later that evening, Marshal withdrew to his chamber and took the counsel of loyal comrades John of Earley, Ralph Musard and his nephew, John Marshal. Though Earley expressed concerns that should the hearts of their supporters fail it could leave them no choice but to flee for Ireland, he was firm in his encouragement to Marshal that by undertaking the regency, even if faced with the worst, only glory and honour would await. On broaching the unlikely possibility that victory over Louis could somehow be achieved, his words now seem strangely portentous: that 'never man of any race won such honour upon the earth'. Earley's counsel warmed the Marshal. It was recorded in his biography, that though he harboured similar doubts, he stated to those present: 'By God's sword, this advice is true and good; it goes straight to my heart that, if everyone else abandoned the king, do you know what I would do? I would carry him on my shoulders, step by step, from island to island, from country to country, and I would not fail him, not even if it meant begging my bread.'[7]

Upon the guidance of God, the papacy and this seasoned crusader would Henry III's kingship rest. Four days after the coronation, Henry built on his oath to the papacy by taking up the cross. That a 9-year-old child would have been in a position to make a trip to the Holy Land, even in peacetime, was, of course, unrealistic in the extreme. Instead, as was recorded by the chronicler of Peterborough, it entitled him to the same protections as promised of one who would journey across the sea.[8]

Shortly after events in Gloucester were completed, Guala organised a council to begin in Bristol on 11 November. The attendance of eleven bishops once again confirmed the support of the prelates. The eight exceptions were Langton, the archbishop of Canterbury and Walter de Grey, the archbishop of York, both of whom were still abroad; Hugh of the Wells, the bishop of Lincoln, as well as the bishops of Salisbury and London, Herbert Poure and William de St Mére-Eglise were all under the weather, while the sees at Hereford, Norwich and Durham were then unoccupied. Election of Hugh de Mapenor in the former still awaited consecration, as did Pandulf's at Norwich. Consecration of Richard de Marisco, the chancellor, in the latter would take place on 2 July 1217.[9]

Concerning the laity, joining Marshal and Chester were Ferrers, the earl of Derby, and William de Forz, the earl of Aumale – one of the twenty-five executors of the original charter – who had switched sides constantly throughout the war. William de Brewer – father and son – were representative of the administrative body; Falkes de Breauté and Savori de Mauléon, the military. Also present were John Marshal, Alan Basset, John L'Estrange, Philip d'Aubigné, Matthew FitzHerbert, Robert de Courtenay and Reginald de Valtort. At the same time, the lay baronage benefitted from a strong following from the Welsh Marches, including the Beauchamps, Mortimers, Lacys, Cliffords and Cantilupes.[10]

Proceedings in Bristol were memorable for many reasons. Falling on another feast day, that of St Martin, the occasion was primarily one of celebration. The formal confirmation of recent appointments saw Marshal officially appointed as regent; in the words of his biographer William was given the *Baillie* of the kingdom and modelled *rector noster et regni nostril*: the literal meaning of which was 'our ruler and the ruler of the kingdom'.[11]

A truce with Louis to halt the siege of Dover Castle allowed Bristol to witness the first appearance of Hubert de Burgh since John's death. There is evidence that Marshal initially called himself justiciar prior to talks with Hubert; however, there is no evidence that Hubert was in danger of being ousted. During Richard's reign, there had been two justiciars, one of whom was Marshal. Similar was true of des Roches's continuation as the king's personal tutor, in addition to remaining on the king's council. Back at Gloucester, des Roches had also been designated the king's carer at times when Marshal was on the road undertaking duties of state.[12]

In addition to the authentication of key appointments, the Bristol council was also significant for other reasons. The first day, with Guala taking centre stage, saw him place Wales under interdict as well as a renewal of the excommunication of Louis and his allies. The following day, matters moved on to more political issues, most significantly the issuance of a new version of the Great Charter. Though initially quashed by the papacy at John's request, the charter presented at Bristol was a far leaner document than that signed at Runnymede. Absent were nineteen of the original clauses, most notably the contentious clauses concerning constitutional reform, such as the appointment of the twenty-five barons. The same was true of the clauses regarding extraordinary taxation. The finer points agreed on, the charter was confirmed in the king's name and sealed with those of the legate and earl of Pembroke. Being but a minor, the king himself as yet had no seal of his own.[13]

As history would later tell, the charter agreed at Bristol would be far more influential than its elder sibling could ever have been. A revision as opposed to a rewrite, its content outlined a more liberal government policy than that experienced under John. The removal of the controversial clauses that had tied John's hands, mirrored by tacit promises from its promoters that certain aspects would be reviewed at a later date, was championed by many of Henry's supporters as the compromise the kingdom needed. On the one hand, it provided a safety net that would allow the inexperienced king a smooth transition into kingship; on the other it extended an olive branch to the rebel barons whose call to arms had occurred in response to John's rejection of those very reasons.

Issued under Marshal's guidance with Guala's backing, the new charter was confirmed the following day. Though several months would pass before the new legislation was circulated amongst the sheriffs, later in November a letter was written in the king's name concerning John's death to the justiciary of Ireland. A promise was also made to Hugh de Lacy, 1st Earl of Ulster and former viceroy of Ireland, who had been ostracised by John in the 1210 campaign, leading to his taking part in the Albigensian crusade, that pledging his fealty would see his rights restored. A copy of the rights charter would be delivered to Ireland in February.[14]

For the young king, it was a case of so far so good. Still to encounter a significant battle or mutiny, there is no doubt that first month had brought many much-needed gains. That such success can be explained entirely by the innocence of the king or the widespread respect of Marshal only extends so far. Even before the reissuing of the charter, nothing in the previous three years had gone further in regard to addressing the rebels' constitutional attitude than news of John's death. Since that time, there is little doubt that a dramatic change was taking place in the way the war was being perceived. The cruel treatment of captured enemies had already largely ceased. The same was true of the widespread wanton destruction of towns and villages.

That this, too, could be attributed solely to the removal of John is an oversimplification. Another critical factor was the late autumn weather. Traditionally, the coming of winter saw a slowdown in European warfare. Hugely unglamorous even at the best of times, thirteenth-century conflict was particularly wearing and haphazard, not least in terms of its organisation. As was famously true of the English Civil War – and in more recent memory, the 2016 Brexit referendum – even the tightest of family circles could quickly become split and subject to long-term feuds. No better example of this concerned the Marshals themselves: when else, but at the height of the age of chivalry, could we find the magnificent earl William fighting tooth and nail for a young boy, only for his eldest son and heir to strive similarly for his boon companion, the dauphin of France.[15]

Equally typical in the winter months, much of the conflict was castle related.[16] Unrelenting in his attempts to take Dover, Louis also attempted to use the uncertainty surrounding John's death to push home his advantage in the south-east. In November – the Waverley annals note the 4th – he finally acquired the Tower of London, the one part of the capital that had refused to yield.[17] On the day that the great charter was reissued at Bristol, the prince began his siege of Hertford, taking it through negotiated surrender no later than 6 December despite the laudable efforts of its commander, Walter de Godardville. Something of a truce was reached in the period prior to Christmas on the condition the royals also surrendered Berkhamsted, which occurred between 13-20 December, again much to the displeasure of its constable, a German knight named Waleran. As usual, such truces proved only a short-term solution and had expired no later than 20 January.[18]

Throughout the winter months, news slowly filtered back to Honorius in Rome. Disappointed by Louis's continued dissent, in early December he again wrote to various parties insisting that the rebel barons put down their swords and swear allegiance to Henry. Understanding in the sense that personal criticisms of John had contributed significantly to the early part of the war, on the matter of Henry's coronation establishing the legitimate rule of his replacement, he took a harder stance. The argument here was an easy one. A young child, innocent of his father's crimes, it was unfathomable Henry could be regarded as in any way responsible for past constitutional failures. Recognising the problem for himself, in a royal letter, undoubtedly written under the close guidance of one of his key advisors, Henry declared, 'We hear that a quarrel arose between our father and certain nobles of our kingdom, whether with justification or not we do not know. We wish to remove it for ever since it has nothing to do with us!' Such tactics were also being employed by Marshal, who highlighted the importance of swaying the earl of Salisbury, the king's uncle and hero of Damme, back to the royalist side.[19]

The pre-Christmas period was a busy one for correspondence. On 3 December Honorius wrote to Guala, assigning him the task of acting not only as guardian of the kingdom but also of Henry's young siblings.[20] As Christmas arrived, the royal household chose to remain in Bristol. After enjoying the festivities with the legate and his new regent, Henry's New Year began with a council in Oxford. Around that time the rebels held a similar meeting in Cambridge.[21] Under Marshal's leadership and Guala's guidance, attempts were made to broker peace on a far broader scale; however, initial talks were unsuccessful. Exactly how involved the young king was in the negotiations is unrecorded. One of the few snippets of information gained at this time is that he benefitted from the tutelage of Philip d'Aubigné, later Warden of the Channel Islands. On 8 January, des Roches was also with the royalist army at Nottingham to witness letters of the new king.[22]

Either ignorant of Honorius's petitions or merely unwilling to listen, Louis's desire for total conquest remained undiminished. After taking Berkhamsted, prior to the Oxford and Cambridge councils, the royal castles of Colchester, Orford, Norwich and Cambridge were all acquired through similarly negotiated surrenders, as were the baronial ones at Pleshey and (following the failed peace talks) Hedingham. The dauphin's hold on the south-east secure, the same degree of conquest was yet to be achieved in the west of England or the Midlands. Worse still, other circumstances were beginning to conspire against him. Not only was the weather making travel extra difficult, leading to a severe shortage of supplies, elements of the baronage were starting to become disillusioned by his harsh taxation policy.[23]

Having opposed John at least partly due to his tendency to favour foreigners, it seems strange to think that the mindset of a French prince would be any different. As expected, the xenophobic feelings that had given rise to clauses 50 and 51 in the original charter had proven a double-edged sword. In terms of the general population, ambivalence towards the foreign troops was no more likely than it had been for John's aliens. Among the barons themselves, feelings of unease had accelerated dramatically on the acquisition of Hertford, not least in the mind of its former keeper, Robert Fitzwalter. When Fitzwalter demanded that the castle be returned to him, Louis flatly stated that no Englishman who had betrayed his natural land could be trusted with such responsibility. Commenting on such matters, the annalist of Dunstable was especially scathing, stating: 'the French became arrogant, repulsed the English nobles from their counsels, began to call them traitors, and retained the castles which they took for themselves, and did not restore their rights to the English'. The Waverley annalist, though far less scathing, was equally straightforward in his views. It was now the preferred position of the English to have a native monarch than a foreigner.[24]

As early signs had already indicated, 1217 would mark a watershed in the direction of the war. Further to events at Bristol concerning interdict of Wales and further excommunication orders against the rebels, Guala had turned the war into a crusade by further awarding the crusader crosses to Henry's followers. Concerning the English rebels, Marshal and the legate adopted a more diplomatic stance. The earl even went as far as to promise that no inquiries would be made into past offences so long as fealty to Henry III was pledged. A guarantee was also given that the penitent men would have their rights reinstated when the war was over. Writing to the abbots of Cîteaux and Clairvaux, Honorius pressed his view that they use their influence to incite action from the king of France to convince Louis to return home; similar was true in his writings to the archbishops of Dublin and Bordeaux.[25]

Further to his correspondence with the prelates, Honorius also wrote to Henry personally, highlighting his hopes for a brighter future once the war was over. Letters to the bishops of Winchester and Chichester as well as the legate outlining the importance of the king's supervision also saw Guala's powers further extended against all ecclesiastics currently swearing loyalty to Louis. Unsurprisingly, Honorius also used the current confusion as an opportunity to attempt to fill vacant sees with his own choices, while touching, albeit somewhat prematurely, on the subject of future marriage for Henry.[26]

A combination of Marshal's diplomacy, developing war fatigue and a clear lack of personal hostility against the young Henry saw the defection of several more barons. Among those who offered their allegiance around this time was William d'Aubigny, Lord of Belvoir, famed for his brave defence of Rochester from John. Imprisoned at Corfe Castle on being captured, in November 1216 he bought his freedom for 6,000 marks and was entrusted soon after with control of the Lincolnshire fortress of Sleaford.[27]

For Louis, the tide continued to turn. Further to the loss of figures such as Aubigny, his earlier gain of the lords of the Cinque Ports had proven only momentary. Around this time, the royalists also obtained a surprise victory in Rye, obtaining the castle 'by subtlety'. Worse still, a revolt in the Weald in the south-east of England led by a squire named William of Cassingham, later dubbed Wilkin of the Weald, saw two nephews of the count of Nevers become captured.[28]

Cut off from France, the lack of allies and supplies became critical, forcing him to request a brief truce. Intent on returning home to gather extra forces and provisions, the loss of the Cinque Ports made departure difficult. As the prince closed in on Lewes on his way to Winchelsea, further setback was encountered when the men of the Weald broke down the bridges. On scrambling his way to the port, the sight of the locals destroying their mills before setting sail under the royal banner threatened to sap what remained of his troops' morale. Left to fend for themselves in a near-empty town with inadequate food supplies, the belated arrival of support from London and Boulogne ended two torturous weeks that had brought his troops to the brink of starvation.[29]

By some means, Louis managed to return to France. Whether or not there is any merit to reports that Marshal had been keen on capturing him, Louis was indebted to the interference of the infamous outlaw and pirate Eustace the Monk. Originally from Boulogne, this colourful character is alleged to have studied black magic before becoming a Benedictine monk only to leave his monastic orders behind him when he set out to avenge his murdered father. By 1202, he was seneschal of the count of Boulogne, after which a life of pirating had seen him serve England intermittently during the period 1205–12 prior to serving the French from his base in the Channel Islands.[30]

Louis's departure was of great benefit to the royalists. Not only did the cessation of hostilities offer the royalist troops well-needed respite, but Marshal also used the opportunity to raise funds through the issuing of a hidage – a tax paid to the king for every hide of land, a hide being an average family's allocation – and carucage – a tax placed on every plough or area of ploughland – in the shires under royal control.[31]

Taxation was still a primitive and somewhat controversial measure in England. Used in 1193 to fund Richard the Lionheart's ransom, as well as part of John's submission to the papacy in 1213, the first actual income tax had occurred in 1207. At the same time John's government demanded one-thirteenth of all income received from rents and moveable property in support of his attempts to reclaim the ancestral lands in France. Somewhat predictably, this had been done with the reluctant consent of the baronage but widespread condemnation of the clergy. As previously mentioned, it was the opposition of Archbishop Geoffrey of York to the tax on moveables that had forced him into exile a year prior to the interdict. Though taxes on income could be highly effective – in John's case the raising of £60,000 was about double his usual annual takings from other sources – widespread unpopularity and the scope for corruption among government officials brought deep resentment.[32]

During the dauphin's absence, the fortunes of the young king also continued to improve in other ways. While Marshal busily prepared his strategies and tactics for Louis's return, the power vacuum at the top of the rebel forces offered a renewed opportunity to convince several more barons to change sides. On 5 March, as the regent left Shoreham-by-sea, he renewed acquaintances with his prodigal son, William the younger, along with the hero of Damme, William Longespée, the earl of Salisbury, both of whom had fought against John during the present war. The meeting was clearly prearranged as the three spent the night at Knepp Castle, during which terms were agreed for them to enter the service of the king. Detrimental as this was to Louis's cause – not least in the eyes of the chroniclers – the defection of perhaps as many as 150 lesser men, mostly supporters of Longespée, was of arguably greater importance still.[33]

Better news still for Henry was the recovery of several castles in the south. In Louis's absence, Rochester, Southampton, Portchester, Farnham, Odiham, Chichester and Marlborough all returned to royal control. The cherry on the cake was Winchester. Though the rebel supporters of the suburbs inflicted considerable damage on the royalist camp at Hyde Abbey, the support of the citizens within the city, coupled with the help of his recent defectors, ensured that Marshal relieved the city after several weeks of siege. Progress was also steadily being made on several other castles. The previously loathed Falkes de Breauté received many plaudits for leading his forces deep into the rebel-controlled Isle of Ely, mirroring the inroads of Ranulf at the imposing Midlands castle of Mountsorrel. In gratitude for his recent service, the industrious Wilkin was made Warden of the seven hundreds of the Weald.[34]

Respite from constant conflict also brought about other important opportunities. Having used the brief peace as a chance to concentrate on short-term administration, in March, the king committed Gascony and Poitou to the archbishop of Bordeaux, while ordering the seneschals to deliver them to him. Truce was also declared between the council and William de Warenne, the previously loyal earl of Surrey who had defected to Louis's side when the cause looked hopeless. At the same time, orders were made for the people of Ireland to make allegiance to the archbishop of Dublin.[35]

Pleasingly for the royalists and Honorius, recent events had left their mark on the king of France. No longer harbouring the ambition of a French empire north of the Channel, Philip's plans had instead moved on to liberation of the Holy Land. Building on his earlier attempts to influence the Angevin bishops of France and Ireland to come to Henry's aid, in April Honorius once again demanded Philip recall his son from England.[36] Whether or not Philip directly complied is unclear. Nevertheless, an indifferent welcome at a royal council at Laon on 5 March confirmed what he must have already suspected. As Marshal's biography rightly recalled, Philip's earlier enthusiasm for an invasion of England had dwindled from the moment of John's passing. Though the lack of support would fail to dissuade the prince from one last try, he must have feared his father's assessment on learning of John's death, Henry's crowning and Marshal being entrusted as regent would indeed come to pass.

'We shall take nothing in England now; that brave man's good sense will defend the land – Louis has lost it!'[37]

Chapter 7

1217
God Helps the Marshal

It was recorded in the Wigorn annals that a series of mock suns lit up the sky on 26 April 1217. The people of Worcester had been unaware at the time that the phenomenon had occurred four days after Louis's return to England, his landing celebrated with the torching of Sandwich. Aided by a mere 120 knights, of far greater consequence was the transportation of a trebuchet. He had also made it back in time for the expiry of the truce.[1]

Despite being in possession of arguably the greatest marvel so far invented in siege warfare, familiar frustrations would again be encountered before the sturdy walls of Dover Castle. On leaving Kent, the prince headed towards Winchester and joined with the earl of Winchester, Saer de Quincy, at the siege of Farnham Castle, which the royalists had taken around mid-March. Learning that Mountsorrel was under attack from Ranulf – who had recently postponed his crusader plans at Guala's request – and William de Ferrers, the earl of Derby, on capturing the outer bailey of Farnham, Louis returned swiftly to Winchester. After reconquering Winchester in less than a week, he divided his forces to continue the siege of Dover and raise the royalist siege of Mountsorrel.[2]

Word of Louis's plans soon reached Leicestershire. Understanding that Louis was heading north, the royalist forces – seemingly under the impression that they were being pursued by the entire might of the enemy – vacated Mountsorrel and, for a brief time, took refuge in Nottingham. With Mountsorrel relieved, the prince continued east to Lincoln in a bid to complete a further ongoing siege. As in Dover, a royal loyalist had held the castle: on this occasion, no officer of high status, but a sheriff, named Nicola de Hay – another female of the Magna Carta era who would soon become something of a celebrated hero in her own right.[3]

66

On learning first hand of Louis's plans – most specifically that the dauphin had split his forces in two – Marshal immediately plotted a counter-strike. On 12 May, the same day Louis resumed the siege of Dover, the regent had been celebrating Pentecost with the legate in Northampton where another excommunication sentence was passed against the French invader. No sooner were the celebrations over, the legate and the king joined Ranulf in Nottingham. The royal forces gathered in Newark 17-18 May, their numbers supplemented by conscripting the garrisons of various castles, following which Marshal led them to Lincoln via Torksey and Stow to the north.

By choosing a route that would allow them to avoid the need to enter the city uphill, Marshal had delivered part one of his masterstroke. His numerically inferior forces numbered only 400 knights and 300 crossbowmen, compared to the 600 knights and 1,000 foot soldiers within the town besieging the castle. Yet Marshal's clever choice of route had brought them to the outskirts of the city almost unobserved. After resting on the night of 19 May, they arrived in Lincoln and prepared to relieve Nicola's garrison. Des Roches, here, was instrumental in deliverance of the key strategies, having learned from a rendezvous with de Hay that the town's blocked western gateway to the north of the castle was potentially accessible. Once Marshal had set up communications with the castle as Chester pummelled the north gate, crossbowmen under the guidance of Falkes de Breauté joined with the garrison via the west gate. They then ventured from the east gate into the street, an effective diversion that allowed Chester to concentrate on the poorly defended north gate.

The clashes that followed quickly spread through the streets and steep lanes that connected the upper and lower town. The worst of the conflicts occurred under the shadow of the cathedral's mighty towers. It was here a spear through his visor severely wounded the French count of Perche despite managing three hard blows against Marshal's helmet. The emergence of the forces led by Chester in the lower town signalled to the French that they faced defeat. Coupled with the Henrician forces descending the hill and another wave led by Alan and Thomas Basset closing in from behind, the rebels' chances of achieving a counter strike uphill became all but impossible.

Disarray among the French forces had been evident from the very beginning. So concerned had the marshal of France and count of Perche become, the commands of the earl of Winchester and Robert Fitzwalter to take the fight outside the city walls were swiftly declined. Any possibility of continuing the siege of the castle within the city walls until reinforcements arrived was also out of the question. Left with no alternative, the rebel forces fled the city in large numbers.[4]

The so-called Fair of Lincoln provided another noteworthy moment in the direction of the war. A royal victory, it had proven remarkably bloodless; some reports place the royalist casualties at only three.

Less true had that been of the city itself. Not content with the spoils of the French nobles and rebel barons, the victorious English went on the rampage. The canons of the cathedral chapter, being deemed excommunicate due to their assisting Louis, were plundered. Following this, the sacking of the town and its churches prompted many women and children to flee. Similar to the situation in the fallout of the fire of Southwark, the rash behaviour of the evacuees in overcrowding their rowing boats on reaching the river sadly led to mass drowning. Incidentally, such things were noted to have occurred after Marshal departed from the city.[5]

The victory secure, a jubilant Marshal rode swiftly for Nottingham to see the legate. Guala again publicly excommunicated Louis and further dubbed the onslaught a crusade by offering an indulgence to Henry's soldiers. Typically, further rewards were offered, including the earldom of Lincoln to Ranulf and control of the city to Longespée. Ranulf was also awarded Mountsorrel, which he immediately razed to the ground on completing the siege. On the rebel side, any lucky enough to avoid decapitation in the battle or taken prisoner fled for the capital. Among those taken were Fitzwalter, de Quincy and several of the 'northerners'.[6]

The cries that echoed from the mouth of the bishop of Winchester as progress was made through the previously sealed gateway, it seemed, had proven right: God really did help the Marshal. Building on the recent momentum, however, would be more problematic. Marshal's hope of delivering Louis the hammer blow fell apart after encountering difficulties in keeping the forces of various garrisons together. In the inevitable pause that followed, Marshal used the opportunity to increasingly restore order by holding a great council at Chertsey in early June. Among the few not to attend was Ferrers, who, further to his being granted permission to take Peak Castle from – ironically – a John supporting castellan, also recovered the rebel-controlled Bolsover

Castle after a lengthy siege. It was notable that the castellan of Peak, Brian de Lisle, had been more than happy to surrender on being awarded Knaresborough Castle as a reward for his role in the Fair of Lincoln.[7]

Back in the south, Louis's position looked increasingly bleak. On 15 May, further problems arose with the siege of Dover when Philip d'Aubigné faced the French convoys with twenty large ships and several smaller craft. Ten days later, while still bloody-mindedly continuing to batter the castle's sturdy Norman walls, he heard the tragic news of Lincoln. Forced to pool his remaining resources, he withdrew to the one place in England that still offered him support: the capital.[8]

On 12 June, the archbishop of Tyre arrived in England, accompanied by the abbots of Cíteaux, Clairvaux and Pontigny to preach a crusade. Keen that the warring factions should put their differences aside and unite under this common banner, their arrival also brought forward provisional articles of peace, and only a day later, an agreement was close. Later that month, as the charter of liberties finally began to circulate among the sheriffs, a safe passage was granted for face to face talks, for which four members of Louis's council and twenty knights met Henry's council between Brentford and Hounslow. Though early efforts failed due to unresolved issues concerning Louis's supporters among the clergy – all of whom Guala steadfastly refused to absolve – and the prince's excessive financial demands, it was now clear to both sides that any chance of a rebel victory could not be achieved without significant financial aid.[9]

On 8 July Honorius wrote to the prelates requesting financial aid for Guala to provide for the governance of the kingdom.[10] North of the border, alliance between Carlisle and the king of Scotland led to an order by Honorius to remove the dissident canons. A suggestion was also made from the papacy that the earl of Chester be made joint regent alongside Marshal, which seems to have been either dismissed or ignored.[11] 21-25 July Marshal hosted a great council in Oxford, followed by another 7-13 August, both of which were successful in further tightening the royalist grip on power.[12]

Though discovery of a final exit strategy remained elusive, any chance Louis had of a successful revival continued to diminish. The defection to the young king's side of Reginald de Braose, son-in-law of Llywelyn and, until recently, his key ally, saw a further turn in the fortunes of the ongoing Welsh campaign.[13] Far worse news for the dauphin was that the diminishing prospects were beginning to make a mark on his family. Following recent defections, Louis's nephew and viceroy, Enguerrand de Coucy, who had previously been placed in charge on Louis's return home in March, no longer maintained his initial indifference to the threat of excommunication for inciting violence against John. Around this time, he too appears to have pledged his loyalty to Henry.[14]

With peace talks stalling, Louis attempted one last throw of the dice. After seeking the assistance of his wife in bringing in reinforcements, his prize came in the form of 120 knights, several hundred men at arms, including William des Barres, the count of Blois and the flagship of Eustace the Monk. On 24 August, St Bartholomew's Day, however, things unravelled for the final time. Having sailed from Calais towards the mouth of the Thames, the complication of a royalist dominated coast left Eustace only one way of approaching London. After allowing the pirate to pass Sandwich, the canny justiciar, Hubert de Burgh, set out on the water and tracked the French vessel upriver. On noticing it for the first time, shouts cried out from the French ship, 'The Hart, the Hart', in mockery of the justiciar.

Taken in by Hubert's ploy, the famed mercenary came unstuck. Low in the water, the massive French command ship, described in some sources as a 'castle' on the water, weighed down by a trebuchet, thirty-six knights and a siege engine proved challenging to manoeuvre, allowing Hubert's ship to get alongside it. A favourable wind gave the French ships containing the soldiers the chance to escape, but for Eustace and his knights, there would be no respite. A combination of that wind and the unleashing of fine lime held in pots on the ship's deck proved detrimental to visibility. Coupled with the ship's sluggishness and a poor decision in rolling up the sails too early, the crew were surrounded. Found hiding in the bilge – part of the hull – the legendary outlaw's final decision was where on his ship he cared to be beheaded.[15]

Crowned in the middle of a war he had played no part in starting, the end was finally in Henry's sights. Greatly encouraged by recent victories, he accompanied Marshal to the siege of London and met Louis at the city gates on 29 August. A week later, on 5 September, a formal conference was held at Kingston, the peace treaty signed at the archbishop of Canterbury's residence in Lambeth on 11 – or possibly 12 – September in the presence of the legate. As later commentators would contend, the peace terms were more than Louis deserved. All of his castles were surrendered and his supporters released from their oath to him, any threat of subsequent punishment withdrawn. Marshal also agreed that the imprisoned should be released without further ransom. As a golden handshake, Louis was awarded 10,000 marks on condition that he would attempt to persuade his father to restore to Henry the lost territories of the Angevin dynasty.[16]

All that remained now was to apply the finishing touches. Two days later, letters of peace and protection of Louis were written up. Five days after that, orders were made in Henry's name that no harm be done to those of Norfolk, Suffolk, Essex and Hereford who had sided with him.[17] On 20 September, Louis and his barons appeared barefoot and dressed in white before Guala at Merton, to be formally absolved of their sins. Two days later, des Roches entered London with Louis at which point he officially handed over the Tower. With this, the rebels' final power base submitted to royalist control. On 29 September, Louis took a safe passage to Dover and left England for the last time.[18]

More than twenty-seven months after events at Runnymede, the First Barons' War finally came to an end: a brief, yet strange time when England variously had two kings and none at all. For the last time in England's history, a Frenchman governed large swathes of the country. Stranger still, the man who effectively ruled the country had never been a king. Instead, he had started as a minor son of a minor lord only to serve five kings so loyally.

A war that had started with a king's refusal to abide by the terms of a charter ended with a young one's forced agreement to abide by another. In such ways, one could argue the cause of the war had been realised. With John dead and the future of the realm in the hands of the new king, the reasons for further fighting had long been lost. Marshal's prudence in dismissing any charges against the English rebel barons allowed for peaceful submission; similar things also allowed London to come to terms. Of those who opposed the king, only the clergy suffered, their cases sent before the pope. As history would recall, the short-term fix had ended a war.

Its long-term legacy, however, would be far more complex.

Chapter 8

1217–1219
Tearful Farewells

A gigantic cross was seen floating through the air over the south-east of England on 27 October 1217. Noted by a canon of Dunstable, its occurrence on the vigil of St Simon and Jude made for an interesting coincidence. Precisely a year had passed since the young Henry III had embarked on his journey to Gloucester to meet the first part of his destiny within the vast nave of its cathedral. That the strange apparition was connected to the monarch, the chronicler was unconvinced. Having moved through the air from west to east, it was the view of all who bore the cross witness that it could only have been a sign from the heavens that the recovery of the Holy Land was at hand.[1]

Signs in the sky were by no means limited to England that year. In May, a similar sight was witnessed above the town of Bebou, which was seen as a precursor to the departure of the crusaders of Friesland and Cologne to Egypt the following year. For the barons of England, a new – fifth – crusade would also be planned for 1218. However, not before the remaining loose ends of the two-year conflict were finally sewn together.[2]

Louis's submission at the Treaty of Lambeth had been a crucial step in re-establishing law and order in England. With the war officially over, life in the shires slowly returned to normal as fears of further rebellion gave way to promises of long term peace. That isn't to say caution became unnecessary. Tournaments, in particular, were viewed as a constant threat as such gatherings had often been used as a springboard for widespread violence. A tournament at Blyth was cancelled in October for such reasons; fortunately for the young king and his new government, this was likely just a precaution.[3] In practice, the departure of Louis had allowed for reconciliation between the warring factions. When Ranulf, Earl of Chester, and William de Ferrers went on crusade with the rebellious Saer de Quincy, Earl of Winchester and Robert

72

Fitzwalter, recent feuds appeared to have been forgotten, and it was similarly the case for a large number of nobles who made the journey to Egypt throughout 1218.[4]

The week the cross was seen above Dunstable was notable for another reason. Having served as a rebel stronghold throughout the war, it was only now, more than a month after the war had ended, that the king entered the city of London for the first time. It was remarked of the occasion that Henry 'was received with glory, and fealty and homage were done to him', a stark contrast from the citizens' crying out Louis's name a year earlier. Throughout the following week, many meaningful discussions took place about the future of the kingdom, the majority of which centred on government procedure. The 10-year-old king had performed admirably in his government's successful overcoming of what had arguably been England's greatest post-Norman challenge to date: a feat that should be considered all the more significant in terms of the context of his accession. Yet only through the implementation of careful short- and long-term policy could peace be established.[5]

On 11 November, almost a year to the day following the granting of the revised Charter of Liberties, the culmination of a great council that had sat since October ensured Henry's government follow through on their earlier promise that specific clauses would be revisited. This would lead to the reissue of the charter for a second time. The more contentious clauses of government already removed a year earlier at Bristol, the most significant change on this occasion concerned forest law. After having failed in 1216 to satisfy this copious subject to complete satisfaction, the 1217 version saw all forest clauses removed. In so doing, the government instead issued a second, more detailed, document alongside what was now dubbed Magna Carta, named henceforth: the Charter of the Forest.

Implementation of such a charter was necessary for several reasons. At the beginning of Henry's reign, nearly a third of England was forest. Though nostalgically that designation might conjure up images of beauty, the forests of thirteenth-century England were often desolate places – the refuge of everyone from the hermit to the outlaw and everything from the wolf to the wild boar. More importantly, the term carried an important legal meaning: all areas classed as 'forest' were placed under the monopoly of the king. Disafforesting older forests – i.e. reducing them to the state of ordinary ground – had proven particularly lucrative for past monarchs. Ever short of cash, John had taken the drastic step of disafforesting all of Cornwall for 2,200 marks as well as Devon for 5,000 and Surrey for 500.

Highly doubtful it may be that thoroughly dealing with the forestry issue in 1215 would have prevented the war, had the barons paid it more attention some discord could have undoubtedly been avoided. Among the barons' demands at Runnymede was that the classification of forests should return to what had been in place prior to the accession of Henry II. In clause 47, John had agreed that any forest created during his reign should be disafforested, but in truth, this did little to affect either the political climate or the physical landscape. Clause 47 was seen as necessary enough to be kept in the charter at Bristol; however, it could also be argued that this was a prime example of what Marshal had in mind when he promised certain things would be revisited. Implementation of the new charter was assigned to his nephew John Marshal. Whereas three clauses concerning forestry were removed from the great charter, the new independent document contained a total of seventeen. In contrast to the original three clauses in the great charter, the Forest Charter made further concessions, including the long-sought confirmation that any forest created since the reign of Henry II would be disafforested. Legislation was also passed that any freeman should have the right to develop his land within the forest and that no man should lose his life for poaching venison, which had been made law during the reign of keen hunter Richard I.[6]

The very day that the charters were issued, a letter was written to the pope in Henry's name, most likely by the hand of Marshal or one of his other key advisors. In addition to offering his warmest thanks to Honorius for his help and guidance in recent times, he also played heavily on the pope's sympathy by requesting exemption from the annual tribute of 1,000 marks agreed by John at Dover in 1213. In the king's defence, not only was the kingdom reeling from two years of persistent conflict, but Marshal's negotiated payment of 10,000 marks to Louis under the peace settlement was ten times the annual tribute.[7]

Peace between Henry and Louis was again confirmed on 13 January 1218.[8] At that time many lords who owed allegiance to Alexander II of Scotland, including the king himself, paid homage to Henry at Northampton. Before Louis's submission, Alexander had gathered his armies and marched as far as Jedburgh in the Scottish borders before learning of the new peace. Absolved of excommunication by the archbishop of York and bishop of Durham at Berwick in December, Alexander subsequently resumed his journey south to Northampton.[9]

Prior to this, the exchequer also reopened. Beginning on 12 November, shortly after the issue of the November charters, Hubert set to work on the arduous task of attempting to draw up accounts for the civil war period.[10] Be it a product of laziness or the sheer impossibility of the task, work was soon abandoned. That Henry was personally affected by the cash flow crisis seems highly likely. Six weeks later, he enjoyed his first post-war Christmas at Northampton in the company of the magnates and the king of Scotland at the expense of recent hero Falkes de Breauté.[11]

Trouble with the French, Scots and his own barons had mostly come to an end by late 1217. In the kingdom of Gwent, in which the beautiful Wye and Usk rivers still flow, a rebellion by local chieftain Morgan of Caerleon forced Marshal to take up arms once again. Unable to prevent the fall of the royal castles of Cardigan and Carmarthen, both of which had been in his possession, broader tensions were dampened when the prince of Gwynedd received assurances that his right to rule his provinces would not be challenged. Though he had initially refused to travel to Northampton in the aftermath of the great council in November, an absolved Llywelyn was then happy enough to make the journey to Worcester in March the following year to pay homage to Henry personally.[12] Safe passage was also granted to King Ragnald of the Isles – which included the Isle of Man, Hebrides and Clyde – yet, perhaps due to geographical difficulties, homage to Henry would not be paid until September 1219. Over in Ireland, the loyalty of justiciar Geoffrey le Marsh – appointed by John in 1215 – was on a far sounder footing, Geoffrey having written to Henry on John's death.[13]

The following year also saw progress in other matters. On 18 February it was announced that all clerks not absolved in the Treaty of Lambeth were to be banished from the realm by mid-Lent. Four days later, the king also ordered the sheriffs to read out the new charter accompanied by an order that all 'adulterine' castles should be destroyed. Such matters and much more, not least the fates of former rebels, would be the subject of significant discussion when another great council met at Westminster on 9 May. Ironically, most of the problems encountered at that time concerned those who had helped sail the young king to victory.[14]

Entrusted with guardianship of Mitford Castle in Northumberland, Philip of Oldcoates was strident in his refusal to give it up to Roger Bertram; the same was true of the lands of the traitorous Eustace de Vesci, which Oldcoates refused to give to the earl of Salisbury. Another hero of the recent conflict, the count of Aumale, was equally unwilling to comply with a new royal command to relinquish Bytham Castle to former rebel William de Coleville and the royal castle of Rockingham to the king himself. Similar was true of Hugh de Vivonne for Barton in Bristol to the earl of Gloucester, Gilbert de Clare.[15]

More considerable frustration for the king and regent at this time concerned the castle in which John had died: Newark. Held loyally throughout the war by castellan Robert de Gaugi, who had been entrusted its care by John, de Gaugi's refusal to surrender control had been a key topic of discussion at the council at Worcester in March 1218. Recovery of Newark was considered of particular importance among the prelates, not least as it was rightfully the property of the bishop of Lincoln. Having made no progress by July, Marshal summoned an army to Stamford on the 15th of that month. By the 23rd the siege appears to have been over. After watching proceedings at Newark in Marshal's care, Henry was also present at Wallingford in Oxfordshire when the errant castellan formally surrendered it. With Guala's agreement, it subsequently passed to the bishop of Lincoln.[16]

By the autumn of that year, new problems of administration were starting to be resolved. Around the time Newark was restored a tournament planned by the king's uncle, the earl of Salisbury, was denied permission to go ahead due to similar fears that had plagued a gathering at Blyth the previous year. That same month, the king ordered that the forests be perambulated and regulated according to the new forest charter. Implementation of the new procedures was a challenge in itself, not least as disafforestation was highly desired at the county level as it brought reversion of royal power to the counties themselves.[17]

Any specific plans for how the procedures specified in the Forest Charter were to be implemented, however, were still to be revealed. In September, a large council confirmed that the charters of the king's minority, including Magna Carta and the Charter of the Forest, would be subject to confirmation when the king reached the age of majority. It is also likely that the king's private seal was used here for the first time. Conditions attached to the seals was expanded upon in November as another council made provision that the great seal – created in the king's image in October – should not be used until the king came of age.[18]

Also in November, the government launched a general eyre. For the first time in Henry's reign, judges once again travelled the country hearing criminal and civil pleas.[19] Such happenings were generally celebrated by the annalist of Waverley, who wrote, 'peace returned and was stabilised in England, and the justices, who are popularly called itinerant, went through all of England after Christmas, reviving the laws and causing them to be observed in the pleas before them according to the Charter of King John'.[20]

In the king's writings to the papacy a year earlier, special praise had been reserved for Guala in gratitude for his invaluable guidance throughout the war. By September 1218, however, his time as legate was coming to an end. Mindful, perhaps, that no legate should ever become too complacent, Honorius wrote to Pandulf Verraccio on 12 September announcing that he would take Guala's place.[21]

The choice was a controversial one. Pandulf was, of course, already well familiar with England being the pope's trusted subdeacon who had received John's submission at Dover in May 1213, helped stave off a French invasion and overseen events at Runnymede. As a reward for his role in proceedings at Dover, Pandulf had also been made bishop-elect of Norwich in 1215 and was blamed in certain quarters for being behind Stephen Langton's suspension. The conflict of interest was indeed a clear one. The archbishop of Canterbury being the primate of England, Pandulf's position at Norwich effectively made him Langton's subordinate. To combat this issue, rather than inherit full control of his see, it was decided that Pandulf's consecration would be indefinitely postponed.[22]

There is some evidence that Pandulf was already in England by this time. Further to his affinity with Norwich, it is likely that he joined Henry in attending the rededication of the recently repaired Worcester Cathedral in June. The necessary choice of final resting place for John, the cathedral had somewhat portentously caught fire when Ranulf and Falkes sacked the city. Further to attending the ceremony, the young king undoubtedly took the opportunity to pay his respects to his father. The rededication would be the final occasion of note for Bishop Sylvester, who died on 15 June, eight days after the translation of St Wulfstan.[23]

Honorius wrote to Pandulf again on 10 November, concerning the recent treaty between Henry's government and the king of Scotland, around which time Guala appears to have taken sail. The outgoing legate's final duty was to write to Marshal voicing his concerns that Louis was yet to release the hostages of the barons of the Cinque Ports as had been agreed explicitly at Kingston.[24] Regarding Pandulf's takeover, the transition period appears to have run smoothly. Other than the usual challenges of day to day kingship, there is little evidence Henry had any pressing concerns during the Christmas celebrations at Winchester as a guest of Peter des Roches.[25]

There is evidence around this time that in Guala's absence des Roches's influence began to develop. Since the creation of Henry's private seal and issue of the royal seal, attestation by Marshal had become slightly less frequent. It is surely no coincidence that Marshal's diminishing presence mirrored Peter's more frequent involvement. From November onwards there was a considerable increase in the number of letters witnessed by Peter, compared to a mere handful before that time. From January 1219 onwards, Hubert also appears for the first time as co-authoriser with Peter.[26]

Then in February, tragedy struck the kingdom. Plagued by old age and declining health, the great William Marshal fell ill. After returning to Westminster from the royal palace at Marlborough around mid-January, Marshal's health declined around the feast of Candlemas – 2 February. For more than three months, the stalwart of five kings was forced to bear the brunt of severe internal pains, depleting his appetite to a point where he survived on little more than sodden bread and mushrooms.[27]

Yet where the flesh was weak, the spirit remained willing. More importantly, the mind invigorated. He had been too ill to attend a council in Rochester in March, during which envoys of the king of France expressed a willingness to extend the truce of Bouvines. His decision, however, to leave the Tower around 16 March and take a gentle four-day river journey to his beloved manor of Caversham, near Reading, allowed a council to be held around 8-12 April. Among those in attendance were the king, legate, and several other senior magnates.[28]

Knowing his time was nigh, Marshal resigned the regency on 9 April. Prompted by concerns of potential cliques, infighting and knowing the next best contender, Ranulf, was presently on crusade, he declared unequivocally that the regency must end with him. No land in the world, he stated to all present, was divided like England. That such words were aimed at des Roches alone is, of course, open to debate. That it included an implicit swipe at the bishop for his attempts at obtaining the king's care seems difficult to ignore.

During the final gathering, the weary warrior took the king's hand in his and formally entrusted him into the care of the legate and to God. He also expressed his most profound prayer that the young king should not follow the example of a 'certain criminal ancestor', most likely a reference to John, but potentially one of many. Worried that the privacy of the gathering might lead to future problems, he courted his son, William the Younger, to present Henry and the legate publicly before the baronage. When this was subsequently done – presumably at Reading – the attempts of des Roches to press home his advantage in Marshal's absence saw him reprimanded by the younger Marshal and Pandulf. His duty done, the great earl held on for another month. It was recorded by Pandulf that the regent visited him in a dream, prompting the legate to absolve him of his sins. William heard personally of this on 14 May courtesy of Pandulf's messenger, the abbot of Reading, who also took his confession.[29]

That day was to be his last. On being pressured on the topic of salvation by Henry fitz Gerald, who supported him through the remaining hours, Marshal's final view seems to have been one of *c'est la vie* – what was done was done, and only God could decide. So strong were his views he rebuked the various clerics for their attempts to achieve custody of his property, commenting: 'the argument of the clerks must be false or else nobody would be saved'. After giving a similar rebuke to his clerk regarding his robes and furs, all of which Marshal had reserved for his knights, the great man died. Just as Howden had written that the Lionheart had conquered cities, even the great knights could not conquer time. His biography ends with the statement, we 'believe that his soul is in the company of God because he was good in this life and in his death.'[30]

True to the vow taken when John bent the knee at Dover, William was interred at the Temple church in London, buried in the habit of a Templar. In future years, Marshal's good friend, Master of the Temple in England, Aymeric de Saint Maur, spoke of his funerary wishes: 'Bury me beside William Marshal, the Good Knight, who has won that surname by his probity on earth and will carry it with him to heaven.'

Such loving testimony was by no means limited to Aymeric. Many years earlier, fellow crusader Richard the Lionheart said of the

'Good Knight', 'I have always held him for the most loyal knight in all my realm. I do not believe he has ever been false.'

Nor was praise limited to English nobility. In his commentary of Marshal, the French king Philip Augustus is known to have commented, 'You have well said – but what I say is that he was the most loyal man I ever knew in any place where I have been.'

Such praise indeed only strengthens the case put forward by Marshal's loyal comrade John of Earley, who in the privacy of the chambers of Gloucester had predicted such greatness at a time otherwise of doom. As history would later recall, Earley was correct in his assessment that in succeeding, 'No man will ever have earned such glory on earth.'[31]

When the funeral train passed from Caversham, many earls, barons, bishops and others, lay or clergy, joined it on its path to the Temple Church in London. At the head of the service was Langton, who performed the final rites. Of all the kind words said of Marshal, it is undoubtedly the archbishop's at the graveside that best expressed the thoughts of all that knew of him.

'The best knight of all the world that has lived in our time!'[32]

Chapter 9

1195–1219
The Three Wise Men

The regency ended with Marshal. As the great statesman had rightly come to realise, the role that no one had wanted during wartime had the potential in peacetime to become the most sought after in the kingdom. The oath he had sworn before a boy of 9 among the plains of Malmesbury to lay down his life for the protection of his charge, had in reality been a tacit acceptance to spend the remaining years of his life as king in all but name. Swayed in his final days no doubt by his most tiresome experiences, many of which he felt vindicated his reservations voiced at Gloucester, he had wisely foreseen that naming of the wrong successor for a boy of 11 could undo all recent good work. If one great lesson stemmed from Magna Carta it was that war came about far more easily than peace; and peace had been bought at a high price.

Despite the exact role ceasing to exist, even in the great void Henry was by no means short of support. Prior to Marshal's death, the increased influence of Peter des Roches and Hubert de Burgh had developed the pinnacle of government into a form of triumvirate, which in effect would replace the regency permanently after June 1219. At its centre was Pandulf, whose position as head was universally accepted. Intriguingly, the Waverley annalist incorrectly placed Hubert's appointment as justiciar to around this time. Though undoubtedly a contradiction of what was agreed at Bristol in November 1216, the suggestion speaks volumes of Hubert's lack of influence up to this point. It is equally notable that in May 1219, des Roches's six-month period witnessing the royal letters ended with Hubert taking over as the principal witness.[1]

Pandulf's arrival had effectively made him the king's chief overseer even before Marshal's death. Now that William was gone, that influence would only increase. The effect such matters had on the government should not be underestimated; not least how the king's key advisors received Pandulf's arrival. Still no friend of Langton, the legate's influence would be better received by des Roches, who was still Henry's tutor at this time. Within days of Marshal's death, the legate wrote to Peter and Hubert on matters of revenue collection, a topic that would be of great consequence throughout the following years. Contrary to the relaxed, yet energetic attitude of Guala, Pandulf took on a more hands on approach and was as free in his opinions on matters of royal appointment and domestic and foreign policy as he was all things clerical.[2]

Unsurprisingly, a developing reputation for meddling aroused further annoyance among the barons. Of particular resentment was his desire that the recent papal edict that no baron could ever hold more than one royal castle at any time be fully implemented. In the early stages of the minority, approximately 100 castles were held in the king's name, about a third of which were royal. For Henry, this topic remained a problem. On the one hand, the keepers had fought so loyally for the royalist cause and the last thing he wanted was to offend his closest allies. On the other, their unwillingness to vacate them ran the risk of the lords continued profiting from local revenues, thus depriving the exchequer of necessary funds and serving to undermine his authority.[3]

One man who had a particular interest in the fate of the royal castles was Peter des Roches. A key member of the triumvirate, even prior to Marshal's illness, no one involved in government at the time was more influential than the bishop of Winchester.

Before he arrived in England, details of his life are sketchy. Born around 1170, Peter appears to have cut his teeth as a cleric in the Touraine area of France before entering royal service in the 1190s. Pinpointing his exact place of birth is difficult. Unlike many of his contemporaries, his commonly used surname, literally translated: of the rocks, lacks a clear point of origin. Named also after the apostle upon which Christ would build his church, the literal meaning of his full name could be discerned as: rock of the rocks, or stone of the rocks. Amusingly, the irony of this wasn't lost on some of Peter's critics, one of which would later warn the king of the need to steer carefully between rocks and stones.[4]

Most likely, Peter was of the same ancestral line as William des Roches, seneschal of Anjou, Touraine, Maine and Poitou at various times, who also hailed from Touraine.[5] Much has been made of Peter's later label, 'the Poitevin', a tag he shared with many others in John's inner circle. The family name de Rupibus was unknown in Poitou.

Nor does he appear to have had any connection with the region either in his youth or from his wider lineage. Intriguingly, this labelling does not appear to have been the work of the contemporary chroniclers and the tradition that he was a Poitevin only dates to the seventeenth century. The term was famously a derisory one, which by the 1230s had become a byword for duplicity and wastefulness.[6]

Similarly, the English were far from beloved in Poitou. Back in the reign of Henry III's grandfather, Henry II had been known there as, 'King of the North'. When Peter first came onto the courtly scene in 1197, it is notable he did so in the city of Tours. Likewise, support for his bid to obtain the see of Winchester in 1205 came from the archbishop of Tours. Undoubtedly the best evidence for his upbringing concerns a poem he commissioned on the life of the Anglo-Saxon St Birinus to which Peter was described as being of Touraine.[7]

In later life, Peter's connection to Poitou becomes clearer. In the years 1200–05, he seems to have been treasurer of the collegiate church of St Hilaire in the region's capital of Poitiers. Exactly fourteen months after first appearing at Richard I's court at Tours in April 1197, he is noted as a member of the king's chamber, witnessing and warranting royal writs. On John's accession, his prospects improved further. In May 1201 he was granted land in Anjou; in February 1203 he received a further land grant as well as being entrusted with the revenues of the abbey of St Martin's Troarn in March. Within a year of his arrival in England following John's loss of Normandy, Peter's stock had already risen considerably. Enriched with benefices and estates including a prebend at Lincoln and being appointed the cathedral's precentor, he was also granted the churches of Cave, Halesowen and Kirby Misperton, a vicarage in Bamburgh and lands confiscated from the countess of Perche and Aimery de Harcourt. There was also talk around that time of his filling the vacant see of Chichester.[8]

Not being elected to Chichester would prove a stroke of fate. Indeed, there is every reason to believe Peter must have felt God was favouring him after the see at Winchester fell vacant in September 1204. In contrast to Chichester, which was by no means renowned for its wealth, Winchester was England's richest diocese having retained much of its pre-Norman prosperity and possessed of a cathedral well on its way to becoming one of the most impressive in England. Curiously, John wasted little time in pushing Peter's case for the bishopric. A man famous for his tendency to profit from vacant sees, it must be viewed a clear endorsement of John's fondness for Peter that within a fortnight of the death of the previous bishop, Godfrey de Lucy, he was already in prime position to receive the support of the monks of St Swithun's. Unlike at Canterbury, the Winchester monks had never possessed any great willingness to promote from within and, despite his battles with the barons and many other key prelates, over the ensuing years Peter's relations with the monks was largely harmonious.[9]

Elected by the monks, consecration by Innocent III duly followed in September 1205, thus beginning a tenure that would prove controversial.[10] When England was placed under interdict in 1208, Peter was the only bishop to remain by John's side and throughout that period he continued to profit from the collection of Peter's pence. Incidentally, the chroniclers also singled him out for being on friendly terms with many agents who did the church lands harm, including the notorious Richard Marsh (de Marisco), later bishop of Durham.[11]

Though there is no evidence that des Roches breached any of the church's customs during the interdict, the fact that he was the only prelate to serve John in a secular manner is intriguing. That he flourished in John's court without any form of major fall also suggests a rare ability to adapt that goes far beyond ordinary sycophancy. As a leading ecclesiastic, he was responsible for providing knights for John's army and was among the few who attended the military campaigns personally – a feat more in keeping with the bishops of the Holy Roman Empire than his English counterparts. A combination of his fighting abilities and his close relationship with John may be highlighted by the fact that, in the war of 1216, John's bastard, Oliver, is recorded as having defended Wolvesey Castle on his behalf.[12]

Largely for such reasons, in the centuries since, des Roches has often been criticised for his lack of commitment, or at least suitability, to his vocation. A capable soldier, he has, in some quarters, been described as a militant in clerics' clothing as opposed to a devout holy man. A well-known lampoon of the time lamented: 'The Warrior of Winchester, up at the exchequer. Sharp at accounting, slack at the Scripture.'[13] In his continuation of the work of Roger of Wendover, Matthew Paris wrote of des Roches that in his youth he was better versed at siege warfare than in preaching of the gospels. The chronicle of Lanercost accused him of taking more pleasure in the suffering of wild animals than that of saving the souls of men. One particularly troubling allegation that would colour perception in the eyes of certain critics was a bull put forward by Innocent III in 1214. In this, the pope accused him of denying the liberties of the church, specifically stating: 'You have said in your heart, "There is no God," since you presume to act against his church ... not fearing to displease God in order to satisfy the demands of man.'[14]

Despite such things, evidence for the contrary is also easily found. Peter's patronage of the religious orders and founding of holy sites ranks on an otherwise unfathomable scale compared to those of the courts of England and France at that time. Undoubtedly his greatest enthusiasm was for the orders of Prémontré and Cîteaux, for whom he founded English houses at Halesowen, Titchfield and Netley as well as le Clarté in France. Also created under his watch were hospitals at Southwark, the Domus Dei in Portsmouth and, during his later crusade, rededication of an earlier one in honour of Thomas Becket in the port city of Acre. Before this, the first Dominican friaries were set up at Winchester. Perhaps most ironically, in addition to his future work on Winchester's Lady Chapel, one of his greatest passions at St Swithun's was to foster the cult of the Anglo-Saxon saints.[15]

Of the man himself and his exact beliefs, details are frustratingly ambiguous.

An influential landowner and financier, his creation of several new parks fits well with his reputation as a devoted hunter. A bizarre story, recorded in the Lanercost Chronicle fifty years after his death, recalls that one day out hunting he met with the legendary King Arthur in a forest. On dining, Peter asked the great king for a memento of their meeting, to which Arthur instructed Peter to close his hands, after which a butterfly flew out from them. The chronicle specifies that after that, Peter could repeat the miracle, earning him the nickname, 'The Butterfly Bishop'.[16]

That such a meeting ever took place is, of course, a matter for conjecture, his love of wine, spices, jewels and gold as revealed by the Winchester pipe rolls could be seen to vindicate his critics that he was more lavish than generous. Conversely, his prolific founding and commissioning of monasteries, abbeys, priories, friaries and hospitals is far more in keeping with that of a man of both deep devotion and artistic taste. His patronage of scholars and poets, coupled with his military capabilities, also makes perfect sense of how he came to be Henry's tutor in 1212. That Henry viewed Peter as something of a Dutch uncle or father figure in John's absence is unsurprising. Having joined John in exile following the loss of Normandy in 1204, along with many of his fellow countrymen, Peter committed himself to John's way of life in a manner few others did.[17]

To conclude that this was out of love for the monarch alone would ignore the challenges of mutual and self-dependency. In a land where aliens were often severely isolated, the greatest chance a foreigner had for survival was to seek government protection. As a consequence, such affiliation brought its own brand of loyalty. No less true was this in Peter's cliques. In the early years, almost of all of his key promotions involved nepotism.[18]

The fact that it was to Peter that John entrusted the young Henry's education also speaks volumes. True, as a neighbour of the Winchester-born prince, it seems logical that combining matters of princely learning with responsibilities concerning St Swithun's was unlikely to be a major burn on his time. It would, nevertheless, have been unthinkable for the ever paranoid John to willingly allow the heir to the throne to become indoctrinated in unwanted thoughts or doctrine. Nor would he have placed him in a position that would have rendered him susceptible to kidnap. That the bishop influenced the young king is clear. In later years, Henry's personality would develop as one whose loves included lavish levels of luxury, patronage of the arts and buildings, simple forms of piety, an attachment to the ancestral French lands, affection for John and a loathing for Magna Carta, all of which were attributes or feelings associated with Peter.

The amount of time that Peter was able to spare the king, at the time a mere prince, may well have changed in the brief period 1214–15 when John appointed him justiciar. How Peter fared in the role has become another hot topic. Following on from the death of Geoffrey fitz Peter in October 1213, evidence for des Roches's commission as justiciar is implied in letters dated 12 January 1214, with formal confirmation occurring in February. It was written in the annals of Waverley that John's thinking behind the appointment concerned subjection of the magnates and to subdue discord. In reality, the appointment of this loathed alien would have the opposite effect.[19]

Frequently a thorn in Langton's side for his tendency to oversee, and often directly influence, the elections of key clerical officials, most notably filling appointments that had become vacant in the interdict, he enjoyed better relations with Pandulf as well as a solid one with Marshal. In February 1214, John also temporarily made des Roches regent as he attempted to reclaim the lost ancestral lands on the Continent. The 100,000-mark tallage for the interdict was also issued during Peter's regency.[20]

A highly able administrator, des Roches maintained the justiciarship until May 1215. According to the Waverley annalist, he was not shy in abusing his power; however, it is unlikely this directly caused his removal. Of greater consequence, the xenophobic articles 50 and 51 in the great charter concerning aliens would have put significant pressure on John to replace him with someone of domestic background. Notably, a short time later des Roches was relieved of his duties and succeeded by the English-born Hubert de Burgh.[21]

A much different man than the 'Poitevin' cleric, Hubert had made his own stamp on the war, not least holding out bravely against Louis during the latter's ongoing siege of Dover. Born around 1170, a younger son of minor landowners of Norfolk gentry, the story of Hubert de Burgh, like that of Marshal, is another of rags to riches.

Far younger than the 'greatest knight' – by his own admission Marshal was well over 70 at the time of Henry's accession – the 46-year-old Hubert had entered John's service in the early 1190s after leaving his home near Norwich in 1185 to travel to London. His first step on the ladder came courtesy of his elder brother, William, who helped secure for him a post at the Angevin court, which at the time was located close to the Thames at Westminster. Though the exact role Hubert was given is unclear and may well have varied, William is recorded as having been on the staff of Prince John at the time of Hubert's arrival. Incidentally, William followed John to Ireland and founded the Irish branch of the family, which would be of profound importance during Hubert's later years.[22]

Inspired by what he saw during his time as an employee of the future king, Hubert's ambitions soared. His interest in castles and acquisition of property evident at an early age, under John he was appointed chamberlain, thus putting him in charge of John's court. During this time, responsibilities would have included maintaining records, paying cash or bills to and from the treasury and keeping the royal castles in good condition and well manned: in short, the perfect apprenticeship for a future justiciar. On John's return to England after marrying Isabella, Hubert was granted the sheriffdom of Hereford, and later Dorset and Somerset. Ever wary of the threat of the Welsh in the Marches, John also empowered Hubert with 100 knights in addition to making him castellan of the three castles of Gwent: Skenfrith, Grosmont and Whitecastle.[23]

How important these moves would be only become clear in the years to come. It is now the consensus of modern historians that coordinated management of the treasury, exchequer and chancery date from around this point: something in which Hubert would have been heavily involved – in certain cases, perhaps the originator. Within two years, the number of civil ranks, properties and alternative income sources Hubert had amassed is quite astounding. Further to those mentioned, he had also become sheriff of Berkshire and Cornwall, custodian of Corfe Castle, castellan of Launceston and Wallingford castles, custodian of the baronies of Beauchamp and Dunster, inheritor of the lands of Emma de Beaufoy in Nottinghamshire and Norfolk and custodian of the forfeit lands of the count of Tregueir in Cambridgeshire, Norfolk and Lincolnshire.[24]

In 1202, Hubert experienced Continental policy for the first time on being sent to Normandy. Already renowned for his administrative talents, it was during these years he also forged a reputation as a capable military performer, most notably during the defence of Chinon Castle from French attack in 1205. However, such things failed to make a mark on the ever-fickle John. Contrary to the wide scale lauding of the local population, John accused him of allowing Chinon to fall and punished him with the confiscation of much of his lands, including the castles of Gwent, which were subsequently granted in hereditary right to William de Braose. By 1218, following which William and Maud were dead after falling foul of John's temper, Hubert demanded of William's son, Reginald, that the castles be returned. A year later, a combination of a court decision and a sensible compromise would see his wish granted.[25]

By 1207–08, Hubert's earlier loss of reputation was on the mend. So great had his stock risen, in 1212 he was appointed seneschal of Poitou, after which he successfully held the county from the king of France. Recalled to England around the time of Magna Carta, his journey to the highest rung of the political ladder was completed on replacing des Roches as justiciar of England. As a consequence of this, Hubert was made castellan of Dover Castle and was still in possession of the mighty citadel when Louis launched his siege. Whereas some saw the death of John as a reason to lose hope, for Hubert the opposite was true. Suggestion by the rebellious William Longespée, Earl of Salisbury, that he surrender it fell on deaf ears. Indeed, when the earl parleyed with Hubert on the dauphin's behalf to inform him of John's death and of Louis's offer of many riches and honours in return for changing sides, Hubert offered his immense response, 'If my Lord is dead, he has sons and daughters who ought to succeed him.'[26]

In seeing off French navies and infamous pirates, Hubert had endeared himself as a hero of the people: a man who, in his own way, invoked the spirit of the emerging English nation more than any other. An ally of Langton, but despiser of foreign lords who abused their power, his continuation as justiciar would do more than anything to frustrate the same onset of promotions of foreign favourites that had occurred throughout John's reign and would later do so throughout Henry's. With Marshal gone, it was to this man, along with the foreign born clerics to whom the future of the kingdom would rely.

The final piece of the young king's magi.

Chapter 10

1219–1220
Rocking the Castles

For the young king, the death of his beloved protector presented what was arguably the most significant problem of his reign so far. True, he had seen off an enemy made up of foreign invaders and rebellious subjects that he had in no way personally offended, yet for each of those challenges it had been Marshal who had taken the lead. Even if the greatest knight were to prove impossible to replace, in the regent's absence it was all the more vital the triumvirate worked together to help fill the void. Now two and half years into his reign, the possibility that an 11-year-old would be capable of ruling alone was unthinkable.

Within the wider community, similar views were held. A particularly derogatory example of this came later that year when the king was labelled 'not a king but a boy' in attempting to resolve the matter of Tickhill Castle in Nottinghamshire, previously held by the count of Eu, Raoul de Lusignan, prior to his death earlier in the year. Similarly, in 1218, clerks at Winchester referred to Henry III's sister as 'daughter of the king', whereas, in 1220, all tin mines in the Cornish stannaries were still being stamped with John's insignia. Possession of his own seal since 1218, though a vast extension of any personal powers he had previously held, remained in the grander scheme of national government little more than a token gesture. In reality, even the local councils possessed more authority than the king.[1]

Attempts at restoration of the national government would continue throughout the summer. Within a month of Marshal's burial, a great council met in Gloucester, during which Hubert was placed in charge of the royal seal. Besides the problems relating to the surrender of the royal castles, one of the most significant challenges remained to curb abuse of power by the sheriffs. A recurring problem had been monies due to the crown being collected but not handed over. Whether it was the talk of such figures that had given rise to murmurings of the king's lack of effectiveness, it was undoubtedly true, even though he had his own seal and with a highly efficient administrator like Hubert put in control of the great seal, many sheriffs and castellans felt safe until he came of age.[2]

In July 1219, commissioners were appointed to settle all remaining disputes with the king of Scotland. In November, Honorius wrote to Pandulf specifically on the matter, ordering him to confirm or annul any treaty that might have been agreed between the two monarchs. Around this time, Henry also requested of the legate protections against his foreign lands. His most pressing fear was the Albigensian crusaders in their war against the Cathars in the Languedoc region of France. Specific directions were given to, among others, John's great foe Hugh de Lusignan with the promises of funds to aid him. The suggestion was also made of a general willingness to prolong the truce of 1214. This, Marshal had been made aware of back in March. As a consequence of his declining health, he had been unable to personally entertain the French envoys at Rochester and deal with the matter in detail.[3]

With the expiration of the truce of May 1214 now upon them, policy with France was a pressing concern. The English coffers were far too depleted from the recent conflict to either embark on or be faced with any further war. Writing to Philip Augustus on 10 May, Honorius thanked him for helping to keep the peace and requested a continuation. In no way willing to see a repeat of events such as at Damme or restart Louis's campaign of three years earlier, a one-year extension was agreed in July, on publication of which Philip condemned Louis's invasion of 1216 for the first time. By January of the following year, secret discussions between Honorius and Hubert paved the way for a longer extension. On 3 March 1220, peace between England and France was agreed until 1224.[4]

Foreign policy would be a significant recurring topic around this time. Earlier in 1219, Geoffrey Neville, seneschal of Poitou, wrote to Henry concerning issues on the Continent. Frustrated by a perceived lack of support, on 1 November he returned to England to formally resign his position.[5]

Poitou aside, the majority of foreign policy concerned the fate of the Holy Land. The death of John's nephew Otho IV had led to the accession of Frederick II as Holy Roman Emperor, a figure who, as history would recall, would both excel and infuriate at various times.[6] Within a year of taking the throne, the Christian armies of the Fifth Crusade enjoyed one of their greatest victories in taking the Egyptian port city of Damietta, thereafter achieving control of the River Nile. It was recorded by at least one of the chroniclers of the time that the river rose miraculously in celebration of the capture of Damietta, as though a Biblical judgement was being exercised.[7] In planning for the crusade, control of Damietta had been considered of profound consequence. In theory, control of the Nile would allow for domination of the whole of Egypt, which in turn could be used as a springboard for total conquest of Palestine and Jerusalem. Fresh from their varying spats in the First Barons' War, the previous October had seen the arrival of the earl of Chester, as well as the earl of Winchester, Fitzwalter and Oliver, one of John's bastards. Despite their initial success, frustrations were encountered when marching on Cairo in 1221 culminated in recent progress being reversed. As a result of the setback, Damietta was soon lost.[8]

Back in England, in mid-December 1219 commissions made up of panels of twenty-four knights and freemen were appointed to determine the bounds of the forests as set out in the Forest Charter. Work was being undertaken in January but appears not to have commenced by the time the king celebrated Christmas with Peter des Roches at Marlborough. That the job was an easy one seems highly unlikely, especially with the added complication of a deterioration in the weather. From the recordings of the chroniclers, there seems good reason to believe that the Christmas court that year was viewed as the highlight of a sodden winter where the heavy rains barely ceased.[9]

With the government now on a far sounder footing, the suggestion was made that the king be crowned a second time. Due to the coronation at Gloucester having been one of necessity as opposed to splendour, it was argued in certain quarters that Henry never got the opportunity to enjoy a proper ceremony. In a bid to remedy this, Honorius wrote to the archbishop of Canterbury pressing the case for a second, grander affair. Having been forcibly absent from the Gloucester ceremony, Langton was understandably delighted on hearing the suggestion. Only recently returned to England after his lengthy suspension, plans were swiftly circulated among the council and the prelates after which proceedings moved forward at a steady pace.[10]

The date set was 17 May 1220. The location, Westminster Abbey: a site whose rebuilding would one day form a key part of Henry's legacy. A day earlier, the young king had taken a direct role in the precursor to the rebuilding, having personally laid the foundation stone of the new Lady chapel.[11] It is quite possible that Henry's affinity with Westminster stemmed primarily from des Roches. An avid builder, the bishop spent large parts of the year at Westminster due to his exchequer responsibilities. It was also in des Roches's time that the nearby episcopal palace south of the Thames at Southwark underwent significant rebuilding.[12]

The contrast between the two coronations was immense. Whereas the first had been memorable for its sparseness and urgency, not to mention the absence of a crown, the second was remarked upon for possessing great awe and harmony. Under Langton's guidance, all of the prelates – apart from the unavoidably absent archbishop of York – and a large number of barons gathered to see Henry recite the coronation oath. Once complete, he once again paid homage to the papacy. A day later, the barons performed a similar one for the king.[13]

Replacing Isabella's basic hoop used at Gloucester, the king was crowned with the diadem of St Edward the Confessor. Precisely what this object was remains something of a mystery. Prior to the coronation, no mention of it seems to have survived. The Bayeux Tapestry famously depicts Edward adorned with a crown. According to the monks of Westminster, Edward's crown was kept there specifically for future coronations. Of the accuracy of the story, proof is impossible to ascertain. That the religious king would have been pleased by Henry's actions seems likely, especially in the light of the young king's developing devotion to him. Incidentally, the coronation would mark the only occasion in England's history where a king was crowned a second time – discounting, of course, that of a queen alongside him. In 1269, when Henry oversaw the translation of St Edward's remains into his new shrine at the rebuilt gothic Westminster, the then-ageing king considered a third to correspond with the date. It was also noted in the annals of Worcester that a further miracle of St Wulfstan occurred on Easter Sunday, which in that year fell around the time of the coronation.[14]

With the king's second coronation officially in the history books, one could argue an important break with the past had been established. Long gone the drums of war, the sound head of Guala and, of course, the great knight who had helped steer him through the choppiest of waters, Henry was at last now able to concern himself with more pressing matters. Satisfied that the new triumvirate of Hubert, des Roches and Pandulf was working productively without need to appoint a direct replacement for Marshal, there also seems to have been a discussion – or at least suggestion – around this time that Henry should be declared of age. Now four years into his kingship, yet still a mere boy of 12 with much about life to be learned, the idea was soon put to one side and would not be raised again seriously for another three years.

Papal interference, of course, continued. Shortly after the coronation, Honorius wrote to Pandulf once again voicing his concerns that certain members of the clergy were using Henry's youth to their own benefit, not least their retaining possession of the royal castles. Not limiting his criticism to the prelates, on clarifying his view that any bishop presently holding a royal castle should relinquish it, in letters dated 26 and 28 May he also specified that no baron should ever hold more than two at any one time.[15]

The cause of the pope's concern was obvious. Just as tournaments were viewed with certain degrees of scepticism due to their potential to organise dishevelled mobs into capable warriors able to form effective armies, it was likewise viewed that a castle's garrison could be used as the springboard for future rebellion. Inevitably, such demands brought varying reactions. Finding support from the justiciar and archbishop of Canterbury, both of whom were adamant that Englishmen should hold the castles, des Roches predictably viewed the demand as being of great peril to his own clique – the so-called 'Poitevin' faction – many of whom still occupied royal castles from John's reign.

As a consequence of such problems, differences between Hubert de Burgh and Peter des Roches threatened to escalate. By no means the best of friends even in John's reign, it was on such matters the pair disagreed most strongly. The natural temptation for any historian is to pin the reason on either des Roches's resentment in losing the justiciarship to Hubert or the underlying trend of nationalism and wariness of outsiders that had become ever more prevalent in England since the loss of Normandy. True to his nationality and values, Hubert was a fierce advocator of pushing key appointments for Englishmen, a stark contrast to the views of the French bishop who had gained so significantly from the favouritism of John towards the 'Poitevin' faction. Likely though it is that differing views on future policy threatened at times to turn into an epic political arm wrestle, it is easy to ignore the universal truth that occasional friction between high up officials is often par for the course. It also seems of equal importance that the absence left by Marshal opened up something of a vacuum at the heart of government.

Just as problems between the pair threatened to reach boiling point, Henry's mother, Isabella, dropped a bombshell. A widow since John's death, the queen dowager had been a notable absentee from her son's early government. While this can partly be explained by the urgency of the war, in contrast to her lack of status in England, her power in her homeland was uncontested.[16] In 1218 she returned to her original county of Angoulême and received the homage of the barons. Still in her late twenties and highly eligible, the former wife of John ended her celibacy with her unexpected marriage to none other than Hugh de Lusignan. A year earlier, he had succeeded his late father, Hugh IX, as count of la Marche.[17]

Marrying without the consent of the king was a risky move for any royal in medieval Europe. For a queen dowager, it was almost unthinkable. Not only did the king and council have complete autonomy over the matter, but it was also highly questionable whether she could marry at all. The identity of her husband was itself surprising. The Lusignans, of course, had long been viewed as controversial characters in the eyes of the English. Significant landholders, it was Lusignans who had captured William Marshal back in 1168, as well as proven valuable allies of John – at least at a price. News of the union was viewed with particular irony, not least as her new husband was the son of the man to whom she had been betrothed when John took the equally controversial step of marrying her as a juvenile.

Inevitably, the event gave Henry a headache. Within weeks of the union being confirmed, the king and Hugh nearly came to blows over Isabella's dowry. As was the right of the council, the initial move had been to dismiss her demands and cut off her pension altogether: an unwise move, albeit well within their powers. Such matters did not go unnoticed in Rome. On growing increasingly frustrated with the unwanted episode of dealing with two shameless self-promoters, in September Honorius wrote to Isabella, demanding she end her harassment of her son regarding her dowry. In a separate letter, he also warned Hugh about his attempts to infringe on Henry's land in Poitou.[18]

The recently wed did, however, have one significant advantage. Henry's sister, Joan, had been present at Hugh's court since 1214, at which time Hugh IX was still alive. Initially sought by Philip II, Joan was later promised in marriage to Hugh X by John as compensation for him having married Isabella. Exactly how it transpired that the mother would walk the aisle instead of the daughter was a complicated affair. Among the reasons cited by Isabella was that on the death of Hugh IX, as well as their kinsman, Raoul I de Lusignan, the count of Eu, that same year, Hugh X's position had become perilous. In need of an heir, the opposition the count faced from his key allies concerning any marriage to the young Joan was fierce. On being advised to marry a Frenchwoman, Isabella interjected, apparently on her son's behalf, claiming such a move would have placed the ancestral lands under severe threat.[19]

Though true to an extent, it would seem that mutual attraction and personal benefit were equally decisive factors. That Isabella saw the move as highly desirable seems unquestionable. When teased – if not berated – by John in her youth following the fall of Normandy with the words 'You see, Lady, what I have lost for your sake,' Isabella is alleged to have responded, 'And for you, I have lost the best knight in the world.' Being more or less the same age as the younger Hugh, and an heir for the new count being desperately needed, the match made more sense than Hugh taking the child Joan. On learning of the marriage, Honorius pressed for Joan's safe return to England, so that matters could finally be settled.[20]

His frustrations inevitably increasing as a result of such challenges, Henry spent much of the summer of 1220 attempting to impose a firm rule on his kingdom. Accompanied by his key governors, he travelled north in a bid to reclaim some of his castles.

First on the list was Mitford, which remained in the hands of the obstinate Philip of Oldcotes. Another of crucial importance was Berkeley Castle in Gloucestershire, which had previously been held by the baron Robert de Berkeley. On Berkeley's death, a new problem ensued when the sheriff, Ralph Musard, discovered the earl of Salisbury had chanced upon the confusion and taken possession of the castle. Contrary to some of the other ongoing issues, the problem was mostly financial. Not only had Berkeley been in debt to the earl, but his niece, Berkeley's widow, was with child.

When news reached the king, the government had been travelling north to discuss a settlement with the king of Scotland. On 12 June, within a day of Henry meeting Alexander II at York, Hubert and the council authenticated a letter for Salisbury's removal. Though, seemingly friendly, correspondence occurred between the pair, Longespée would not be present at York due to illness. Over the coming days, better progress was made regarding Scotland. An ironic by-product of Hugh and Isabella's marriage was that it allowed the two kings to enter an arrangement for Alexander to marry Joan, recently cuckolded by her own mother in Poitou. There is evidence to suggest talk had also included Henry's other sister Isabella, with the Scottish king initially agreeing to marry one or the other.[21]

Matters in York completed, at least for now, the government moved south. Their differences seemingly put aside, Peter and Hubert moved from Nottingham to Northampton via Leicester 20-25 June, only to backtrack fifteen miles to Rockingham where one more matter from John's reign remained unresolved. According to the Barnwell chronicler, on being crowned a second time, Henry began a tour of his kingdom, seeking the peaceful surrender of the royal castles, only for Aumale's Rockingham to be the only fortress to deny the king entry. Though later historians, not least the eminent David Carpenter, would question this, arguing instead that Aumale was a unique victim of government pressure, and that the tour of his kingdom was merely the route to and from York, for Aumale the refusal would spell trouble. Despite having arrived in England during des Roches's time as justiciar, by no means in the bishop's inner circle and having twice changed sides in the First Barons' War, Aumale was regarded as profoundly disloyal.[22]

Concerning the papal demand that the royal castles be surrendered, Henry had so far encountered mixed fortunes. Refusal by William of Aumale to comply with the order led to a series of brief, but unwelcome, military onslaughts, starting with Rockingham. A combination of Aumale's absence and the lack of sustenance presently being enjoyed by the soldiers of the garrison – apparently they only had three loaves of bread between them – soon saw their resolve wear thin. Backed by a £100 investment by Falkes de Breauté, Rockingham fell on 28 June. A few days later the same was true of Sanney – or Sauvey – in Leicestershire, as well as the earl's manors in Northamptonshire.[23]

At some point before 7 July, Henry arrived in Canterbury in preparation for the long-awaited transfer of the remains of St Thomas Becket into the cathedral. Martyred in 1170 by four knights on the loose commands of the king's grandfather, Henry II, 'who will rid me of this turbulent priest', Becket's original interment in the crypt soon saw Canterbury become one of the most popular pilgrimage sites in medieval Europe. No longer able to cope with the constant demand, permission had been granted the previous January for a new shrine to be created in the cathedral's long east section, the translation of which coincided with the fiftieth anniversary of the archbishop's murder. Following the opening of a site that would soon welcome tens of thousands of pilgrims and give rise to stories that would famously inspire Geoffrey Chaucer – thus in its own way giving birth to the modern English language – on 7 July, Henry personally witnessed the relics being moved into their new home. At the request of the prior of Christ Church, Honorius granted an indulgence of 40 days for all who assisted in the translation.[24]

The ceremony itself was remarked upon for its radiance. Overseen by Langton, just as he had the coronation, the occasion was attended by countless foreign prelates including from Hungary and Rheims. Others, however, were conspicuous by their absence: not least Lusignan, who had declined the invitation, but whose messengers continued to press home the same argument concerning his wife's dower.[25]

One less welcome guest had been Berengaria of Navarre, widow of Richard I, whose visit also concerned her dowry. In keeping with Isabella, John had been reluctant to authenticate release of her funds, despite being ordered by Innocent III to restore Berengaria her due in 1213. In early September 1215, John sent at least two documents to Innocent acknowledging the agreement, to which Berengaria was content. However, in a letter dated 8 June 1216, John asked of Berengaria to forgive non-payment due to the rising costs of the war with the barons. Later in July, Henry finally acknowledged the overdue agreement between her and the crown, forcing him to borrow 1,000 marks from Pandulf as a down payment.[26]

Of the person behind the name, again, facts are sparse. Described by at least one modern-day historian as more 'prudent than beautiful', she had gained England an ally in Navarre but failed to provide Richard with a legitimate heir. Concerning the former, the marriage had proved a political success, not least because of the brilliance of her brother, Sancho the Bold, in defending Aquitaine while Richard lingered at Duke Leopold's pleasure. Placating her now was of similar importance, due to Navarre's proximity to Gascony and her support from the king of France. Since Richard's death, she had stayed in her property at Le Mans – Philip had granted her Le Mans in exchange for her loyalty – and was a generous almsgiver to the local priory.[27]

By the end of August, an agreement was concluded with the legate and the king of Scotland after a safe passage was granted for Alexander to entreat with Henry at York for a second time. Around this time, Henry also wrote to the justiciar of Ireland, Geoffrey le Marsh – also known as Geoffrey de Marisco – concerning the government of the Emerald Isle.[28]

With matters in England, Scotland and Ireland progressing, decisions also needed to be made about the ancestral lands on the Continent – not least those of concern to Isabella. In September, at which point the king and his triumvirate had reached Exeter, Henry committed Gascony to his seneschal, Philip de Ulecot, following which letters were issued to his castle holders in Poitou and Gascony to deliver them up. Around this time, word reached Pandulf that a tournament was due to go ahead despite the present ban, enticing him to request the issue of royal letters prohibiting it.[29] A further request was also made of Hugh for the return of Joan so that her marriage to Alexander might finally take place.[30] That same month, des Roches also announced to Hubert the death of the archbishop of Bordeaux, which probably goes some way to explain de Ulecot's profit. In December, the French knight Hugh de Vivonne was given the task of serving the king as seneschal of Poitou, Aquitaine and Gascony.[31]

Violence in Wales had again threatened to rear its ugly head earlier in 1220. When trouble arose in the middle March, Pandulf had been quick to defuse the tensions with a truce. Shortly before the coronation, the four key officials Hubert, Peter, Langton and Pandulf had parleyed with Llywelyn at Shrewsbury. On 5 May, an agreement was struck. Among the business conducted was for Llywelyn's son Dafydd, by wife Joan, illegitimate daughter of King John, to be recognised as his heir, thus cutting out older, illegitimate son, Gruffudd. This further solidified the agreement made with John in 1212 whereby all of Llywelyn's kingdom would escheat to the English Crown if he had no heir by Joan. Though the truce was confirmed, this would fail to solve all matters. Of great concern to Llywelyn's rule in Gwynedd, the decision was foolishly made to allow the Welsh prince's ally, Morgan ap Hywel, the lord of Gwynllwg, to reopen his case for Caerleon, a Marshal land. In exchange, Llywelyn would relinquish Maelienydd, which he had held since the First Barons' War.[32]

On William Marshal's death in 1219, his estates had fallen to his sons. This included lands in Wales, Ireland and Normandy. Chief amongst the sons was William Marshal the Younger, now second earl of Pembroke. Born in 1190, William had already excelled himself in John's care before initially fighting for Louis on the back of acting as a surety for Magna Carta. Intriguingly, when staying at Worcester Castle, the regent had forewarned his son prior to it being taken by Ranulf of Chester. Following this, father and son had met with the earl of Salisbury at Knepp. After seeing action at the siege of Winchester, the younger Marshal had also fought for Henry's cause at the Fair of Lincoln. Predictably, it was William who commissioned his father's excellent biography, *L'Histoire de Guillaume le Mareschal*, just a few years later.[33]

A meeting for 2 August at Oxford was arranged to bring peace between the prince and the Marcher lords. Truces were also agreed at Shrewsbury until Michaelmas. In reality, only five days passed before Llywelyn reneged on any promises concerning Maelienydd, his justification that he had only agreed to surrender the homage of the nobles there and not the land itself. Worse still, his later claim that homage belonged to the princedom of Wales put him in direct breach of the 1218 Treaty of Worcester that decreed homage of the princes of Wales was due to Henry.[34]

When the council met on 2 August at Oxford, Llywelyn failed to attend. In his absence, the government offered another date, 30 September at Westminster, after which talk focused on taxation for Poitou. Though the truce of 5 May had at least ensured the coronation, business with Alexander and the translation of Becket's relics all passed by without a hitch, Llywelyn remained active in Wales. In July, Henry's government had ordered Rhys Gryg, prince of Deheubarth, to surrender to Llywelyn what he had gained during the war: namely, the castles at Kidwelly and Swansea and lordship of the Gower. It was against Gryg, acting as the king's agent, that Llywelyn marched his forces on 21 August leading to the surrenders of Kidwelly and the Gower. In reality, the campaign was a personal vendetta against Marshal, not least because of Llywelyn's belief that he was due ransoms for Marshal's men captured during the war. Around 29 August, the prince invaded Pembrokeshire, attacking the castles of Narberth and Wiston before burning Haverfordwest. In the words of the Brut Chronicle, 'he inflicted immense slaughter on the people every day'. So dominant had Llywelyn become in the area only a bribe of £100 spared Pembroke.[35]

Throughout the summer, a strangely unprepared Marshal had been stationed mainly in France, dealing with severe debts and in no hurry to raise an army. In a letter to Hubert, he requested justice be meted out at the September council in Westminster. In response, Marshal was ordered to surrender the royal castle of Fotheringhay, which would form part of Joan's dower for her marriage to the king of Scotland. As late as October, the debate remained ongoing between Llywelyn and Marshal concerning infringement of Marshal's lands and only on 3 December was Fotheringhay finally handed over.[36]

While good news concerned Joan's being given up to the king's envoys at La Rochelle, further tensions with William of Aumale proved an unwelcome distraction to an otherwise magnificent Christmas court that was celebrated at Oxford.[37] Still angry at the loss of Rockingham and Sauvey, the justiciar's intention to carry out a 1217 order for the submission of Bytham Castle saw a petulant William storm away from the court and begin a revolt in Lincolnshire. Plundering the neighbouring towns and churches, he threw down the gauntlet by holding several prisoners in Bytham's strong dungeons. Described by the Whig historian and Anglican bishop William Stubbs as 'a feudal adventurer of the worst type', Aumale's recklessness reached new heights when he was summoned to a council at Westminster, only to march on the city with a large force. Seemingly perturbed, he changed plans and marched instead on the recently given up Fotheringhay Castle in Northamptonshire.[38]

In Aumale's absence, the council met to discuss a scutage to defeat him, following which Pandulf officially excommunicated him. Accompanied by the legate and Ranulf – since Marshal's death, the most senior earl in the kingdom – Henry arrived at Bytham on 2 February. Whether aware of the king's coming or not, Aumale would not be there to meet him, having instead sought sanctuary at Fountains Abbey in Yorkshire. Minus their leader, Fotheringhay surrendered, and after a six-day siege, Bytham was also back in royal hands. Left no option but to remain in sanctuary or take up the cross, Aumale surrendered and was pardoned by both king and legate. It is a testament to the chaotic kingdom England had become that within a month he was back in favour at court. A precursor to Bishop Stubbs's comments, the contemporary chronicler Roger of Wendover wrote of Henry's lack of punishment that it set, 'the worst of examples, and encouraged future rebellions'.[39]

Precisely who was at fault here has also become a cause of contention. Though in ordinary circumstances, criticism must lie with the king, in the case of a boy still not 14, it is difficult to lay the blame on Henry entirely.

To take the chroniclers at face value, much of the frustration lay with the forgiving legate, which could itself be viewed as a jibe at Pandulf's key ally, Peter des Roches. That William was forgiven on taking up the cross is true; however, his willingness to agree did at least put down any continued rebellion.

Whether directly affected by the minor rebellion or not, Pandulf's time in England was coming to an end. Less than three months after having placed the first stone of Salisbury cathedral on 28 April 1221, Langton's journey to Rome the previous year, lamenting the legate's interference, ensured his legateship would come to an end. Around the same time, Rome also received a visit from the bishop of Durham, Richard Marsh, concerning an inquiry into his conduct in the see, eventually leading to his acquittal. Pandulf officially resigned the legateship in July and in October departed on a mission for Henry to Poitou. In May the following year, he was finally consecrated bishop of Norwich. Langton's reassurance that no more legates would be appointed in England in his lifetime would be honoured. Already minus his wise regent, the king would also be forced to take the next step without his closest ecclesiastical advisor too.[40]

Chapter 11

1221–1223
War and Peace

Canonisation of the late Hugh, Bishop of Lincoln was confirmed in February 1221. Born in France, a man of noble bearing, Hugh had enjoyed renowned status for his holy actions, not least his role in the construction of Lincoln Cathedral in the new gothic style after the earlier building suffered earthquake damage in 1185. Like his great contemporary, St Francis of Assisi, as well as earlier saints such as Columbanus, a touching element of Hugh's story was his love of animals. Emblematic of the bishop is the tale of a wild swan, who became his most prominent disciple and protector. A sign of Hugh's purity, it was told that the swan would eat out of his hand, yet bite that of any other. According to one of the chroniclers, Hugh occupied the see of Lincoln for fifteen years and fifteen days, his illness on 1 November 1200 preceded by terrible thunder and lightning. On his death on 1 December, an unusually penitent John forewent usual royal pomp and traipsed through the mud for a time as a pallbearer.[1]

Religious matters would be ever present on the political landscape of 1220–21. Merely a year after the conquest of Damietta, the annals of Dunstable lamented a prophecy of the loss and recovery of Palestine, something, one could argue, the subsequent loss of Damietta went some way towards fulfilling. On 22 November 1220, Frederick II had been officially crowned Holy Roman Emperor in Rome, some eight years after being first crowned in Mainz.[2] Yet barely a year later Honorius personally blamed him for the loss of Damietta. His delay in leaving for the Holy Land was undoubtedly of profound consequence for the crusaders in Egypt, all this occurring despite the efforts of the king of Jerusalem, John de Brienne, to obtain aid for the crusade. Of similar lament, February 1221 witnessed the passing of the earl of Arundel, William d'Aubigny. Namesake of the lord of Belvoir, Arundel was a former favourite of John, who had defected briefly on John's death before pledging his loyalty to Henry after the Fair of Lincoln. In 1218 he had been one of many to join the Fifth Crusade, only to die in Italy on his way home.[3]

At a time when the Christian armies needed a miracle, it seemed that amid noise and confusion, they might have found one. A strange letter that had circulated Europe that year made its way to the court of Henry III courtesy of one Cardinal Pelagius. Its timing coinciding with the completion of the giant tower of St Paul's Cathedral, the letter told of a legendary king, known as Prester John, who had recently subdued the king of Persia. Exactly who this king was has long been the topic of considerable research. A somewhat King Arthur-like figure, the legends of Prester John have seemingly covered all boundaries. They have placed him anywhere from India to Ethiopia, his kingdom reputedly the home of everything from the Lost Ark and the graves of the Magi to the mythical Gates of Alexander and Fountain of Youth. Unlikely to have existed in the sense of being the head of a vast Christian empire, it is notable that same year the infamous Mongol emperor Genghis Khan gathered his forces in Persia, and is undoubtedly the man behind the myth.[4]

One who appears to have been preparing a crusade at this point was Peter des Roches. It was recorded by many of the chroniclers, namely those of Winchester and Dunstable, that both Peter and the bishop of Hereford travelled to Santiago de Compostela in April 1221, leaving shortly after Easter, which had been celebrated in Woodstock.[5] Alternate theories have since abounded their destination was Paris or Rome for reasons that will soon be explained. Interestingly, his departure also seems to have coincided with Pandulf's resignation. In a further blow for the bishop of Winchester, Marshal's voluntary relinquishing of Marlborough Castle to the legate, as part of his marriage contract with the king's sister, saw him become further aligned with the legate and Hubert. In March 1222, Pandulf continued to display loyalty to the English cause by arranging a truce with Lusignan. There was also renewed talk on Pandulf's departure of declaring the king of age; however, this again came to nothing.[6]

Soon to join des Roches in agreeing to journey to the Holy Land was the influential Poitevin, Peter de Maulay. Appearing in England for the first time in 1204 after granting his lands close to the Poitou/Touraine border to his brother Aimery, Peter had supported John through good times and bad. Deemed an 'evil counsellor' by John's great critic, Roger of Wendover, he had been accused of being responsible for the murder of Arthur and, like Falkes de Breauté, he was often regarded as something of a soldier of fortune. A close ally of des Roches, who he regularly visited at the bishop's properties at Taunton and Fareham, the fortunes of the pair soon became inexorably linked. So great was John's trust in him, he was arranged in marriage to a wealthy heiress and granted custody of John's favourite residence of Corfe Castle. Within these walls, he housed the king's second son, Richard, as well as the queen and Henry whenever they were present. In addition to the royal guests, de Maulay's responsibilities at Corfe extended to the keeping of several important prisoners: most notably the controversial princess, Eleanor, the fair maid, of Brittany.[7]

Cited by some past commentators as a genuine threat to Henry's right to rule, as the daughter of John's late brother, Geoffrey, Eleanor was the sister of the disappeared Arthur and, in her brother's absence, heiress to vast swathes of the Angevin Empire. Despite a clear lack of interest among the baronage in pressing her claims to the throne, she was the most obvious candidate for insurrection against Henry. Although it is highly likely that Eleanor was already in John's custody by the time Arthur was seized at Mirebeau – at which time Henry III was still to be conceived – she had known Corfe Castle as her home since around 1206. Joining her had been twenty-five of her loyal French knights, twenty-two of whom John had starved to death after a gaolbreak culminated in recapture. A shopping list that survives from the time demonstrates she was generally well provided for, despite being forced to endure the longest period of captivity ever experienced by a royal in England.

Still in control of both Eleanor and Corfe in 1221, de Maulay had met opposition for his alleged abuses of power, not least his own refusal to surrender the royal castles in his possession. The reason, so he claimed, was simple: by relinquishing his castles, he would be breaking an oath to John not to do so until Henry reached the age of majority. In Peter's defence, there is some evidence that John had imposed some form of oath on the castellans to hold the castles until Henry was at least 14. Guala, himself, had also entrusted the castles to the recipients under specific terms.[8]

Things began to change in October 1217 when Peter was summoned to the royal court to answer charges concerning a private war against the earl of Salisbury for control of Somerset – a matter that was eventually resolved. Subsequently, de Maulay received some 6,561 marks as ransoms for sixteen prisoners held at Corfe. Yet curiously in the previous two years he had paid nothing into the Exchequer from his properties from Somerset or Dorset. Sometime after presenting Henry's younger brother Richard at the king's second coronation, accusations of extortion saw Richard leave Corfe.

From there, things deteriorated. On 30 May 1221, Hubert and a minor West Country knight named Richard Mucegros accused de Maulay of treason. The charge concerned the royal princess for whom he had long been responsible – more specifically that he plotted to hand her over to the king of France. Whether there was any truth in the rumours or whether this had arisen from a shared plan put forward by Hubert and Mucegros, whose lands de Maulay had recently taken due to his failure to pay a royal fine in de Maulay's sheriffdom, is unclear. When brought before the Winchester-based court at Whitsun ten days later, along with his contemporary Engelard de Cigogné, the pair were humiliated, stripped naked and put in prison.[9]

Des Roches was back in England in July, accompanied by what would prove the nation's first group of Dominican friars. His return from the Camino – assuming he had actually gone to Santiago – came just in the nick of time for de Maulay. Though Corfe was lost, de Maulay was allowed to keep the sheriffdom. Later that year, he also took up the cross with des Roches and Falkes only to postpone their departure on the loss of Damietta. Prior to that news, there appears to have been talk of des Roches being made archbishop of that city, a project – if not a pipedream – that was subsequently shelved. The following year, de Maulay was acquitted and for the time being retired to his estates.[10]

Henry's tutelage under des Roches would officially end around this time. Though there is evidence that elements of their previous arrangement continued until as late as October, there is also reason to believe Henry's formal education was in decline before the bishop left for the Camino. Of the reasons for its end, it seems various influences were at play. A key factor undoubtedly was the extended influence of Hubert. A man capable – at least during this particular period – of maintaining solid working relationships, but no great friend of des Roches, Hubert would have been as concerned as anyone of the king falling into bad habits: not least Henry repeating the mistakes of his father in placing too much of his trust in certain cliques made up primarily of foreign lords.[11]

A secondary reason appears to have been Henry's boredom, which most likely stemmed from his adolescent frustrations at being king in name only. In his regular absence from government, Henry had been granted his own court at Wallingford or Havering, the former of which was held by his illegitimate half-brother, Richard fitz Regis, the costs of which were covered by des Roches.[12]

Precisely what Henry's education consisted of is also sadly lost to time. Besides the roles played by des Roches, as well as Ralph de St Samson and Philip d'Aubigné concerning riding and military matters, his tutor, one Master Henry d'Avranches, was known to have implemented a rigorous routine for the king's grammar. Not yet 13 at his second coronation, Henry was still a young man and by no means the complete scholar. Even in the thirteenth century, a scholar's education rarely ended prior to the age of 14, something that would have been especially true in a royal household. In April 1221, Henry was deprived of Philip d'Aubigné, who appears to have departed on crusade.[13]

Another factor in the termination of his pupillage may well have been the rising influence of Stephen Langton. Having travelled to Rome to seek Pandulf's removal, the archbishop had been absent for the legate's final nine months in office and had only returned in July 1221.[14]

Born in England to a family of minor knights from Lincolnshire, Langton had at one time been associated with the household of Henry II's bastard Geoffrey Plantagenet – the very same man who would later inherit the archbishopric of York. By the 1180s, the future archbishop of Canterbury had made his name as a scholar in Paris, lecturing on the Bible. No friend of Peter – along with Pandulf, the bishop had been blamed for Langton's suspension – Langton, as archbishop of Canterbury, was Peter's spiritual superior. Yet there had been no place for him in the triumvirate. It is highly likely that Henry's devotion to Edward the Confessor stemmed at least in part from Langton. A magnificent scholar whose writings have gone mostly unpublished, Stephen is generally accepted as the person responsible for dividing up the Bible into the modern layout of chapters we know today. Throughout his time in Canterbury, he had been as vociferous as any in his attempts to curb absolute monarchy: something of which his discovery of Henry I's Charter of Liberties was a prime example. He would remain steadfastly in favour of reform for the remainder of his life.[15]

Foreign policy again came to the fore in May 1221. More than three years since the joyous scenes that followed Louis's departure from England

and the end of the First Barons' War, Henry formally acknowledged the prince's joint crowning alongside his father Philip Augustus by sending representatives to France for the ceremony. Undoubtedly motivated by matters of diplomacy and potential gain as opposed to that of personal celebration, the king also had other issues on his mind. Since leaving England more than three years earlier, Louis was still to relinquish some English territories, a flagrant disregard of the terms agreed at the Treaty of Lambeth. Now joint king, the English magnates hoped Louis's influence on his father would be more rewarding. Sadly for Henry, he would have a long wait.[16]

Ever keen to cement peace with Alexander, Henry spent four days at York in midsummer, during which he witnessed the previously agreed wedding between the Scottish king and his 10-year-old sister Joan at York Minster. That same month, assignation of the king of Scotland's dower to his wife was also confirmed. From there, Henry and the justiciar moved south to Shrewsbury where a council that included Llywelyn was held between 27 June and 3 July. Later that year, most likely October, the twice-widowed Hubert de Burgh married for the third time. The lady in question, the king of Scotland's eldest sister, Princess Margaret, who Henry had earlier overlooked.[17]

For a second year in a row, Christmas was a tense affair. Moving south from Oxford to Henry's home city of Winchester, the divisions between his key advisors continued to widen. The setting on this occasion had been the castle. As bishop of Winchester, Peter des Roches's local home was Wolvesey Castle, a now romantic ruin to the rear of the cathedral. Though Christmas had often been kept there, the nearby, and more impressive, Winchester Castle, where the king had been born, was prepared as his lodgings. On this occasion, the hostile air was born of a quarrel between Ranulf and Longespée, with the latter's position backed up by the justiciar. Precisely what was said is unclear, only that Ranulf's heated words were taken as a threat of violence. A recurring pattern in the young king's reign, it took the calm mediation of Langton to return things to normal.[18]

Just as the fourth Lateran Council of 1215 had been of considerable significance to ecclesiastical matters in Rome, the same would be true in 1222 with regard to implementing such measures in England. Fresh from his visit to Rome, in April Langton oversaw one of the most important events in English religious history. Held at Osney Abbey, near Oxford, the provincial synod was quite possibly the largest gathering of its type to be held in England. Attended by all the key prelates, proceedings saw the publishing of a new constitution comprising some fifty chapters, concerning the roles and responsibilities of the clerics in addition to religious and monastic observance. On his return, Langton had instantly picked up his friendship with the justiciar, something that was of little benefit to the bishop of Winchester.[19]

Throughout the year to come, problems again arose in the surrender of the royal castles. Chief among them was the situation concerning the Welsh hilltop castle of Dinas Powys, at the time in the hands of the Earl Marshal despite being the property by right of Gilbert, Earl of Gloucester. In Gilbert's presence, Marshal willingly surrendered it to the king on the assumption that it would, in turn, be delivered to Gloucester. However, rather than wait for the usual procedures to be followed, Gilbert took up arms in July to ensure its return, much to the king's surprise. A month earlier, in June, protests were recorded in Yorkshire over the forest eyre. Resumption also occurred, around this time, of royal demesne, thereby tenants of land owned by the crown were again required to pay a tithe.[20]

A far more significant disturbance in the summer of 1222 concerned the city of London. Capital of England since the eleventh century, medieval London was a strange place in many ways. The site where William the Conqueror ordered the construction of his, now infamous, Tower, it was also here William was met with the greatest backlash from 'hostile inhabitants'. Indeed, prior to the Norman invasion, it was within the walls of the ever-expanding city that discontent at the feudal overlords had taken root. Now the largest city in England, by the thirteenth-century London had developed into an affluent trading hub abundant in merchants and royal officials, yet also a dangerous place to venture out after dark. Drink as the greatest English vice is mentioned explicitly in William fitz Stephen's description of the city.[21]

Effective government may have succeeded in keeping the peace in the country at large, but within the walls of the capital, a series of minor insurrections blemished its record. As usual, drink aside, a simplified explanation could be placed on a lack of affinity with the king. Yet, also as usual, much of the hatred was reserved for his key advisors. On 25 July – St James's Day – tensions spilt over during a wrestling match between the citizens of the city and those of the suburbs in fields near the Tower. After the defeated tenants of the abbot of Westminster asked for a rematch on 1 August – the feast of St Peter ad Vincula – the decision by the defeated team to bring in professional ringers – as well as hidden weapons – for the second encounter caused tensions to flare. Capitalising on the rising troubles, former sheriff of London, Constantine FitzAthulf, did his best to fan the flames with an attack on the precincts of Westminster. A passionate supporter of the dauphin in the recent war, reports abounded that FitzAthulf's men cried 'Montjoie! May the Lord assist us and our Lord Louis!' which heightened rumours that a renewed invasion by the French prince was imminent.[22]

Somewhat predictably, it was Hubert to the rescue. Successful in securing the assistance of former royal favourite and one of the heroes of the Fair of Lincoln and the siege of Rockingham Castle, Falkes de Breauté, the rising was quelled and Constantine brought before them in shackles. The following day, Falkes and a large force took the former sheriff and his two key supporters to Southwark to be hanged without trial. Falkes was also influential in obtaining the peaceful surrender of the Londoners. As was precedent in such occurrences, the crown seized the guilty man's property. As punishment for his ineffectiveness, the mayor was fired.[23]

If the wind of change that was blowing through England in 1222–23 wasn't hard enough, the weather itself was proving particularly turbulent. Heavy rainfalls, winter frosts and the occasional dry summer had been usual for the farmers of England and Wales since time immemorial. Yet just like the strange omens witnessed in the skies, abnormal weather was seen as another judgement from God. On 8 February 1222, there was dreadful thunder, the worst of which was felt in the town of Grantham in Lincolnshire, whose church caught alight amidst the accompanying lightning. Though large volumes of holy water – and according to Roger of Wendover, the lighting of the holy candles – brought the conflagration under control, it was remarked that a peculiar smell endured long after.[24]

In Surrey, as recorded by the chronicler of Waverley, a hard frost in April was followed by a harsh drought that summer, the effects of which had severe repercussions for the harvest.[25] On 30 November, the feast of St Andrew, a terrible storm was recorded throughout the whole of England, destroying several churches and towers, as well as many secular buildings including castle ramparts. So bad was the tempest in Warwickshire, that the destruction of the house of a knight of Pilardeston (modern-day Pillerton Hersey) resulted in nine deaths before apparently drying a local lake. On the eve of St Lucy the Virgin, 13 December, a storm of even worse magnitude achieved even more destruction throughout the country. Recorded by, among others, Roger of Wendover and the annalist of Bermondsey, it was mused by the former that it 'threw down buildings, as if they were shaken by the breath of the devil'.[26]

If terrible tempests capable of bringing down buildings were not enough to instil the fear of God in the heart of the thirteenth-century european, earthquakes certainly could. In Italy the following year, such rumblings brought widespread calamity to Brescia, with further effects being felt in Venice and Rome. That same year, for the second time in its history, the archives of Pershore Abbey were destroyed by a fire.[27]

Of even more significant long-term consequence than building damage and infernos was Stephen Langton's developing influence on Henry's government. Holding a great council at Westminster in early January 1223 on the back of another Christmas at Oxford, the archbishop convinced the king to comply with the terms of the great charter. Ironically, around this time Henry ordered an inquisition into the customs and liberties enjoyed by John before the First Barons' War, an indication, perhaps, that he felt compliance with the charters of his minority had left him short-changed.[28]

Rather than solving the matter, the decision led to accusations from the royalist baron William Brewer that the rights had been exhorted by force. Agreeing to further acknowledgement of the charter, Henry wrote to the sheriffs confirming his decision. On hearing the news, Honorius issued a papal bull in April declaring that Henry should henceforth be allowed to assume the full reins of government. On the 13th of that month, the pope also wrote to the chancellor, Ralph Neville, now bishop elect of Chichester, confirming the bull, while also stating his views that the 16-year-old was officially still a minor.[29]

Four years had now passed since the extension of the peace of Bouvines. With less than a year remaining before expiration, the mood in Rome was becoming unpredictable. Five days after writing to Neville confirming Henry's unofficial coming of age, Honorius penned another letter to Philip regarding the truce's renewal. As usual, the other key issue on his mind was the Holy Land. In the last century, nothing had impaired the crusader cause more than war in Europe. Hoping to persuade all minds to focus on the bigger picture, Honorius also wrote to Henry on the possibility of joining Frederick II on a crusade, while requesting any who made a crusader vow be made exempt from paying tolls to help fund their journey.[30]

Privately Henry backed the idea of a crusade. That this stocky teenager of a largely peaceful temperament was ever serious about following in the footsteps of his uncle and regent in launching his own endeavour seems doubtful, particularly while still in his minority. Even the slimmest of possibilities, however, were eliminated when Llywelyn went on the rampage in Wales.

Since the previous truce in 1220, life in Wales had been anything but peaceful, yet even by past comparisons, Llywelyn's latest actions were extreme. Few of his crimes could rate more seriously than his holding of Marshal's animals and livestock and razing the buildings to the ground, spreading terror throughout the local populations and causing Marshal significant financial loss. William the Younger's inability to prevent Llywelyn's devastation of the Pembrokeshire lands had brought him to the verge of financial ruin. One source placed the damage at a cost greater than Richard I's ransom to Leopold of Austria.[31]

Llywelyn's success had brought misery not only to Marshal. Growing resentment at the prince's actions had brought with it the disillusionment of many key supporters, as well as putting him in direct conflict with his eldest son, whom he had previously had removed from the line of succession. For Marshal, the familial infighting would prove something of a Godsend. After Llywelyn launched an assault on Shropshire in early 1223, laying siege to, taking and subsequently razing the Fulk FitzWarin castles of Whittington and Kinnerley, Marshal landed at St David's in April with a large army raised from Ireland. Aware that Pandulf's truce had been renewed for another year in April 1222, Marshal waited until its expiration before striking hard. So effective was the tactic that by the end of that month, the earl of Pembroke had forced Llywelyn from Cardigan and Carmarthen. When Llywelyn sent his son to subdue Marshal, Gruffudd was defeated at Kidwelly. A council at Ludlow 6-10 July was set up to listen to the mutual grievances and dissolved without reconciliation. As a consequence of the disagreement, Langton excommunicated Llywelyn and placed Wales under an interdict.[32]

For Henry, Welsh insurgency brought new problems. Being forced to deal with the most significant military challenge since the First Barons' War, his perceived lack of support for Marshal when several of the other earls and barons had come to his aid threatened to endanger their already precarious relationship. Perhaps inspired by the late regent's penchant for diplomacy, Henry accepted the council's proposal that the previously agreed wedding between William and Henry's sister, Eleanor, should take place. At the time of the wedding in April 1224, Marshal had been 34 and Eleanor only 9.

Prior to that time and with an invasion of France deferred, the king hosted a great council in Worcester. Once finished, he headed for Gloucester to lead his forces across the Marches. On 19 September 1223, the justiciar accompanied him on the journey from Hereford to the recently fortified castle at Builth, held by Reginald de Braose. On relieving Builth from Llywelyn's latest siege, they headed for the town of Montgomery, arriving on 30 September. The castle there was an old one located in a strategic position over the Severn crossing which made it susceptible to attack. Intent on strengthening their hold on the Marcher lands, discussions began immediately about building a new castle in a more secure location.[33]

With proceedings in the field reaching something of a stalemate, the mediation of the archbishop of Canterbury and earl of Chester ensured peace with the Welsh was reached on 8 October, following which Langton lifted Llywelyn's excommunication. Consistent with the approach that Henry would adopt throughout his life, the king put great emphasis on defence and over the next few years had the town and new castle heavily fortified. By building the new castle on Llywelyn's route from southern Powys into England, it was hoped the latest developments would, at last, bring peace to the lands of March.[34]

Predictably, the reality would not be quite so simple.

Chapter 12

1223–1224
An Englishman's Home is His Castle

Shortly prior to the peace agreement, talk of a crusade had been revived. Already on the receiving end of countless requests from the pope, in September 1223 the king made his way to Canterbury to personally receive 'solemnly and with great honours' John of Brienne, King of Jerusalem, who had ventured throughout Europe in an attempt to gather support for another crusade. As usual, Henry was personally affable towards his distinguished guest. Less clear is whether the crown or clergy pledged any funds. Incidentally, Brienne had previously visited Rome, Germany, Spain and France, during which he seems to have received similar promises.[1]

Wishes of a liberated Holy Land, peace with Wales, Scotland and France would again encounter the usual distractions concerning guardianship of the royal castles. Though surrender of the castles by the present castellans remained a matter of clear importance, several letters dated between September and December offer a startling insight into the loss of urgency. Indeed, one from Honorius to Henry in November confirmed that it was up to the king whether or not they were acted on.[2]

As usual, the brunt of the castle holders' frustrations was aimed more at Henry's key advisors, namely Hubert, as opposed to the king himself. Fresh from his return to London after the Wales campaign that had culminated in events at Montgomery, Hubert cemented his ever-strengthening alliance with the earl of Pembroke during the first week of November by formally granting him the castles at Cardigan and Carmarthen. A week later, according to Falkes's *Querimonia* – a fourteen-page document Falkes wrote later in his life for reasons that will soon become apparent – the justiciar summoned the sheriffs of Hereford and Gloucester, Walter de Lacy and Ralph Musard, respectively, to appear before the king's court and not be allowed to leave until their castles were handed over. Coincidentally at the time, Walter's brother, Hugh, was leading a revolt in Ireland. In contrast, Musard, a key ally of the younger William Marshal, seems to have been aware of Hubert's plan.

The assumption in the eyes of the other castellans, of course, was that deprivation of Musard and de Lacy would prove the first of many in the implementation of the papal letters. Of particular concern here to Henry's government were the background grumblings of key holders Ranulf, Falkes de Breauté, Engelard de Cigogné and Peter des Roches, as well as the already riled William of Aumale. One could argue Llywelyn's recent submission was itself a blow for Ranulf, who had long been something of a mediator between the king and the prince of Gwynedd but again no friend of Hubert. Holding between them such a vast swathe of castles, eight held by Falkes, two courtesy of de Cigogné and four, which were under the control of the bishop of Winchester, it was feared that any anti-government alliance could quite easily culminate in further civil war.[3]

Later that month, matters reached something of a tipping point when some of the barons became embroiled in a conspiracy to overthrow the justiciar. At the heart of the plot seems to have been an attempt to gain entry to the Tower of London – Hubert's key citadel. Less clear is whether or not they attempted to gain control of the Tower or merely unsettle the justiciar. Of the key participants, namely, Chester, Aumale, Falkes and Brian de Lisle, it is also unclear whether Chester was the main ringleader or all were equally involved.

On hearing of the projected coup, Henry was livid. At the time the news reached him he had already set off from Gloucester to London, thus enticing the rebel barons to retire to Waltham on the 28th.[4] The archbishop of Canterbury did his best to broker peace, but that did not end the discontentment. So infuriated had the barons become that a deputation approached the king in person and demanded Hubert's removal. When Langton organised a conference to commence around 4 December, attended by the key lords, accusations were made that Hubert had been squandering finances. Predictably, an argument also ensued between de Burgh and des Roches as Hubert retaliated by accusing the cleric of being the main instigator. Again, the peacemaker was Langton, who helped mediate a truce until 20 January.[5]

Still intent on reclaiming his castles, on 8 December the king successfully liberated Colchester. Contrary to Honorius's earlier decree that no prelate would benefit from their occupation, the grateful recipient was none other than the bishop of London, Eustace of Fauconberg.

Eustace had replaced the previous incumbent, William, in the see in 1221. Of particular importance at this time, from 10 December onwards, a change in the testing clause of the king's letters confirmed the age of majority was fast approaching. Whereas past letters were worded, 'Witness Hubert de Burgh, my justiciar', the latest included the markedly different, 'Witness Myself'. The first of these occurred in Hubert's presence; also present had been Langton and the bishops of Bath and Salisbury, the former of whom hoped that the granting of the royal seal to Henry would put an end to recent tensions. Although there is no evidence to indicate that the king was declared of age at that time, Langton's mediation must undoubtedly be seen as a firm indication that the failed endeavour to see Hubert ousted had at least made a mark.[6]

Later in December, Henry wrote to Honorius concerning the state of England. To this, Hubert added his desire that certain mischief-makers in Rome should not be allowed to return – a reference to the rebel envoys. Clearly the pope was aware of recent events. Henry wrote to Honorius on 19 December, thanking him for his help, as well as asking for his continued assistance in maintaining the peace. There is some evidence that Henry suspected the barons had created their own papal-directed literature around this time, all of which only succeeded in further souring the Christmas mood.[7]

Keeping the company of Langton at Northampton, many of the other prelates and rebel barons kept theirs at Leicester. What conversations and decisions transpired, one can only imagine: only that in the aftermath Langton threatened the Leicester crowd with excommunication. Unlike developments during the First Barons' War, such threats would have the desired effect. On 30 December, Chester and his fellow rebels appeared at Northampton at which point the papal letters from April were presented before them. Satisfied that the command was authentic, Ranulf set the tone and his castles including Shrewsbury, Lancaster and Bridgnorth were surrendered in exchange for legal tokens of acknowledgement. Falkes did the same for Hertford as well as the castles and sheriffdoms of Oxford and Northampton. Engelard relinquished Windsor and Odiham; de Lisle Knaresborough, Bolsover and Peveril. Henry's steward, William de Cantilupe, did the same for Kenilworth and the sheriffdom of Warwickshire-Leicestershire.[8]

In total, between then and the following April, orders were issued for the transfer of property of all thirty-three royal castles. This also

Above left: Fulk IV, Count of Anjou. (Artist Unknown)

Above right: Fulk V, Count of Anjou, I King of Jerusalem. (Artist Unknown)

Right: Geoffrey Plantagenet, Count of Anjou. (An illustration that once adorned his tomb in Le Mans' Cathedral. Museum of Archaeology and History, Le Mans, France)

Henry II family tree. (Royal MS 14 B VI, British Library)

Henry II, Richard I and John, as they appear before the west front of Lichfield Cathedral. (Photo: Mike Davis)

Above: Duke Arthur of Brittany paying homage to Philip II of France. (*Chroniques de St-Denis*, British Library)

Right: Tomb of Eleanor of Aquitaine at Fontevraud. (Christopher Knight's, *Popular History of England*, 1856)

Below: King John out hunting. (Cotton MS Claudius D II, British Library)

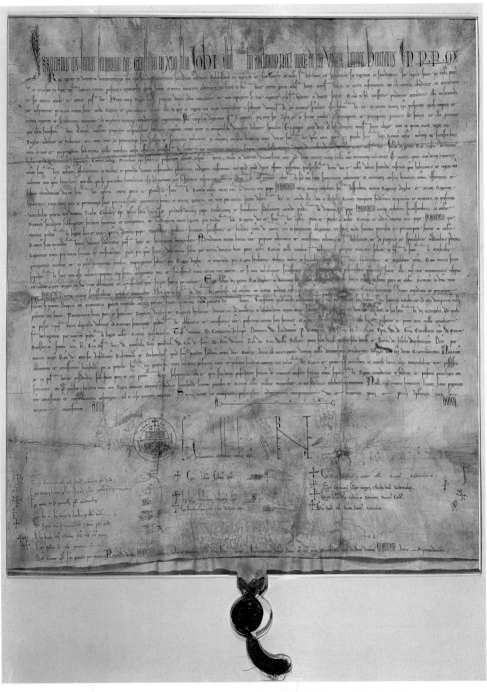

The Papal Bull that officially made England a Papal Fiefdom. (British Library)

Templar Church near Dover, where, according to tradition, John submitted England
to the Papacy in May 1213. (Photo: Mike Davis)

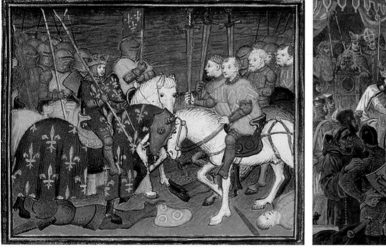

Above left: Philip II's victory at Bouvines in July 1214. (Vincent of Beauvais, *La
Miroir Historial Vol IV*, 1410)

Above right: John signing the Great Charter at Runnymede in June 1215. (John
Cassell, *Illustrated History of England*, 1864)

The Original Magna Carta 1215. (British Library)

The Papal Bull that annulled Magna Carta in August 1215. (British Library)

Prince Louis of France sailing to England in 1216. (Matthew Paris's *Chronica Majora,* 1259)

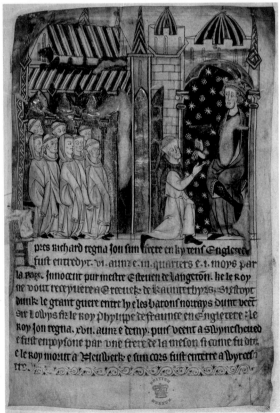

Above: Dover Castle. (Photo: Mike Davis)

Left: The alleged poisoning of John at Swineshead Abbey in October 1216. (Cotton MS Vitellius A XIII, British Library)

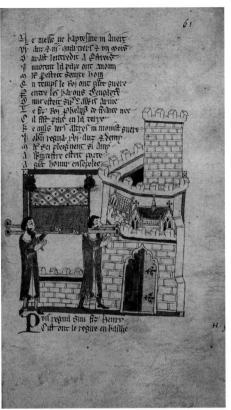

Above left: John's body being transported to Worcester in October 1216. (Egerton MS 3028)

Above right: Arms of William Marshal, 1st Earl of Pembroke. (Matthew Paris, *Chronica Majora*)

Right: Château de Tancarville in Normandy, where William Marshal began his journey to knighthood. (Artist Unknown, 1822)

Above: John's family tree. (Royal MS 14 B VI, British Library)

Left: First coronation of Henry III, at Gloucester Cathedral on 28 October 1216. (Cotton MS Vitellius A XIII, British Library)

The Fair of Lincoln in 1217. (Matthew Paris, *Chronica Majora*)

Above: The Battle of Sandwich in August 1217.
(Artist Unknown, 1873)

Right: Pope Honorius III. (*Acta Sancti Petri in Augia*.
Kantonsbibliothek, Vadianische Sammlung, St Gallen,
Switzerland)

Above: The Capture of Damietta 1218–19. (Cornelis Claesz van Wieringen, 1625. Frans Hals Museum, Haarlem, The Netherlands)

Left: William Marshal's tomb. (From Knight)

Second crowning of Henry III, on 20 May 1220 at Westminster Abbey. (Matthew Paris, *Chronica Majora*)

Above left: Canterbury Cathedral. (Photo: Mike Davis)

Above right: Statue of Stephen Langton, Archbishop of Canterbury under John and Henry. (Photo: Mike Davis)

Corfe Castle in Dorset, for a time under the control of Peter de Maulay. (Photo: Mike Davis)

On the left, Pope Innocent III excommunicating the Cathars. On the right, the Albigensian Crusade. (*Chroniques de St-Denis*, British Library)

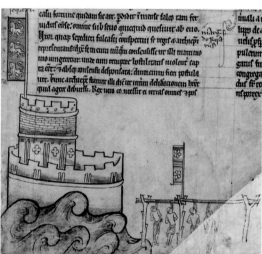

Above left: Coronation of Louis VIII and Blanche of Castile in 1223. (Miniature from the *Grandes Chroniques de France*, 1450s, Bibliothéque Nationale)

Above right: Siege of Bedford in 1224. (Matthew Paris, *Chronica Majora*)

Magna Carta 1225. (British Library)

The Charter of the Forest 1225. (British Library)

Above left: Louis IX. (Artist Unknown)

Above right: A meeting between Frederick II and the Sultan of Egypt, Al-Kamil Muhammad al-Malik, during the Sixth Crusade. (Artist Unknown)

Montgomery Castle. (Artist Unknown, 1785)

Left: The West Façade of Winchester Cathedral. The domain of Peter des Roches, it was here where Henry III and Richard, Earl of Cornwall were baptised. (JPD)

Below: The outside wall of Wolvesey Castle in Winchester, former palace of Peter des Roches. (JPD)

Netley Abbey in Hampshire, founded by Peter des Roches. (J. B. Harraden, 1814)

Above left: Henry II, Richard I, John and Henry III. (Matthew Paris, *Historia Anglorum*)

Above right: Henry III, as he appears along the west front of Lichfield Cathedral. (Photo: Mike Davis)

Above left: Henry III. (Cassell)

Above right: Henry sailing to Brittany. (Matthew Paris, *Chronica Majora*)

Above left: First Great Seal of Henry III. (Author's collection)

Above middle: Second Great Seal of Henry III. (Author's collection)

Above right: Second Great Seal of Henry III – reverse side. (Author's collection)

Above left: Peter of Dreux, Duke of Brittany, Count of Richmond. (Artist Unknown, Bibliothéque Nationale)

Above right: Llywelyn ap Iorwerth and his sons, Gruffydd and Dafydd. (Matthew Paris, *Chronica Majora*)

Right: John's new tomb in Worcester Cathedral. (John Harris the Elder, John Harris the Younger, 1816, British Library)

Above left: Hubert de Burgh in sanctuary. (Matthew Paris, *Chronica Majora*)

Above right: Usk Castle in Monmouthshire. (JPD with kind permission from the owners)

Left: Whitecastle Castle in Gwent: one of three castles in the area to have been owned by Hubert de Burgh. (Photo: Mike Davis)

Above: Grosmont Castle in Gwent. (JPD)

Right: Monmouth Castle. (JPD)

Richard Marshal unhorsing Baldwin of Guînes in 1233. (Matthew Paris, *Chronica Majora*)

A view across the Curragh of Kildare where Richard Marshal was defeated on 1 April 1234. (Public Domain)

included surrender by Hubert of Dover, Canterbury, Rochester, Norwich, Hereford and Orford; the same would be true of the earl of Salisbury and William Brewer of Salisbury and Devizes. Their distribution to new owners would primarily be the choice of Langton in accordance with the papal instructions that no baron could hold more than two at any one time. While Windsor and Odiham fell into his hands, of greater consequence was the surprise agreement by Hubert for the return of Langton's brother Simon, exiled for his support of Louis and accused as having 'gloried in being the cause of John's death'.[9]

Success had finally been achieved, at least for the short-term. More significant problems, however, would arise for maintaining the peace long-term. Of particular importance were the king's relations with his former tutor, Peter des Roches. Following the example of the barons, early in the new year, the bishop of Winchester would do the same for Southampton, Porchester and Henry's birthplace of Winchester. Further to relinquishing his own castles, Henry's coming into possession of the royal seal would leave Peter absent from government. The final writ authorised by Peter occurred on 8 December. He would not authorise another for nine years.[10]

His relationship with Hubert at a low ebb, Peter instead turned to Pandulf. Building on the trust and harmony that he had with the former legate, he secured a letter from Honorius reminding Henry what his father owed the papacy as well as offering a polite notice against interfering with the see of Winchester. It is quite likely that a minor dispute arose; however, if so, the effects of that are unclear. The letter, in some ways a contradiction of the pope's earlier order that no bishop shall hold a royal castle, could also be viewed as an indirect suggestion in favour of the disgruntled bishop being empowered. His complaints, concerned with safeguarding his own position following the castle surrender and his personal feud with the justiciar, made no accusation of problems with the king personally. Any reply Henry offered, if indeed there was one, does not seem to have survived. There is some evidence at this time that the royal agents on being sent to Rome were largely ignored.[11]

A fiery-tailed comet illuminated the skies above France in early July 1223. Reminiscent of the arrival of another icy celestial body in the skies above Hastings in 1066, its coming was viewed with great significance by the royal astrologers. Seemingly portentously, Philip II passed away on 14 July 1223, bringing with it the beginning of the reign of his son and joint king: now Louis VIII of France in his own right.[12]

Hoping Philip's death would not see a repeat of the events of 1216, Honorius wrote to Louis before the year was out praising his accession, while also reminding him of the importance of peace with England. As the following three years would demonstrate, Honorius had every right to be worried. Whatever the exact words of wisdom the chronicler of Waverley believed Philip offered his son on his deathbed, their effect seems to have been limited. Louis had never forgotten his humiliation on leaving England. Nor was he prepared to let sleeping dogs lie.[13]

No sooner was Philip's body lowered into his tomb in the Basilica of Saint-Denis, Henry ordered that his navy be made ready on the south coast to mount an expedition to restore Normandy. As John had been aware, not only did the duchy offer a tangible connection with William the Conqueror, but, in financial terms, it was more valuable than the rest of the Angevin Empire put together. So serious had Henry been when taking it that back in July, the king had promised the barons of Normandy that fealty to him would be rewarded with whatever they lost in England under John.[14]

Sympathetic to Henry's cause, Pandulf wrote to the pope from Paris suggesting Louis's coronation be postponed until the Normandy issue was settled. Whether Louis was aware of this or whether personal experiences influenced him, he immediately put preparations in place for a quick coronation, and was crowned on 6 August. Unperturbed, Henry dispatched his ambassadors on matters concerning the Treaty of Lambeth, leading to further impasse. Of far greater consequence for Henry, the French king threatened his 'just' earlier invasion would be repeated.[15]

Any plans Louis had for a renewed invasion, however, would be deferred due to Honorius's continued pleas for the liberation of the Holy Land. Complicating things further, the lack of urgency for a campaign against the Cathars in the Languedoc saw Louis change his plans and prepare an attack on Henry's lands in Poitou. As with Normandy, unanswered questions concerning the wider remnants of the Angevin Empire remained of great significance in England. By no means popular in the eyes of the English people, many of whom saw the likely scutage or military call up in aid of the endeavour as an unwelcome burden, the lands to the south were of immense sentimental value to Henry, not least as they offered a direct link with his lost ancestry.

Unlike Normandy, Poitou was yet to be lost. Despite nearly falling in Philip's reign, by 1223 only the capital city of Poitiers was in Louis's control. On paper at least, Henry's authority as count of Poitou remained intact. So far, just as had been true of the reigns of Henry II, Richard and John, the feudal lords had been happy to pay homage to their lord in exchange for a quiet life free of interference. During Henry's early minority, this had been of great benefit. Not only had it saved him the financial burden of an unnecessary war, but in allowing first Marshal and later the triumvirate opportunity to concentrate on domestic issues, it had allowed the government to take a firm grip on administrative matters. The latest problems, however, threatened to reopen Pandora's box. Among them was the county being the domain of his mother and stepfather.

Relations with Hugh remained cold for Henry. Barely six months after Pandulf left England, Honorius had been called upon to intercede in another dispute between the pair about Isabella's dower. Prior to John's death, Isabella had been granted no lands in England, and the dower that did come mostly concerned areas once held by Eleanor of Aquitaine. At the time that Joan was brought to La Rochelle, Henry's government had decided to authenticate the release of his mother's dower, including transfer of the castle at Berkhamsted.[16]

Contrary to promises made to Pandulf that the restoration of the royal castles and other lands in their possession would occur, by June 1222 even the best attempts of the dean of Bordeaux had failed to make any progress. Equally unforthcoming had been orders to the archbishop to excommunicate the count if things were not adequately dealt with. Frustrated with the lack of progress, Honorius wrote again to the archbishop of Poitiers, threatening to excommunicate Hugh as punishment for injury inflicted on the king as well as the prelate for failure to comply with a papal demand. Inspired no doubt by Philip's death and an opportunity to cement control of Normandy and Poitou, in August 1223, Geoffrey de Neville was sent out to provide Hugh with a new offer, which by October had led to Hugh offering some form of compromise. Matters were finally resolved in January 1224, and new arrangements were scheduled to last four years.[17]

By April 1224, discussions with Henry and the pope concerning a crusade remained ongoing. Talk of another extension of the peace of Bouvines with Louis also remained on the agenda. In preparation for this, inquiries were made into injuries committed on both sides during the truce. Officially, the truce between England and France remained in force at least until April. Only too aware of the legalities, Louis played for time in replying to Henry's demands concerning the Angevin Empire and the agreement at Lambeth. By waiting until 8 November 1223, thus allowing the truce to enter its last six months, Louis had ensured that the earlier agreement would not be altered prior to the expiration and would remain in effect until April.[18]

Both Henry and Honorius must have known what Louis was planning. The pope wrote to the French king at least twice between February and April, his requests for peace falling on deaf ears. Worse news for Henry concerned the latest actions of Lusignan. Despite Isabella's earlier reasoning to Henry that the marriage between her and Hugh would be of great benefit to the king, in practice the marriage had gained Henry nothing. Ever one to profit from the disloyalty of others, Louis wasted no opportunity in attempting to purchase Lusignan's loyalty. As Henry's advisers and the pope negotiated for a further truce, Louis made treaties with the barons and Hugh reneged on the January agreement. In May 1224 the king of France invaded Poitou.[19]

Back in England, the seal had been left in the hands of the earl of Salisbury at Westminster as Henry and Hubert set out to Shrewsbury to discuss matters with Llywelyn. The pair had reached Oxford on 9 May, when news of Louis's refusal to renew the truce brought more pressing matters to a head. On hearing the news, the mood was grim. Deeply concerned by what was transpiring, Henry held a council in Northampton the following month where a discussion took place in earnest.[20]

Across the Channel, meetings between Louis and Henry's envoys at a great council in Paris had confirmed the worst. Louis stridently advised that French reclamation of John's land was just: the forfeiture by John had been absolute, thereby depriving the offspring of John of the right to rule as king of England or duke of his French possessions. Unsurprisingly, Henry's explosive Plantagenet temper was reaching boiling point. Styled since his coronation – like his father – Duke of Normandy, Duke of Aquitaine, Count of Anjou and Count of Poitou, Henry refused to acknowledge Louis's rule over these territories. Though now at war, with the truce expired, it was technically a fact that, for the first time since the Norman Conquest, a king of England now ruled over parts of France without any feudal subjection to the king of France.

Louis's forces met at Tours on 24 June 1224. On leaving the city, they continued on foot through Thouars to the seaport of La Rochelle, renowned not only as the strongest of the Poitevin cities, but also the one that had the closest affinity with England. Since 1221 the seneschal of Poitou had been Savori de Mauléon. Renowned for his efficiency as a fighter for John, and still possessed of estates in England, Savari was familiar with the role. A mercenary of the great house of Thouars and son of the late viscount, Savari had been captured by John at Mirebeau after he supported Arthur before being released from Corfe Castle and appointed seneschal of Poitou by John in 1205. In 1216, Savari had been present at Guala's council in Bristol having previously been designated by John one of the regency. On leaving England in 1218, he saw action in Spain before joining the Christian cause at Damietta. His return to the role had come as a result of Pandulf's mission to Poitou after resigning the legation.[21]

Due to the lack of military support, Louis's march put the port in grave danger. Though so far the seneschal had shown similar loyalty to Henry as he had for John, the French king's superior strength forced him to relinquish the small town of Niort after a two-day siege. By 3 August, La Rochelle had also fallen. For the first time since the days of Arthur, the seneschal was now fighting on the side of the French.[22]

As was so often the way, the taking of a major port delivered something of a domino effect. Town by town, all of Aquitaine north of the Dordogne swiftly followed. True to previous form, Lusignan's treachery was rewarded with a grant for the small English-ruled Isle of Oléron, located off France's west coast. Louis, meanwhile, continued his march. Setting his sights on Gascony, he led his forces south, taking all but the loyal city of Bordeaux. For now, the only support for the Angevins had been courtesy of each other.[23]

Had Henry acted, it seems likely some of the lands in Poitou and Gascony might well have been saved. Sadly for the king, a more pressing issue at home complicated military action abroad. Once again, the spectre of surrendering the royal castles had come back to haunt him.

Chapter 13

1224
The Baying of Bedford

At the same time that the king's lands in Poitou and Gascony were under unremitting attack, in England Henry was encountering other problems. Re-establishing law and order, though good progress had been made in recent years, remained an ongoing task and continued to pose complex problems.

One of the most challenging aspects related to dealing with acts of 'novel disseisin': defined in English law as the unlawful appropriation of another man's land. Throughout the spring of 1224, the king's justices travelled the country hearing individual pleas. Among the most significant cases, no less than thirty such accusations had been made against the controversial Norman, Falkes de Breauté.

Exactly who Falkes was has become something of a bone of contention. French-born and of Anglo-Norman ancestry, there is considerable doubt as to whether he was the illegitimate son of a French knight – most likely of the village of Bréauté in Normandy – or whether, like Hubert, he had risen through the ranks after entering the world as a commoner. In the view of the majority of the chroniclers, it was almost certainly the latter; however, xenophobic prejudice clearly influenced their overall perception. An example of the contempt in which he was held is their conclusion that his Christian name was a consequence of the scythe he had once used to commit murder. Similar retorts were uttered from the lips of Archbishop Langton, who remarked of Falkes and his fellow aliens: 'Here is the scourge of the earth! Here the affliction of the natives, to whom the people of England were so often given over as booty!'[1]

Regardless of his background, since his arrival in England, Falkes had done well for himself. It was the view of Bishop Stubbs, who had been so critical of Aumale, that Falkes was a clever refugee of the adventurous kind who had attached himself to John. That John had been grateful for his subsequent devotion is indisputable. Since entering royal service no later than 1206, Falkes had served the king in Poitou and became entrusted with the wardenships of Glamorgan and Wenlock on his return a year later. Around this time, he was knighted, as well as made constable of the Marshal lands of Cardigan and Carmarthen. Control of these developed him a reputation among the Marches as something of a despot. That he deserved it is easily illustrated. On being sent to destroy the Cistercian abbey of Strata Florida in Ceredigion for its opposition to John, only the hefty price of 700 marks ensured the building's survival.[2]

By the end of the First Barons' War, Falkes's authority had reached near unprecedented heights. In control of six sheriffdoms by 1215, John further rewarded his loyalty by appointing him steward of the king. Throughout the conflict, he performed well: capturing Hanslope in Buckinghamshire and holding Oxford before joining with Ranulf at the sieges of Worcester and Mountsorrel. On the death of the fourth earl of Devon, he was awarded the hand of the wealthy countess, *ipso facto* gaining him the earldom of Devon and Wight, which he would hold until his stepson reached his majority. Significantly enriched and now officially of noble status, John's trust in Falkes is further illustrated by the fact that he was made executor of the king's will on John's death. Under Henry, this pattern would continue. Entrusted with the command of an additional shrievalty, his loyalty to the royal cause remained unequivocal. A fierce opponent of events at Runnymede, he supported Marshal's claims to be regent and also backed the earl's reforms at Bristol.[3]

Despite his many successes, his reputation among the clergy suffered. While the loss of Hertford and Cambridge on his watch both blemished his otherwise distinguished military record, of greater regret had been the terrible atrocities experienced at his command by the people of St Albans in retribution for the city's coming to terms with Louis. In reality, the citizens had only done so under duress from the dauphin after Louis breached the truce of Berkhamsted. Sadly, events at St Albans would not be isolated. A similar attack occurred on Wardon Abbey in Bedfordshire, yet without the broader implications. An extraction of 100 marks from the monks of Thorney was also demanded for restoration of their lands. Both examples, however, paled into insignificance in the context of his treatment of the monks of Worcester when he sacked the city with Ranulf. In order to raise the monies demanded as punishment for their loyalty to Louis, the monks were forced to melt down the shrine of St Wulfstan. The events at St Albans, however, had upset Falkes's wife to such an extent that he later paid compensation to the people of the city in a bid to appease her.[4]

Better success awaited Falkes in the latter part of the war. Having captured the Isle of Ely for Henry after which he fought alongside Ranulf at the siege of Mountsorrel, he played a significant role at the Fair of Lincoln in carrying out the diversion that helped Marshal win the day. When the war was over, it was at Falkes's honour at the royal castle of Northampton that the king was entertained that Christmas.

As the following years clearly illustrated, Falkes had reached the peak of his success. Influential though he may have been in helping the justiciar put down the Westminster troubles of 1222, his dealings with the more radical senior magnates were often strained. By the time of the conspiracy to infiltrate the Tower, his relationship with Hubert had been damaged beyond repair. Undoubtedly a result, at least in part, of snobbery and a general distrust of outsiders, many of Falkes's other dealings both during and after the war had become causes for concern. His refusal to return four manors pawned to him by William Marshal had been the cause of private tensions that spilt over into his relations with the younger Marshal. A similar dispute arose between Falkes and the earl of Salisbury over Lincoln Castle, a site for which Falkes provided large parts of the garrison.[5]

Of greater consequence still, his impressive military performance during the war appears to have instilled in him a false sense of invincibility, especially concerning possession of the royal castles. While one might argue the same was true of Ranulf and the other keepers, as recently as 1223 Falkes remained in possession of eight royal castles. Due to their close geographical proximity to one another, this made him quite easily the most powerful lord of the Midlands. Like Ranulf and Aumale, his reluctance to lose what the king and legate had earlier assigned him is unsurprising. Nor is a motive lacking for his involvement in the Tower conspiracy of November 1223. Whether he was directly involved or merely not opposed to the failed coup, the result remained the same. Left no choice but to comply with the papal orders, by January the castle at Hertford and the shrievalties and castles of Oxfordshire and Northamptonshire had all been relinquished.[6]

For the majority of the royal castellans, deprivation of their castles between December and March would prove the worst of their problems. For Falkes, on the other hand, the earlier surrender was just the beginning.

Possibly motivated by a general wariness of Falkes, the potential use of his remaining resources to mount future insurrection or to embark upon a more personal vendetta, in February Hubert went further and demanded he give up his recently acquired Plympton Castle as well as his one remaining royal castle. For all his losses at Northampton, Falkes still held the mighty Bedford, which he had liberated for John during the war.[7]

Met with the new demand, Falkes refused to cooperate. Well aware that the papal letters granted any baron permission to keep up to two castles at any one time, in the case of Plympton he argued the fortress had entered his estates by way of his wife's previous marriage and was not the property of the king.[8] To this, Hubert rejected the argument and proceeded with the original demand. When Falkes again refused to give them up, the justiciar changed tactic and charged him with 'novel disseisin'. Though many later commentators have condemned the accusation as an invention by the justiciar, of the thirty cases put forward, no less than sixteen were deemed serious. Already severely in debt and by no means a regular contributor to the exchequer, the consequences of the guilty verdicts threatened a severe financial blow.[9]

On being brought before the king's justices at Dunstable, rather than face the charges, Falkes entered a conspiracy with his brother, William, to kidnap the justice of the bench. As well as serving as Falkes's commander of the garrison at Bedford, William had other motivation for his involvement: not least as his own properties, including one at Kirtlington in Oxfordshire, were also due to be seized.[10]

Dunstable had been carefully chosen for Falkes's hearing. In addition to being located close to Falkes's manor at Luton, where he was allegedly guilty of disseising several freemen, he had also been accused of damaging property of the abbot of St Albans. Of no less significance, the justice chosen to sit at Dunstable was none other than Henry de Braybrook, who had held the castle at Mountsorrel from Falkes in the First Barons' War before barely escaping the Fair of Lincoln with his life. After William caught de Braybrook on 16 June, the siblings proceeded to hold him up in Bedford Castle, along with two others.[11]

Unfortunately for the king, Falkes's insurrection would prove only the start of an exhausting process that would have significant repercussions for the future of Poitou. As news of developments at Bedford filtered through, a furious Henry summoned a council in Northampton to discuss the matter. Concerned that Falkes's actions may prove a catalyst for further civil war, rather than amass a force to head to Portsmouth, the king instead sent one to Bedford. After three days of peaceful requests achieved no sign of submission, Henry was forced to resort to more drastic measures.[12]

The siege that followed was undoubtedly the most challenging the royals had faced in England since Rochester in 1215. In its own way, the greatest of its type Henry would ever be involved in. Renowned for its heavy stone defences, John had personally overseen fortification of the castle precisely to withstand such a siege. Quadrangular in shape and originally consisting of an old tower and inner bailey, Falkes had added a new barbican and keep – possibly a shell keep – as well as an outer bailey and a series of stone-lined palisades and ditches, the latter of which were rare in England.

Breaching such defences required vast resources. Siege engines were brought in from no less than three counties, while others had to be manufactured on site. Especially impressive was the presence of at least two wooden towers manned by archers and crossbowmen. Roger of Wendover stated of the constructions that none of Bedford's garrison could remove their armour for fear of being wounded. At least one trebuchet was present, along with a minimum of five mangonels: a slicker, smaller version of the same instrument that required multiple men to operate it. The king's wages bill alone for the entire siege exceeded £1,300, even excluding other expenses such as provisions. Though the exact size of the king's army is unrecorded, it has been estimated to have been 1,600-2,700 in any one day.[13]

Hopeful that the delay would buy the brothers time, Bedford's strong towers and baileys kept the king's forces at bay for two months. The attack commenced on 20 June; Braybrook was finally liberated on 14 August.[14] According to the annals of Dunstable, the royalists gained control firstly of the modern barbican, from which they entered the outer bailey where much of great value was stored. After mining their way into the inner bailey, the final objective was Falkes's recently constructed keep, which was breached by a combination of mining and explosives. If the account of the chronicler Ralph of Coggeshall is accurate, more than 200 royalist soldiers and labourers lost their lives in the campaign, as well as six or seven knights.[15]

What Falkes had been hoping to achieve here defies belief. Though his apologists have argued that he was never the originator of William's kidnapping plot, but merely agreed to go along with it, the idea that he genuinely believed the castle could survive long enough for a papal reprieve or bring the country to civil war seems ludicrous. Sadly for all concerned, in contrast to the lenient sanctions imposed upon Aumale, the punishments ordered for the culprits were ruthless and swift. Or at least they would have been had Falkes not fled to Wales amidst the confusion.

Having made his getaway before Bedford was captured, Falkes turned to Ranulf and Llywelyn for help. While Llywelyn's correspondence with the English government suggests a degree of sympathy with Falkes, citing the real disturbers of the realm as those who had burdened Henry with useless plans, fortunately for Ranulf, the experienced earl recognised the stupidity of Falkes's endeavour and took Henry's side at Bedford. Left with no other option, Falkes conceded defeat on the advice of the bishop of Coventry after taking sanctuary in a local church. True to his usual form, Langton publicly excommunicated de Breauté for his insurrection against a papal vassal; Rymer recorded that the bishop of Coventry had earlier done the same.[16]

Worse news for Falkes would come on learning that his wife had left him, arguing the wedding of eight years earlier had been against her wishes. Having also lost his brother, William – interestingly Henry refused to lay any blame on another brother Colin, a clerk, for the insurrection – he showed less willingness to hold on to his lands, using them instead to bargain with the king. Of the eighty prisoners, only three knights, who were accepted as Templars, were spared execution. In contrast to the lack of retributions in the aftermath of Bytham, and perhaps consistent with his earlier threat in anger that all involved would pay with their lives, Henry had the entire garrison hanged.[17]

Concurrently with events in England, Falkes retained the support of the papacy. On 17 August, Honorius wrote to Henry on Falkes's behalf, imploring he end the siege. Whether or not Honorius was fully aware of what had transpired is unclear. As fate had it, Braybrook had been freed by the time the letter was written. Nevertheless, its content is noteworthy. Having previously been firm in his views that the royal castles should be given up, Honorius now advised Henry not to test the loyalty of his subjects. Around this time, he also wrote a far sterner letter to Langton, shortly after which Henry received independent correspondence from a chaplain in Rome. In contrast to Honorius's views, the chaplain keenly pressed Henry to make his point known, perhaps further evidence that Honorius was unaware of the bigger picture.[18]

Henry was furious. Besides the loss of over 200 of his own troops, the king was unwavering in his view that Falkes's attack had ruined any short-term chance of countering Louis's charges in Poitou. To help combat the costs, Henry issued a new scutage – as previously recalled, a tax issued on an area of land able to support a knight. In addition to issues of cost, time and effort, Breauté's actions here were significant for other reasons. Going back to the days of the Norman Conquest, xenophobia towards foreigners had been a developing issue in England. That the average man in a meadow, toiling with his plough, had an invested opinion in patriotism may stretch a point; however, evidence of the new sense of national identity was clearly taking root among the baronial classes.

During the First Barons' War, the usual murmurings of dissent had escalated. Although born in England, together Richard and John had both experienced the loathing of many an English-born subject. Famously quoted as having said he cared 'not an egg' for England, Richard's regular absence had left a gaping hole in the hearts of many of his subjects. His heavy taxation had impoverished England; something John continued. Richard's one redeeming quality was that he made far better use of the revenue. Though John's tendency to remain in England was a notable contrast, the pair were far more alike when it came to favouring foreign subjects at court. Coupled with John's determination to tax in aid of recovery of the Angevin territories, in 1215 such things had reached a point at which it was left to Magna Carta to deal with such issues. Of Falkes's claim that he had made so many enemies in England out of love for the king, there may be evidence to support him. Equally, however, Falkes's personal benefit had been greatest.

By 1224, resentment against the king's choice of advisors was again in danger of creating significant splits among the magnates. When the war was over, Louis's departure, coupled with the removal of John's most hated ministers from high office, had been seen as a victory against a foreign invader as opposed to the quietening of dissident rebels. While such matters would contribute in no small part to specific problems Henry would encounter later on in his reign, in cases such as Bedford pinning the blame on the foreign rebel also made for convenient scapegoats. Without question, de Breauté's actions had caused a delay to any Poitou mission and wasted significant resources and lives. Less convincing, however, is an argument that pinning total failure on one troublemaker takes appropriate note of the broader problems.[19]

In the minds of the population at large, however, there was no coming back. Two years earlier the hero of the London riots, Falkes quickly became the victim of fresh hatred. Realising his predicament, Falkes surrendered his Templar-kept finances to the king and ordered the transfer of his, non-royal, castles in the West Country. His excommunication lifted, he was temporarily banished to the Continent. On his arrival in Normandy, Louis briefly imprisoned him in retribution for his part in the war of 1215–17. During his time abroad, he would write a fourteen-page justification of his actions, now known as Falkes's *Querimonia*. That the king ever read it is doubtful. In his heart of hearts, the Norman adventurer must surely have known that the fading views of England's south coast would be the last of it he would ever see.[20]

Chapter 14

1224–1227
The Poitevin Potential

With the Bedford fiasco finally dealt with, Henry's thoughts returned to Poitou. Having failed to prevent Louis's rampage the previous year, the pope wrote to the French king again in August in a bid to negotiate peace. Around that time, he also wrote to Henry to update him on the matter. Somewhat predictably, troubles with Lusignan had also resurfaced. A day before writing to Henry, Honorius penned letters to the bishops of Saintes and Limoges, as well as the dean of Bordeaux, ordering Hugh's excommunication unless he restore Joan's dowry.[1]

Thankfully for Henry, no worse fortune would await that year. On a rare positive note, peace was made with the former earl of Ulster, Hugh de Lacy, thus helping to appease elements of dissent in Wales. Since his return to Ireland in 1223 after thirteen years fighting the Cathars, Hugh had been constantly at war with Marshal. Peace in Wales would also benefit that year from the marriage of the king's beloved sister, Eleanor, to the younger William Marshal, who in turn received lavish gifts from the king. In this favourable climate, and what must have seemed a welcome break from the previous two years, the Christmas court at Westminster passed without incident.[2]

With the old year out, the new brought fresh opportunity but also familiar frustrations. Correspondence between Henry and the duke of Austria concerning a marriage to his daughter, Margaret, led to nothing. The same applied to negotiations with other European rulers. When a council convened in January, one of the key issues was that of raising additional funds. Helpful though the scutage issued to replenish the coffers diminished by the liberation of Bedford had been, it did not solve the problem entirely. Worse still, news from Poitou and Gascony was becoming increasingly desperate.[3]

As usual, Hubert focused his efforts on arousing the generosity of the magnates. He also proposed a levy of one-fifteenth on all movable property in England to ease the burden. When the same proposition was put to the clergy, Langton offered encouragement at the price of granting of further liberties. £40,000 richer – approximately £30 million in modern money – Henry agreed to a third revision of the great charter and a second of the Charter of the Forest. When news of this reached Rome, Honorius wrote to Henry asking that he be just in every way, most likely an implicit order to honour his word. He also wrote to the prelates of England asking them to offer assistance as best they could.[4]

For Henry, the total amount was probably more than he had dared hope. Just as had been the case for his father and uncle, taxation in England had proved highly unpopular. The issue of a carucage in 1220 had gone down so badly in certain quarters that many sheriffs met with aggressive opposition. Elsewhere the assessors were refused access to the land of the lords and failed to make the collection. Intriguingly, imposition of the carucage was restricted on church lands, a matter that seems to have been administered by des Roches while Hubert was up in York conducting marriage negotiations. Affected, perhaps as well, by its being attempted within a year of Marshal's death, a big problem was the nature of the tax: a carucage being a levy on immovable property: i.e. land. Except for a carucage of the clergy obtained in 1224, the equivalent of 1220 would be the last of its type to be attempted in England. Throughout the reign of Henry III's son, Edward I, the new measures would become the norm. Despite raising far more money than scutages and carucages, taxes on moveables would only be attempted four times in Henry's entire reign.[5]

In February, commissioners were appointed for collection of the tax. The following month, enriched by at least some of the promised funds and minus the distractions of the previous year, Henry was at last in a position to commence his long-awaited action south of the Channel. Warned again by Honorius of the importance of keeping his subjects onside, Louis's continued unwillingness to comply with the pope's wishes saw the first steps taken to reclaim the lost lands. His invasion forces gathered, in March Henry was finally ready to launch his ships for Gascony.[6]

At the head of the fleet was the king's 16-year-old brother, Richard, the *de facto* heir to the throne. Having enjoyed a mostly sheltered childhood, most of which he had spent in the south of England at Corfe Castle under the supervision of the now-ousted Peter de Mauley, Richard was already somewhat experienced in the field, as well as knowledgeable of the Angevin territories. His first experience appears to have come recently, accompanying his brother on the Welsh expedition of 1223 prior to its postponement as a consequence of the attempted coup on the Tower. As later years would demonstrate, Richard's military talents far outweighed his brother's. Even at the time, there is evidence that Richard's potential was viewed with the greatest respect. The decision to place Richard at the head of the king's forces was made at a council in London in early February. Henry knighted him on 2 February and eleven days later granted him the lucrative earldom of Cornwall. Henry may have bestowed on him the county of Poitou as well. To complicate matters, John had already fathered a son of the same name with a mistress prior to his second marriage. Whereas the new earl had been specially named in his brother's memory, it would not have been out of keeping with John's character at that particular time had he chosen the name ironically: the lad being born out of wedlock. It was this Richard who had participated in his father's failed Poitou mission of 1214, as well as been made governor of Chilham Castle.[7]

On 23 March 1225 Richard set sail from England with a strong fleet that included his uncle, the earl of Salisbury and Henry's old tutor, Philip d'Aubigné. Still famed for his heroics at Damme, Longespée undoubtedly controlled the expedition, just as the late William Marshal had done for Henry less than a decade earlier. As a reward for his involvement, Longespée was granted wardship of the lands of the earl of Norfolk, who had recently died. Equally battle hardened was the former governor of the Channel Islands, d'Aubigné, who had led the royalist forces in Kent and Sussex during the First Barons' War before piloting a ship at the Battle of Sandwich. At the time his tutoring of Henry ended around April 1221, he seems to have been planning a crusade.[8]

On reaching Gascony, Richard was warmly welcomed in the port city of Bordeaux, at the time the only Gascon city still in English control. Over the coming months, he captured the communes of St Macaire and Bazas, leaving just the town of La Réole in Louis's command. On receiving correspondence that the army was severely in need of funds, Hubert came to their aid by launching a second fleet on 6 August carrying a war chest of 6,000 marks of silver as well as many fine jewels and cloths. Another would follow with 3,000 twelve days later. In total, 52,341 marks would be spent in Gascony's defence. When La Réole finally fell on 13 November after a siege that had lasted most of the summer and autumn, the lord of Bergerac hailed Richard as lord of all of Gascony.

How much of this Henry was personally aware of is unclear. On taking Bazas on 2 May, Richard wrote to inform him that all of Gascony, except for one town, was back under English control. Though arguably true, attempts by Hugh de Lusignan to relieve La Réole threatened to undo all of the previous work. The astute Richard saw this coming, however, and caught his treacherous stepfather in an ambush that prevented him from crossing the Dordogne. Over the coming weeks, Hugh was also forced to give way on his backup plan of saving Bergerac.[9]

Of more significant complication to Richard, the interference of Savari de Mauléon's navy occupying the Bay of Biscay saw a dramatic slowdown in communications and trade between England and Bordeaux. Once a loyal subject, de Mauleon proved to be especially influential in stopping the fleet in Rochelle roads. Though he refused Richard's offer to revert again to the English side, a change in the wind saw the English fleet escape with a large vessel of Bayonne. For the second time in the young king's reign, the Cinque Ports were of vital importance. As trips between Bordeaux and the English ports became ever more common as wine trade between the two areas increased, clashes between English and French at sea became commonplace.[10]

Success at sea proved less easy for the earl of Salisbury. Forced to return home due to illness, William's ship was nearly lost, forcing him to take temporary refuge on the island of Ré, close to La Rochelle. After reaching his destination the following spring, he passed away at Salisbury Castle in March.[11] Whether Longespée's decline was of direct connection to his earlier illness and near-death experience or whether other factors contributed, conjecture has been writhe. It was the belief of Roger of Wendover that William succumbed not to the fortunes of war or sea, but poison by the hand of Hubert de Burgh. Prior to the earl's death, during the period when he was thought lost at sea, Hubert's nephew, Reymond, made the foolish decision to propose marriage to the countess. Not only did Longspée soon turn up alive, the young Reymond was no earl. Furious at the perceived lack of respect Reymond had shown her, the enraged wife and returned earl took up their grievances with Hubert, who was forced into an embarrassing apology.[12]

Now indisputably the head of the king's forces and navy, Richard's responsibilities ranged far beyond ordinary military and naval matters. Victories and truces required diplomacy; the latter of which could make or break a relationship or campaign. Alliances of particular importance included those made with the counts of Auvergne, neither of whom were friends of Louis. Another of note was Richard's far more awkward union with his first cousin Raymond of Toulouse, renowned for both his military might yet also for his sympathy for the Cathars in the Languedoc. Heresy, of course, was serious business. So much so that in 1213, Raymond's father of the same name had been exiled to England, only for the legate, Nicholas, to expel him.[13]

Good relations were achieved with the regent duke of Brittany, Peter of Dreux. Having coveted the earldom of Richmond back in John's reign, Richard put forward firm promises that he would receive it in exchange for his submission: a small price to pay considering Peter's fealty would bring Brittany back under Plantagenet rule. Negotiations around this time also concerned a marriage between Henry and Peter's daughter, Iolenta.[14]

As Louis's continued onslaught on the Angevin estates continued to incite Honorius's wrath, Henry received a letter from the pope before Christmas informing him that a nuncio named Otho would soon arrive for a visit. It has long been speculated that at least part of the reason concerned an intercession for Falkes de Breauté, who had since made his way to Rome. Shortly after the fall of Bedford, Robert Passelewe, once a clerk of both Falkes and des Roches, and one Robert de Kent had earlier visited the Vatican on Ranulf's behalf.[15] Whether the reason the chronicler Roger of Wendover referred to as 'urgent business of the Roman Church' included Falkes or not, the promise of renewed papal interference in English affairs did little to amuse the clergy. Coincidentally, over in France, the Legate of the Apostolic See, Romanus, had earlier attempted to use his influence to ensure that Louis handed over Normandy, Anjou and Aquitaine to Henry as tacitly promised in the Treaty of Lambeth. On hearing the latest news, the legate promised Henry's agents on the Continent that he would attempt to hinder Otho on his journey.[16]

In June, Romanus wrote to Henry to assure him that Louis would allow de Breauté to travel freely in France, rather than be imprisoned. For Falkes, this would be as good as it got. Once free, he continued with Passelewe to Rome where he passed away in 1226. Of the exact cause, the chronicler Matthew Paris offered only two clues. The first was an account of him retiring after dinner and being later found dead and poisoned. Accompanying the text was an image of the devil feeding him a fish.[17]

Otho most likely arrived in the autumn of 1225. A nuncio as opposed to a legate, his powers did not carry the same weight enjoyed by Nicholas,

Guala or Pandulf, yet that did not stop him from pressing his suggestions. Among the worst were requests that the pope be assigned a prebend in every cathedral. Similar ideas concerning equivalent offerings from every bishopric, abbacy and monastery did little to placate the doom-mongers. Ever hopeful of good relations with the papacy, Henry stalled for time, stating the matter would be discussed with the magnates.[18]

Such an opportunity would arise on 13 January at Westminster. After spending Christmas at Winchester, Henry moved on to his palace at Marlborough and swiftly called the council to deal with Otho's requests – requests he said that concerned the whole nation. While staying at Marlborough, the king fell mildly ill. In his absence, some discussion appears to have taken place concerning de Breauté before Otho extracted two marks of silver under the head of procuration (fees in support of papal officials in England), which was undoubtedly vastly less than the visitor had hoped. Concerned that Otho's arrival potentially breached the earlier promise that no legate would again be assigned to England in Langton's lifetime, the papal visitor was recalled to Rome soon after, most likely at Langton's suggestion.[19]

Richard's success in Gascony had been a notable benefit for Henry, yet for all the good work, advancement into Poitou was still not achieved. Writing to Lusignan on 8 January 1226, Honorius vented his usual anger at the count of la Marche for his disloyalty to Henry and once again threatened him with excommunication. Of far greater disappointment for Henry, however, was Honorius's correspondence in April demanding he refrain from interfering with the Albigensian Crusade, of which Louis was now contributing. In addition to deferring the already delayed French campaign, the prospect of a crusade in the south brought about other unwanted complications. Only a year earlier Richard had successfully created an alliance with Raymond of Toulouse; however, this was now under serious threat because of Honorius's request that no pact exist due to Raymond's heresy. Around this time, the pope also made an identical demand of Louis regarding Henry's territories.[20]

Reluctantly, Henry agreed to postpone his expedition until the Cathar situation was resolved and, as such, passed on the news to Richard in Gascony. Also in January, and most likely as a reward for his compliance, Honorius granted Henry the right to tax the Irish clergy. That such measures also formed part of the pope's hope of receiving financial aid from England also seems highly likely. A council met around 4 May at

St Paul's to discuss the current state of affairs, prior to which Honorius had been particularly careful to adopt a conciliatory, if not Pauline, approach to monetary matters. Acknowledging the church's past evils, he also argued that such problems lay in poverty and that it was the duty of good Christians to see to the church's needs.[21]

Langton was scornful of the requests laid out in the latest papal letters, citing that the magnates of France had already rejected similar demands. Undoubtedly buoyed by the suggestion, Henry responded that England's reply would be 'no more backward in obedience' than any other country. No later than May, in a bid to curry extra favour with Henry, Honorius wrote again to the king to inform him that both he and Richard were exempted from excommunication unless done by specific order of the Apostolic See. In June, Honorius went even further by offering Richard future guarantees that the papacy would provide for both his welfare and that of his brother.[22]

This same guarantee would not apply for the prince of Gwynedd. When a meeting with Llywelyn in April 1225 was again postponed, further violence threatened to break out. Throughout that year, Llywelyn unleashed great anguish on the people of Glamorgan, burning several towns and villages. This uncertainty remained until October when the discussion took place between Henry and the pope concerning excommunication of Llywelyn and interdict over his lands. By July 1226, there were at last signs that the deadlock was close to being broken when a safe passage was granted for Llywelyn and Joan to meet with the king at Shrewsbury on 27 August.[23]

Snow on 24 June had come as a great shock to the monks of Winchester.[24] Never likely to be regarded as the best of omens, such things were viewed with particular concern when news reached England that Louis VIII, in continuing his crusade against the barons of southern France, had laid siege to the city of Avignon. Declared an independent state at the end of the twelfth century and now unequivocally sided with Raymond of Toulouse, the citizens of the city had unrepentantly closed their gates on Louis and the papal legate, leading to the commencement of the siege on 10 June. After three hard months, Louis finally took the city on 12 September, culminating in an order that the city walls be parted with their ramparts and the moat filled in. Ironically, September also ended with dreadful flooding, which proved a significant threat to the city's welfare.[25]

16 September marked the death of Pandulf. Since leaving England, the faithful legate had continued to aid the English cause in France

before ending his days in Rome. As per his wishes, his body was taken to Norwich to be interred in his cathedral.[26]

Less than two months later, a similar fate befell Avignon's conqueror. True to his word, Henry had made no effort to interfere with the Albigensian Crusade; however, as with John and Henry the Young King, death in conflict was merely one way a king could meet his maker. Aged just 39, Louis VIII passed away in Auvergne on 8 November as he attempted to make his way back to Paris. Whether the astrologer who correctly predicted Louis's failure to return had also been aware that he shared John's susceptibility to dysentery is another matter.[27]

Further in common with his great foe John, in vacating the throne Louis had left the crown in the hands of a minor. Aged just 12, the challenges facing the future saint, recently crowned Louis IX, in many ways mirrored those that had been confronted by the young Henry III. His coronation similarly lacking in jubilance, their mutual devotion to religion would far outweigh their love of war. Though Louis had been saved the complication of a violent civil war, a combination of the resumption of Holy Wars in the south, a determined Richard leading a campaign of reclamation in the centre of the country and a court of countless meddlers would have been enough to give the young king instant headaches. Deprived an ally of Marshal's aura and capability, his regency instead fell under the spell of his vocal and capable mother, Blanche of Castile.[28]

Somewhat predictably, discontent against Blanche raged in certain quarters. Seeing the confusion as an opportunity to salvage the lost Angevin estates, Henry made contact with the nobles of Anjou, Normandy, Brittany and Poitou in a bid to drum up support for an English invasion. Exactly what Henry promised the lords is unclear, only that the suggestion seems to have gone down well. Barely six weeks after the death of Louis VIII, many of those who had conquered Poitou for the late king had aligned themselves with Henry. Among the losses for the young Louis were the ever-treacherous Lusignan and the Poitevin seneschal, Savori de Mauléon, both of whom had been taken in by Richard's charms. Placation of Lusignan finally saw Henry restore Isabella her dower in England, which he had revoked in the light of their defection. Grants were also provided to the city of Saintes, including an agreement to support the viscount of Thouars against the king of France. He was also granted the castle at Loudun.[29]

Christmas in 1226 was kept at Reading, the same town where Henry's great-great-grandfather and namesake, Henry I, had been laid to rest in 1135. On arriving at the capital early in the New Year, he immediately aroused the citizens' displeasure by demanding 5,000 marks of silver. Of Henry's exact justification, much has been speculated. His perpetual need of funds had, of course, been further exacerbated by the financial burden of his plan to retake the Angevin lands. Yet argument has also been made that the citizens had gifted a similar amount to Louis on his departure in 1217.[30]

Strident in his views the money was owed, Henry's new swagger remained visible as he headed north to his personal court at Wallingford and from there to Oxford. Now in his twentieth year, he was, for the first time in his life, something of an experienced statesman, at least by comparison to the 12-year-old king of France. Clearly sensing an opportunity to readdress a balance that had been tipped in the magnates' favour since the first reissuing of the charter at Bristol in 1216, the young king entered the city of dreaming spires ready to lay down a mark. On holding a council on 9 January, Henry declared that, by the consent of the archbishop of Canterbury and common council, from this moment onwards he would issue charters under his own seal.[31]

The consequences of this council were potentially limitless. Not only did it throw fresh doubt over the future of the charters, of more short-term importance, it raised several questions concerning the makeup of Henry's government. In the eyes of Peter des Roches's critics, the news was highly fortuitous. For Hubert, in particular, the promise of the bishop of Winchester's complete removal left him free to guide the king as he pleased. Indeed, dissolution of the old triumvirate – arguably a duumvirate since Pandulf's departure – without appointing replacements left Hubert in sole control of the government. Likewise, it is unlikely that many tears were shed from Langton's eyes that the butterfly bishop was moved ever further from power.[32]

Of far greater consequence was the mindset of the king himself. More than ten years after taking Marshal's hand among the planes of Malmesbury, Henry III had emerged from the shadows of youth a full-bodied Plantagenet. Four times he had agreed to reforms: bringing about three reissues of the original charters. For the first time since the second charter at Bristol, everything Marshal had worked so hard for – everything the rebel barons had initially fought for – now rested on a political knife-edge.

Get this wrong, and it would lead England to the teeth of a further civil war.

Chapter 15

1227–1230
A Steep Learning Curve

Contrary to the views of many previous commentators, Henry's actions did not in themselves bring about an official end to his minority. Nor could they. Although in his twentieth year, he would not reach the age of majority (21) until 1 October 1228. Of specific importance on this matter, the 1216 issue of the great charter had a new clause about barons obtaining majority at 21. That said, by taking charge of his own seal, from this moment onwards, Henry was able to lead from the front and no longer subjected to the guidance of overseers.

True to Honorius's promise of 1218 that any charter made before he obtained the great seal would be subject to later confirmation, the charters of his minority were questioned. That Henry had doubted his authority up to this point is hardly surprising. Further to the rebukes he had encountered concerning the case of Tickhill Castle in 1218 that he was a mere boy, a year later, Philip II had similarly remarked, 'the children of King John have neither as much money nor as much power to defend themselves as had their father'.[1] For arguably the first time in his reign so far, the dark side of his father and grandfather clearly shone through. In a bid to impose his authority, Henry demanded that a heavy tallage – feudal duty or land tax – be laid on the towns in exchange for the Forest Charter's renewal. On a related note, the pledge of two years earlier by the clergy that a fifteenth on movable property be handed over in return for the reissue of the Great Charter was finally dealt with.[2]

It seems strangely fitting that this new chapter in Henry's life would also see the departure of certain figures who had been influential in guiding him through the greatest challenges of his youth. That des Roches was ousted was no major surprise. In reality, his powers of persuasion had waned considerably since the confiscation of the royal castles back in 1223. For Hubert, the prospect of being the sole guiding influence over the king with no legate, no Peter or Marshal to operate alongside him may have been seen as a reward in itself. Yet more considerable fortune would bless him on being made earl of Kent.[3] While Hubert revelled in his newly reached heights, Peter's fortunes had all but evaporated. Effectively in the political wilderness, he subsequently entered the geographical one by way of the Holy Land. Among his final acts before departure was a reconciliation on Henry's behalf at Farnham with Savari de Mauléon after which the former seneschal of Poitou accompanied the bishop on the early stages of his crusade.[4]

Joining des Roches in departing Henry's journey was the much-loved Pope Honorius III. Now 77 and in his twelfth year as Holy Father, Honorius breathed his last on 18 March. Like most who occupied the throne of St Peter in the crusader age, two dominating forces had driven his policy: reform and a liberated Holy Land. One of his final acts was to issue a plea for aid in support of the Sixth Crusade. Sadly for Honorius, he would never witness the dream of peace in the Holy Land. Some would argue such a dream was impossible.[5]

Regarding matters of reform, Honorius had continued along the path initiated by Innocent III. He added considerably to the corpus of canon law and also oversaw the reorganisation of papal finances. He remained passionate in his support of the evangelisation of Moor-dominated Spain, eradication of the Cathars and the spreading of Christianity to the Baltics; the Franciscan and Dominican orders were also created on his watch. Both contemporarily and in future years, he was famed for his scholarly writings: his time as a tutor to Frederick II in the Holy Roman Emperor's childhood being of particular importance. A native of Rome, his election as Vicar of Christ was celebrated throughout the city and his death widely mourned. Though his critics in England lamented his interference in domestic policy, his apologists will argue he was a calm influence on Henry and was beloved for his kindness and love of peace.

Taking Honorius's place was Cardinal Ugolino dei Conti di Segni, who adopted the name Gregory in honour of assuming the pontificate in a monastery dedicated to that saint. Exactly how old he was at the time of his consecration is unclear. So vague are sources concerning his upbringing, his date of birth has been placed anywhere between 1145 and 1170.[6]

Born in the ancient town of Anagni in central Italy, the election of Gregory IX was not so much the culmination of a mighty rise, but a journey influenced by nepotism. A nephew – if not a great-nephew – of

Innocent III, Gregory had been made a cardinal at Innocent's pleasure and was promoted at least twice by his relative. His performance as dean of the Sacred College of Cardinals, on the other hand, must have made a mark on Francis of Assisi, as he was earmarked by Francis to be made cardinal protector of that order in 1220.

Picking up where Honorius left off, Gregory wrote to Henry shortly after his election on matters concerning another crusade. In possession of his great seal Henry may now have been, it did not change the fact that England was still a papal fiefdom. For this reason alone, Gregory's backing would continue to be of great importance to Henry. In April 1227, Gregory renewed Honorius's bull of 1223, decreeing that the 19-year-old was able to rule by himself without subjection to the magnates.[7]

A further sign of the king's journey into maturity and majority was the stepping up of marriage negotiations. In a bid to widen his present choice – namely Iolenta, daughter of Peter of Dreux, and Margaret, daughter of Leopold VI, Duke of Austria – talk commenced about one of the daughters of Premysl, King of Bohemia. Warm wishes were also offered to the key lords of the Holy Roman Empire, most notably Frederick himself and Louis I, Duke of Bavaria. Whether all such correspondence was sent in the pursuit of marriage is now unclear. Having struck out on his own and still intent on reclaiming the lost ancestral lands, the forging of new alliances in Europe was of increasing priority.[8]

Bad news had recently been brought to the king on the return of his ambassadors from France. The situation there ever complicated, things had taken a further turn with news that the lords, including Lusignan, had made peace with Blanche, culminating in the Treaty of Vendôme. The reasons for the agreement were obvious. Military and financial support from England for the Angevin states never consistent, the presence of the French army south of the Loire had left Poitou susceptible to easy conquest. As a consequence of Peter of Brittany's coming to terms with Blanche, the suggestion of a marriage between Iolande and Henry was immediately dropped. With Henry's chances of achieving restoration of Poitou now looking increasingly precarious, it was thanks almost solely to the perceptive movements of Richard that allowed peace to be made with Louis's regency in July for another year. When the earl of Cornwall returned to England, he did so with the county of Poitou still technically under English rule.[9]

Remarkably, rather than return to a grateful court and awaiting a long list of honours, Richard actually walked into a heated argument.

The cause on this occasion was an ensuing quarrel over Richard's rights to a certain manor that had previously made up part of the earldom of Cornwall. In recent times the manor – if not eight – had been allocated to the German knight Waleran: the same loyal castellan who had held the royal castle at Berkhamsted so valiantly during the First Barons' War. In response to Richard's ejection of a royal bailiff from the Cornwall lands, Waleran countered that the property had entered his possession by royal grant. It was the view of the annalist of Dunstable that Richard received the earldom there for the first time; however, most likely, it was only now that he finally benefitted from the possessions.[10]

Severe famine and terrible thunderstorms would set a morbidly appropriate scene for an English summer that would be high in drama. On Richard's being forced to reinstate Waleran, as well as give up the honour of Berkhamsted that had formed part of his mother's dowry to Reymond de Burgh, a stormy meeting between the two royal brothers culminated in Richard being threatened with exile. To make matters worse, Hubert appears to have made plans for Richard's arrest. Outraged at his mistreatment, Richard fled Henry's court on 9 July and joined with William Marshal the Younger at Marlborough. A short time later, the pair rendezvoused with the earls of Chester, Gloucester, Surrey, Hereford, Derby and Warwick at Stamford in Lincolnshire. For Henry and his government, the developing intrigue must have seemed like déjà vu. Only four years earlier had the attempted coup of 1223 threatened to bring England to the point of civil war. Chief among the rebel earls' complaints were the increasingly tyrannical behaviour of Hubert and the dreadful condition of the Forest Charter. Nor did the nobles alone voice such criticisms.[11]

Undoubtedly fearful that rebellion was at hand, a meeting was arranged for 2 or 3 August in Northampton. Fortunately for all concerned, Henry's willingness to give in on some of his demands ensured that talks progressed well. In acknowledgement, the nobles and barons agreed to support Henry with an additional £1,200 on the back of the original one-fifteenth granted in 1225. The threat of rebellion quietened and approximately £800,000 in modern money richer, a year of mixed fortunes would end with floods reaching unprecedented levels but a peaceful Christmas court at York.[12]

Throughout the following year, relations with France continued to be complicated. Henry's position in Gascony secure and the lands of Poitou still far from permanently lost, the great frustration for Henry at that time was that the current truce prohibited him from extending his hand towards his lost dominions. Nor, at least until the Albigensian Crusade ended, was that likely to change. Continuing in the same vein as his predecessor, Gregory pressed Louis and his government to restore all of the ancestral lands due to Henry. True to another promise made by the late Honorius, the legate Romanus was forbidden from excommunicating Henry or Richard without papal approval.[13]

All the while, the future of the Holy Land remained at the forefront of Gregory's mind. Before Christmas, a further letter reached the king, this time courtesy of the Patriarch of Jerusalem, highlighting the imperativeness of a new crusade. The likelihood that one might finally take place had escalated somewhat in the light of developments in France. Nor does Henry appear to have been against the proposal. Yet whatever thoughts he privately held came to nothing throughout 1228. In August of that year, news reached the royal court that Llywelyn had attacked the recently fortified castle at Montgomery.[14]

Responsibility for Montgomery's defences lay primarily with the justiciar. Already castellan of the three castles of Gwent, as well as having acquired lordship of Cardigan, Carmarthen and the Gower Peninsula, it was only logical that Montgomery be added to his jurisdiction. In his bid to relieve the castle, Hubert threatened to incur the wrath of his peers by levying the charges on the kingdom. Never popular, even at the best of times, the grumblings on this occasion were far more understandable due to Llywelyn's attack being on Hubert's personal property as opposed to being issued in support of a war concerning the nation at large. On mounting his attempt to combat the Welsh prince, Hubert marched west with a large army of some 500 knights that included, at its head, the king himself.

Buoyed by a Welsh retreat and a successful siege, the English forces maintained their course throughout Powys to the nearby village of Kerry. On reaching the monastery there, the usually benign king unleashed his fury on the monks and ordered it be razed to the ground as punishment for their siding with Llywelyn. Key to his decision might well have been his learning that the Welsh had been using it to store arms. No sooner was it destroyed, work began on building a castle in stone.[15]

Sadly for Henry and the justiciar, what had begun as a campaign of great potential was now heading for disaster. One of the main problems was a personal dislike of Hubert among the Marcher lords, notably

William Marshal the Younger and William de Braose – son of Llywelyn's son-in-law Reginald who had served alongside Llywelyn against John before making peace with Henry. A more recent addition to Hubert's list of enemies was the earl of Cornwall, something that can be largely explained as a consequence of the feud regarding Waleran on Richard's return.[16]

All involved in the present circumstances knew only too well that this was never so much a campaign of national importance but a defence of Hubert's lordship. Plagued by a lack of incentive and a ubiquitous Welsh force constantly interfering with English supply lines, on one occasion the English troops were caught off guard. In a stunning turn of fate, William de Braose, one of the stronger Marcher lords, was captured. A combination of Llywelyn's regained strength, Henry's perpetual lack of funds to afford the completion of the new castles and the earlier lack of motivation among his troops left the king little option but to sue for peace. The king celebrated his 21st birthday on 1 October, after which he agreed a 'disgraceful' truce with the prince of Gwynedd. Not only had the campaign been truly wasted, but it had ended with the loyal William still in captivity.[17]

Across the sea, events in France continued to take surprising turns. Successful in uniting the French lords, implementation of the Treaty of Vendôme had so far lived up to its purpose in delivering a major blow to Henry's chances of augmenting his rule over Poitou. Worse still, the agreement potentially threatened this further through the promise of future marriages between the Lusignans and French royals. Research into the legalities of the 1227 truce between Richard of Cornwall and Blanche offers a particularly striking illustration of how Henry's French possessions had reduced dramatically since John's peace with Philip following Bouvines in 1214: something that Louis VIII's move into Gascony had temporarily worsened. Nevertheless, the agreement was not without benefit for Henry. From a domestic perspective, favourable terms for Isabella went some way towards ending the ongoing dispute over her dower from John. Also of great consequence was Hugh's willingness to surrender any rights to Bordeaux as had been disgracefully promised to him by Louis VIII.[18]

Better news for the king was the easing of tensions at court. Especially true was this concerning requests for military aid. Discontent on the home front had cooled since peace had been made between the two brothers, limiting any personal animosity to Hubert. That this alone was treated with appropriate concern can be found in the content of many contemporary papal letters. Never one to encourage illegal gatherings, around this time, Gregory wrote to Henry directing that certain tournaments should be banned as some of the barons and nobles were using them as opportunities to make compacts to resist the king's policy.[19]

Further to baronial grumblings, it was recorded in the annals of Dunstable that a serious rift had opened up between Henry and Archbishop Langton. The catalyst, just as it had been with John, had concerned the privileges of the see of Canterbury. Only when Henry agreed to abide by the rights of an ancient royal charter were things finally resolved.

Unfortunately for the archbishop, the agreement would mark the end of his affiliation with the king. While staying at his manor at Slindon in Sussex, his health deteriorated, and he passed away on 9 July. His body was brought back to Canterbury for burial in the Chapel of St Michael – often referred to in the modern day as the Buffs' Chapel – that lies close to the great south door of Canterbury Cathedral. A bizarre epilogue to his story, when the chapel was rededicated in the 1400s, Langton's body was moved and reinterred a short distance away. A strange extrusion runs through the east wall of the chapel, from which half of the late archbishop's body now lies. Perhaps influenced by a sense of personal loss, a short time later, Henry made peace with the late archbishop's brother, Simon, as well as papal agent Robert Passelewe.[20]

As Langton's election of twenty-one years earlier had illustrated only too clearly, the coming of a new archbishop of Canterbury in Plantagenet England was rarely a straightforward affair. Nor, alas, would the election of his successor be any different. On receiving the news that the monks of Christ Church had elected their fellow brother, Walter of Eynsham, to the see, Henry copied his father and sought to quash the election. While the king may well have secretly coveted the see for one of his allies, on this occasion, there were other factors at play. Whereas Langton had been celebrated in his own life as a great Biblical scholar who had impressed the great learned minds of England and France, Walter, by no means a young man himself, was far less respected in this department.[21]

Henry's first choice to replace Langton was one Richard le Grant. A native of Essex, Grant had been chancellor of Lincoln for around nine years. A renowned writer and teacher, albeit no Langton, it has also been speculated that he was chancellor of the University of Cambridge, noted in the records as Richard of Wetheringsett; however, there is no clear evidence for this. Support in his bid for the see of Canterbury came from the bishops of Rochester and Coventry – other sources say Chester. On sending his agents to the Vatican in an attempt to obtain support for Grant's candidacy, Henry bizarrely granted Gregory permission to take one-tenth of all property in England in aid of his dispute with the Holy Roman Emperor. Earlier that year, Frederick had been excommunicated in retribution for his delay in journeying to the Holy Land – something that Frederick had blamed on illness. When news of Henry's intentions reached Rome, Richard le Grant was accepted into the See of Canterbury on 19 January, seemingly without the need of an election.[22]

An election was needed that year to fill the see at Salisbury. After William Scot's election to the see of Durham was quashed, the role was taken up by Richard le Poure after his transfer from Salisbury. At the time, this had angered Henry, who wished the vacancy for Hubert's former chaplain, Luke of St Albans, who replaced Peter de Rivallis as head of the royal wardrobe in 1225. He even threatened to tear down the walls of Durham Castle if he failed to get his way. Around the time of the Canterbury election, two canons of Salisbury were chosen to go to Rome, to seek papal confirmation of the monks' choice of Robert de Bingham. Not only was the outcome greatly received by the cardinals in Rome but the canons were also especially warmly welcomed by Otho.[23] In July, correspondence between king and pope concerned other matters: namely, Henry's request to have his father's body moved to Beaulieu – the originally intended location for his burial – as well as joining the sees of Waterford and Lismore in Ireland. For unknown reasons, the transfer of John's remains to Beaulieu never occurred. In 1232, his body was instead moved to a new tomb in Worcester Cathedral, which bears the imposing effigy that stands today. On 27 May 1229, Bingham's consecration was confirmed, followed by Grant at Canterbury on 10 June.[24]

In 1229, England welcomed the fourth papal visitor of Henry's reign. Named in the records as Stephen, apparently a papal chaplain and messenger as opposed to a legate, his mission seems to have more or less mirrored that of Otho: most specifically collection of the tenth that Henry had promised Gregory the previous year. That this Stephen was the same papal chaplain who had corresponded with Henry so favourably over the Bedford fiasco seems likely, albeit impossible to prove convincingly.[25]

On 29 April, a short time after Stephen arrived in England, Henry called a council to meet at Westminster. Among the business conducted, Stephen read aloud his collection of papal letters relating to the previously promised tithe. Across the sea, much had happened in the last twelve months. In the king's earlier writings, specific mention had been made of Gregory's feud with Frederick, yet since that time Frederick had left Apulia for Cyprus and led his fleet from there to Acre. So great was antipathy towards him that an attack was made on his followers under the banner of the king of Jerusalem, John of Brienne, the legate, Cardinal John of Colunna and Count Thomas of Apulia.[26]

Around the time of Stephen's visit, news had reached England that Frederick II had triumphed in the sixth crusade of 1228–29. Despite taking Jerusalem through negotiated surrender, the recapture of the Holy City did little to win over Gregory. Highlighted in Stephen's letters were an extensive list of Frederick's misdemeanours, including entering the Church of the Holy Sepulchre on the feast of the Annunciation, being crowned in the church despite being excommunicated, and ordering Christian girls to entertain Saracen men at his palace. There was also an accusation that Frederick held the sultan with whom he had negotiated the return of Jerusalem in higher esteem than the pope, a suggestion that may have had some truth.[27]

Regarding the financial aid, Henry had, of course, secretly agreed to the papal demands – the price of Grant's appointment – though nothing had been discussed with his council. Fortunately for the king, the magnates reluctantly agreed to come to Rome's aid; however, how it was collected was utterly shocking.[28] According to the chroniclers, many of the papal collectors were joined on their rounds by usurers, as a result of which those who were unable to pay the tithe from their own funds had no choice but to borrow the money at extreme levels of interest. Not only was the practice illegal – usury was, of course, banned by the church – it also left many clergymen impoverished. How the 'little poor man', Francis of Assisi, would have viewed such practices one can only imagine. Since he died in 1226, Francis's fame had continued to soar. This led to his canonisation in 1228, news of which was recorded in England around the time of these collections.[29]

Successful crusades and canonisations would prove the highlights of what were otherwise tricky years on the Continent. In 1229, a student strike at the University of Paris led to the suspension of classes. For a time, the university relocated to the city of Angers. Not until the following year would the matter be resolved. Hoping to capitalise, Henry appears to have offered the affected certain privileges should they transfer to Oxford.[30] Prior to the peaceful restoration of Jerusalem, war broke out between the Lombard city of Bologna – supported by the pope – and the imperial city of Modena.[31] Back in England, a personal visit by the king to the priory of Dunstable did little to resolve a feud between the monastery and townspeople. Just as had been true throughout the country, most of the outcry concerned tithes and tax collection, with many among the towns' folk affirming they would rather go to hell than enrich the greedy monks.[32]

Relations with France was again one of the main topics of discussion around the Christmas table in 1228. Of compelling interest to Henry, certain letters had arrived at the Oxford court, courtesy of the lords of Normandy, Gascony, and Poitou hinting at the possibility of future English dominion. Also present as the king's guest was the archbishop of Bordeaux, Gérard de Malemort. News that the previously good relations between Blanche and the lords of Normandy, Brittany and Poitou were showing signs of breaking was music to Henry's ears. Only too aware that no renewed mission would be possible prior to the expiration of Hubert's latest truce, due to run until July, Henry instead set a course for long-term preparation so that a sizeable force would be ready for the summer.[33]

As usual, Gregory was ardently against war between the two nations and once again wrote to both kings in the hope of a peaceful solution. Better news for Gregory and Blanche would occur in April following a great triumph over Raymond of Toulouse in the Albigensian Crusade. In the Treaty of Meaux that ensued, Raymond, blessed with a daughter, Joan, but no sons, was left little option than allocate his dominions for the king through Joan's marriage to Louis's younger brother, Alphonse. In restitution for his Cathar sympathy, Raymond reluctantly took up the cross in return for absolution. Around the time of the Treaty of Meaux, he also earmarked the abbot of Cîteaux as the ideal mediator between Louis and Henry.[34]

Throughout the year, Henry's desire to reclaim the lost lands had showed no signs of abating. Satisfied that relations between Blanche and the lords were little improved, Henry pushed ahead with plans to invade. Despite initially aiming for a summer departure, a combination of the truce and Hubert's advice saw him continue to bide his time until the autumn. On 9 October, and with the time of departure drawing ever nearer, a ship carrying the regent of Brittany, Peter of Dreux, docked in Portsmouth harbour. On disembarking, Peter formally paid homage to Henry as king of France. During the talks that followed, Henry granted the duke his long-coveted earldom of Richmond and officially acknowledged him 'Duke of Brittany'. The launch date was set for 15 October; however, this was immediately postponed due to a lack of resources and insufficient ships. After becoming aware of the miscalculation, a furious Henry drew his sword and threatened to execute Hubert on the quayside, while slandering him with the claim that he had accepted 5,000 marks from Blanche to delay the mission. His temper eventually cooled, on Peter's advice, Henry agreed that the expedition would be postponed until the spring.[35]

A terrible thunderstorm on 25 January 1230 aroused familiar dread in the hearts of the citizens of London. Particularly true had this been for the congregation gathered at St Paul's Cathedral for the anniversary of Paul's conversion. As the bishop celebrated mass before the high altar, a deafening thunderclap was recorded as having shaken the very foundations, following which a bright lightning strike from the darkness created the illusion that the cathedral itself had become engulfed in the fires of eternal damnation. Whether the lightning bolt had been a direct hit or a near miss is now uncertain. Only that the emergence of an accompanying stench prompted all, except the bishop and a deacon, to flee. Not until the foul odour cleared did the congregation flock back and completed the mass.[36]

That the dreadful thunderbolt could have been deemed a sign from the heavens of God's annoyance of the malpractices of Rome seems a reasonable assumption, not that the metaphor was lost on other matters. High among the explanations of the soothsayers must surely have been the king's frustrations at the failure of the Poitou launch the previous year; not least his developing anger at his justiciar. Henry had been slow to forgive Hubert for the shambles he had witnessed in October. Throughout the recent Christmas proceedings in York, relations between the pair had turned frosty like the weather.

Of greater merriment to the king had been the arrival of his sister, Joan, as well as brother in law, King Alexander II of Scotland, marking the first meeting in the city between the kings of England and Scotland since Alexander's wedding with Joan in 1221. Apart from the usual pleasantries and political business with Scotland, Henry had only one thought on his mind: to right the wrongs of past failures on the Continent. Unrecorded is Alexander's exact reaction on being obliged to offer a financial contribution for his upcoming venture.[37]

In the spring, lessons from October, it seemed, had finally been learned. When the invasion force cast off from Portsmouth on 30 April, the fleet consisted of an impressive 230 ships, with a capacity of 4,000 men and no less than sixteen horses per vessel. With Henry, Richard, Earl of Cornwall and Hubert all taking up positions in the fleet, Henry appointed chancellor, Ralph Neville, to act as regent with the help of judge Stephen of Seagrave as temporary justiciar.[38]

The expedition was noteworthy. Not only was this the first campaign on foreign soil to have occurred since John's calamitous expeditions of 1213–14, but it was also Henry's first recorded trip abroad. On crossing the Channel, the English forces stayed in Guernsey on the night of 2 May. The next day they were welcomed by Peter of Dreux on docking at the walled city of St Malo on the Brittany coast. On 8 May, they proceeded south to Dinan, the predesignated meeting place for the army, and from there continued past the city of Rennes to Nantes. Henry had intended to meet his mother and stepfather there, but not for the first time Isabella let him down.[39]

Better news for Henry had concerned the timing of other matters. War between the French magnates and Theobald, the poet-count of Champagne, had forced Louis to split his forces to deal with the war on both fronts. Realising his best chance at keeping Henry out of Poitou was to block his progress through Anjou, Louis assembled a large army at the region's capital of Angers. He subsequently moved to Oudon, a castle about sixty kilometres to the west. A suggestion was mooted among the king's Norman allies at this time for Henry to go to war in Normandy, though this was dismissed as a step too far. Throughout Brittany and Poitou, the lords mostly paid Henry homage, except for a handful who fortified their castles against him. By midsummer, Henry had received the allegiance of all the lords in Poitou except for the ever-treacherous Lusignan and Raymond, Viscount of Thouars, whose brother Aimery had long ago become disillusioned by John's behaviour in the aftermath of the capture of Mirebeau.

For Henry, never a king destined to go down in the annals of history for sharing his grandfather and namesake's penchant for warcraft, as the summer progressed, he demonstrated his inexperience. Whatever dreams he had of conquering lost lands were not implemented. An unopposed march through Anjou, and from there into Poitou, displayed all the characteristics of a European tour as opposed to any form of well structured military campaign. His forces crossed the Loire to the south on 1 July after which the only action of note was to recapture Mirebeau. The castle, of course, had been of great significance to Henry's father. Located in the Upper Saintonge, the siege that began on 21 July was over within nine days, thanks mainly to the arrival of the knights of Gascony with a siege train from Bordeaux.[40]

With Mirebeau conquered, Henry's forces continued to Bordeaux where he stayed for about a week enjoying the wine and cuisine. Now at the most south point of his kingdom, the only logical option was to return north. The route chosen was more or less the same ground already covered. They crossed the Loire again to the north and on 15 September, all loose ends were tied up in Nantes. In the same month, Henry penned a letter to his half-brother, Geoffrey de Lusignan, confirming his intention to return home, citing illness among his men – bouts of which were also experienced by himself and Richard – as a reason for cutting the endeavour short.

With this, Henry's first cross Channel sortie came to a disappointing end. On departing the port of St Pol de Léon, they arrived back in Portsmouth in October. Whereas the voyage out had preceded a solar eclipse, the return was marked with a lunar one. On Henry's orders Ranulf, William Marshal the Younger, William of Aumale and Peter of Dreux remained behind with a force of some 500 knights and 1,000 men at arms for the ancestral lands' protection.[41]

Twelve years would pass before Henry would see the green of France again.

Chapter 16

1230–1231
The Awakened Dragon

Invasions of Scotland and the Isle of Man by raiding Danes and Norwegians would impose significant hardship on the monarchs of those lands throughout this time. After inflicting the type of losses for which their Viking forebears had become renowned, the enemy attacks were eventually repelled after a combination of fierce skirmishes on land and at sea.[1]

South of Hadrian's Wall, things improved for Henry with the long overdue news that the cold war between the pope and Holy Roman Emperor had, at last, come to an end. On returning to Italy from the Holy Land, Frederick's troops had clashed violently with the papal forces, the result of which threatened to lead to a major conflict. Fortunately for all concerned, a truce was agreed in August, after which Frederick received absolution from Gregory at the pontifical palace. Also that year, the Elector of Saxony, Albert I, was reported as having landed in England; due to Henry's earlier absence in the Poitou campaign, the journey appears to have occurred after his return.[2] 23 December marked the death of Richard I's widow and Henry's aunt, Berengaria of Navarre, aged around 60. A minor player in European politics even at her prime, her final act of note was the founding of the Cistercian abbey of L'Épau near Le Mans.[3]

Christmas was celebrated at Lambeth that year, less than two months after Henry's return from overseas. Control of his kingdom resumed having retaken the reins from Neville, Henry wrote to Louis hoping that diplomacy, as opposed to further warfare, would culminate in the return to English ownership of the remaining territories lost during John's reign. Among the magnates, meanwhile, the recent expedition's lack of progress had drawn sharp criticism, leading to further tension between Henry and the justiciar. Henry's lack of progress had proven just as great a problem financially as it had in military terms. So severe had the situation become that within his army, some of the less wealthy knights had been left little option but to pawn their armour and horses for provisions.[4]

On 26 January a council met at Westminster to deal with the fallout. As previously recalled, since reaching the first stage of his majority back in 1223, Henry had gained possession of a small private seal; however, this was used only for chancery and exchequer business that didn't require the legal approval of the magnates. Acting within the capabilities of the private seal, Henry put forward a request of three marks on all fiefs – laity and clergy – to help balance the books. In a move that made Henry's decision to pursue the consecration of Richard le Grant as archbishop of Canterbury all the more ludicrous, Grant opposed the decision, only to be moved when Henry issued letters that further guaranteed the liberties of the clergy. Most likely in reward of this, later in January Henry received a further notice of excommunication exemption from the papacy. A similar waiver prohibited the royal chapels being placed under interdict except by specific order of the apostolic see.[5]

Undoubtedly hopeful that the gesture of affection would go on to inspire further generosity in the king himself, Gregory wrote to Henry in April, encouraging him to make a lasting peace with Louis. Though a permanent resolution would remain elusive, the challenges encountered in the previous year's campaign had all but removed any idea of subsequent expedition into the lands of his forebears from the king's agenda. The obvious financial problems aside, there is reason to believe Henry found the experience both chastising and exhausting. As history would tell, the rudderless expedition that had just ended would be Henry's last in France until 1242.[6]

Of far more imminent concern to the king of England and his magnates around this time was that the deteriorating relations with Hubert were spreading to other factions. Throughout the following year, a bitter feud ensued between archbishop le Grant and the justiciar concerning the property of the young Richard de Clare[7] – later 6th earl of Gloucester. On the death of Richard's father, Gilbert de Clare, 5th Earl of Gloucester – also the husband of the late William Marshal's daughter, Isabel – from the very same illness Henry had himself experienced prior to returning home from Brittany, Hubert was appointed the 8-year-old's guardian as well as the keeper of Richard's property. There is some evidence that Hubert and his Scottish royal wife planned a wedding between Richard and their daughter, Meggotta, who was around the same age; however, this came to nothing. That the possibility appealed to Hubert seems highly likely. Had this been achieved, the joining of the lands of the two families would have made the justiciar one of the richest men in the kingdom.[8]

Of particular significance in this was Tonbridge Castle in Kent, which due to its location fell strictly within the archbishop's jurisdiction. As Richard de Clare was a minor, and unable to obtain his lands in his own right, Grant took issue with Hubert's hoarding, leading to accusations that the justiciar was interfering with the privileges of the see of Canterbury. When Henry took the justiciar's side, a furious Grant left England and took his case to Rome. Among the charges brought against Hubert were of his extraordinary levels of power in England, his marrying a wife to whom his first wife had been closely related and his frequent infractions on the see of Canterbury. Although Grant was well received at the Roman curia and granted an audience with Gregory, the journey ultimately did him little good. On 3 August the following year, while still in Italy, he passed away and was buried in the commune of San Gemini in Umbria. With this, for the second time in four years, the Chair of St Augustine fell vacant.[9]

Concurrent to such events, the spectre of war with Wales continued to threaten the security of the borders. Still in captivity as a result of the mangled 1228 campaign, William de Braose had negotiated his freedom on the perilous condition that Isabella, one of his four daughters, be wed to Llywelyn's son. In fulfilment of the dowry obligation, William would also part with the impressive castle at Builth.

No sooner had the agreement been made, when travesty struck. From sources unknown, word had reached the prince of Gwynedd that during William's time in captivity he had been discovered alone with Joan – Llywelyn's wife and Henry's bastard half-sister – in the prince's own bedchamber. In a fit of rage, Llywelyn seized William from Builth at Easter time and hanged him from a tree before some 900 witnesses. While Joan would suffer a year's house arrest as punishment for her apparent infidelity, revenge against William would fail to calm Llywelyn's rage. In the weeks that followed, the truce of 1228 was tested to the limit when the Welsh prince laid waste to much of South Wales, concentrating his efforts mainly on the Marshal lands of Pembrokeshire and Gwent. Three years after the burning of St Nicholas, the village suffered again, along with that of St Hilary.[10]

In April 1231, less than a fortnight after the highly anticipated wedding had taken place between Gilbert de Clare's widow, Isabel Marshal, and the king's brother, Richard, Earl of Cornwall, the situation in Wales threatened to deteriorate even further following the shock passing of William Marshal the Younger. What caused the 41-year-old's death remains a mystery. Later conjecture by Roger of Wendover's famous successor, Matthew Paris, pointed the finger of blame squarely at Hubert de Burgh through poison. Despite Wendover having earlier made a similar allegation against the justiciar concerning the late earl of Salisbury, Paris is the only chronicler who made such a claim.[11]

While England lamented, Wales rejoiced – so wrote the annalist of Waverley.[12] Having fathered no children with first wife, Alice de Bethune, nor with Henry's young sister, Eleanor, William bequeathed his lands and titles to his younger brother, Richard, now henceforth 3rd Earl of Pembroke. There is a bizarre legend here that William's lack of an heir had been due to a curse put on the family by the Irish bishop of Ferns, Albin O'Molloy, in retribution of the first earl's seizure of two of the bishop's manors between 1207 and 1213. Having earlier excommunicated Marshal, to which the regent had argued such things had occurred in a time of war, their feud reached a pinnacle in April 1218 when the bishop was banned from prosecuting his plea against him. Two months later, Pope Honorius was himself forced to intercede, leading to requests of the archbishop of Dublin and Pandulf to attempt a reconciliation between the pair. Their attempts futile, O'Molloy arrived in London on Marshal's death and petitioned Henry fruitlessly for the manors' restoration. Failing in his own efforts to convince the bishop to absolve the late Marshal of his excommunication, O'Molloy apparently foretold the end of the family line in retribution for his sons' refusal to restore the manors. In April 1231, William Marshal the Younger was laid to rest alongside his father in the Templar church in London. Curse or no curse, the king was deeply saddened to hear of his death. When told the bad news, Henry is reported to have cried out, in reference to his grandfather's knights slewing of Thomas Becket, 'Woe, woe is me! Is not the blood of the blessed martyr Thomas fully avenged yet?'[13]

Hoping to gain some degree of control over the Marshal lands, Henry moved quickly. Successful at least in forcing a Welsh retreat, no sooner had he departed than Llywelyn invaded Hubert's estates in the Marches. A key concern once again was the fate of the recently fortified

Montgomery Castle. As violence flared, the English garrison charged with defending Montgomery marooned the Welsh by cutting off their escape route and took many of their enemies captive. On Hubert's orders, a number of the prisoners were executed, their heads brought before the king.[14]

Learning of the vulgar occurrence, Llywelyn hastily assembled a large army and unleashed his fury on the borderlands. The carnage that followed was almost unprecedented. Stories abounded of churches being locked with hordes of women inside and burned to the ground. Nor was the anguish inflicted limited to the common folk. Accusations were also made that neither nobility nor clergy were immune from his wrath. Particular damage was wrought that year upon the Braose-owned Radnor Castle, as well as the castles at Brecon, Hay and Caerleon. Though the prince of Gwynedd had failed to take the fortresses, he later took the de Clare castle at Neath and the Marshal one at Kidwelly before burning the town of Cardigan. He was more fortunate with the rulers of the mines. It was recorded in the annals of Tewkesbury that knowledge of their existence in England was only uncovered around April 1228.[15]

Hearing of his enemy's latest rampage, Henry's true Plantagenet temper was unleashed in full. By 13 July, a sizeable force had gathered in Oxford; according to the chroniclers, it comprised all of England's nobles, priests and bishops. From there, he negotiated the return of Caerleon and Cardigan before his forces of around 600 proceeded to Hereford. Llywelyn, meanwhile, had gathered his troops in a meadow close to Montgomery Castle and set up surveillance of the English movements. Due to the general wetness of the surrounding area, he had so far sought to avoid open warfare; instead, choosing to bide his time until the English soldiers left the castle.

It was at this time, so wrote Roger of Wendover, that a bizarre occurrence took place. In a bid to deceive the garrison, Llywelyn convinced a Cistercian monk from the nearby Cwmhir Abbey to enter a conspiracy. On arriving at Montgomery Castle, the monk is alleged to have told the castellan of the castle, Walter de Godardville – the same man who had defended Hertford Castle so valiantly for the royalists during the First Barons' War – that he had seen Llywelyn in a nearby meadow awaiting reinforcements. On planning a surprise attack, the soldiers were told, in response to their question regarding whether their horses could safely cross the river, that the Welsh had destroyed the bridge but wading through the river on horseback would be safe due to the enemy's insufficient numbers.

Believing the holy man to be true of word, Walter summoned his men on horseback and spotted the Welsh a short time later heading into the nearby woods. Only when it was too late did they realise their enemy had lured them into the marshy riverbank. From there, the cunning Welshmen emerged from cover and put all who were unable to flee to the sword – including the horses. On hearing news from the Marches, the famously devout king's reaction again drew comparisons with that of his forebears. In retribution for the monk's deceit, the tithe barn of the abbey was looted and razed. Had it not been for the abbot's willingness to part with £200, the same would have been true of the monastery itself.[16]

Of the ensuing conflict, the campaign was once again strangely directionless. In a further repeat of history, Llywelyn's onslaught was punished with excommunication before matters ended with an unsatisfying truce. Henry's only achievement of note was the rebuilding in stone of the previously destroyed Maud's Castle, located in the modern day village of Painscastle between Builth and Hay-on-Wye. After consolidating the English presence around the border, one might also argue that strengthening the fortress named in honour of the formidable Maud de Braose – who had defended the castle so resiliently years earlier before being starved to death by John – acted as a psychological block over the Welsh. Its importance was deemed less impressive in the eyes of the annalist of Dunstable, who made the claim that while Henry rebuilt one castle, Llywelyn destroyed ten.[17]

During his stay at Maud's Castle, Henry received a visit from Peter of Dreux and Ranulf, Earl of Chester, who brought with them news of a truce with Louis.[18] Also present at various times were de Mauley and William de Cantilupe. Since leaving France a year earlier, attempts by Ranulf and the new earl of Pembroke, Richard Marshal, to make inroads in Anjou and Normandy had been unsuccessful. Worse still, cessation of Louis's war with Theobald of Champagne had allowed the French king to pool his resources in the regions' defence. Knowing that their chance of conquering Poitou had passed, at least for the time being, the earls concluded a three-year truce with Louis on 4 or 5 July. Also present for the negotiations was Henry's former tutor, Peter des Roches, who had recently returned from the Holy Land.[19]

Exactly how des Roches had performed during his crusade has not been recorded in one continuous account. Clues, however, can be found in the piecing together of various snippets from other sources. In contrast to 1218–21, no Englishman of lay magnate status joined the sixth crusade. Of des Roches's colleagues Peter de Maulay and Falkes de Breauté, the former decided against making the trip, whereas Falkes had died in Rome in 1226. When Peter made his peace with the king and prepared to leave the realm, the only major names in his company were Savari de Mauléon and the bishop of Exeter, William Briwewe. Making up the remainder of the party was a mixture of minor players including local landowners, clerics and those of his own household.[20]

That great glory awaited the Butterfly Bishop had been a matter of some amusement, if not prophetic musings, in the minds of certain contemporaries. Still to be paid for the poem des Roches commissioned him to write on St Birinus, the king's former grammar tutor, Henry d'Avranches, penned the intriguing lines around the time of his departure, 'Now you doubly adorn Syon, O Peter, and labour to raise and sustain its rocks and stones. The walls of Jerusalem rejoice that destiny prepares such a rock for them who shall be both their foundation and their crowning monument.'[21]

Joining the main fleet in sailing for Palestine in October 1227, Peter wrote to Gregory concerning Frederick's absence and its impact on the hearts of many of the pilgrims who immediately left for home. For the next year or so, the bishop remained in Palestine, concentrating on improving crusader defences, most notably within the port cities of Sidon and Jaffa. The annalist of Dunstable also singled him out for regaining Christian control of another coastal city in Ascalon. At the same time he re-established Richard I's hospital dedicated to St Thomas Becket at the port city of Acre.[22]

Buoyed by such early achievements, momentum in the Christians' favour swung rapidly on the arrival of the Holy Roman Emperor at Jaffa on 15 November 1228. Contrary to the attitudes of many prominent figures who rebuked Frederick, Peter seems to have had less qualms about dealing with him. Indeed, just as he had stood by John throughout the excommunicate and interdict years, Peter appears to have been a valuable player throughout the negotiations of 1228–29. The same would be true of the bishop of Exeter in treating with the sultan of Damascus.[23]

In March 1229, after several months of constructive negotiations, Peter joined with the central Christian forces as they entered Jerusalem for the first time. With major questions still unresolved regarding the legitimacy of Frederick's actions – not least an excommunicate making peace with an infidel – he opened up negotiations with Peter regarding refortification of the city. Ironically, Henry d'Avranches's earlier prediction that 'The walls of Jerusalem rejoice that destiny prepares such a rock for them who shall be both their foundation and their crowning monument' would be somewhat realised. Though undoubtedly intended as a slight, under Peter's guidance, the gate of St Stephen and the Tower of David were both rebuilt.[24]

In April, after Frederick's departure, Peter returned to Acre, around which time Gregory suspended him and Briwewe from office for collaborating with an excommunicate. Frederick set sail for Italy on 1 May. Peter probably sailed with him. If the musings of the annalists of Tewkesbury and Dunstable are accurate, he was influential in bringing the Holy Father and prodigal son to peace. A year later, similar would be true on leaving Rome for France at which time he played a pivotal role in cementing the truce with Louis.[25]

Contrary to the common perception of the bishop at the time of his departure, des Roches had returned to England a hero: the very man who had helped restore the Holy Sepulchre. It is quite possible that Peter founded the abbey at Titchfield, close to Fareham, at this time in thanksgiving for his safe return. Though the sixth crusade had been by no means a complete success and not without squabbles, on 15 July, he had been welcomed home. A grand ceremony at Winchester followed on 1 August before being warmly embraced by former pupil Henry on 10 August.[26]

The summer of 1231 was also the first time that England had seen Richard Marshal since the death of his elder brother, the younger William Marshal. Of Richard's exact movements prior to this time, sources are again frustratingly scant. The only thing that can be discerned for sure is that he had been tending to the ancestral lands in Normandy before joining with the English lords who had remained in France after Henry's departure. As the second son of the 'greatest knight', he had inherited some of his father's lands, most notably the Normandy lordships of Longueville and Orbec, which William the younger had signed away to him in June 1220. As the first earl's second son, on William's death without issue, Richard became the next in line to the Pembroke estates, including the family lands in both Wales and Ireland. This also made him heir to the title Lord Marshal of England.[27]

Of Richard's life, again, there remain significant gaps. Born in 1191, he was married to Gervaise de Dinan, daughter of the powerful Bretonese baron Alan de Dinan, at some point prior to 1224 and was still to father a child. Due to his wife's inheritance, Dinan had been chosen as the meeting place for Henry's forces in May 1230. At that time Richard almost certainly played host to the king and the senior magnates, including brother William. Married into Bretonese nobility, Marshal was also a keen supporter of Peter of Dreux. Ironically, Gervaise was a kinswoman of the former seneschal of Anjou William des Roches, which may have extended to the lineage of the bishop of Winchester. There was some accusation that Richard Marshal was involved in the, probably fictitious, Eleanor of Brittany plot that had seen the demise of Peter de Maulay. If the plot had been a real one, this, of course, would have cast doubt on whether des Roches left for Santiago on Camino and would also have put Richard on des Roches's side.[28]

On hearing of his brother's death, Richard made his way to England and joined up with the campaign against Llywelyn. Around this time, Wendover states that a dispute followed with Henry over the king's apparent reluctance to grant Marshal seisin over his brother's rights. Again the chronicler's finger of blame was pointed squarely at Hubert, whose poor advice led Richard to journey to Ireland to raise an army. Whether this disagreement actually happened is unclear; again, Wendover is the only source. The key concerns seem to have been a rumour that William's widow, the queen's sister, might be pregnant, as well as Richard, a landowner in Normandy and Brittany, in inheriting the Pembroke estates would be destined to suffer the same problems as his father concerning fealty to the kings of England and France. One way or another, Richard paid the king homage at Painscastle, and he was invested in his family lands sometime between 3-8 August.[29]

As the October weather began to make its presence known, Henry departed Wales and returned to England. With talk of marriage once again on the agenda, Ranulf persuaded the king against marrying Alexander II's second sister on the grounds that Hubert had married the elder sister – someone Henry had passed over. Christmas was spent at Winchester in the company of the recently returned bishop, his former tutor and advisor and now hero of Jerusalem, Peter des Roches.[30]

Question marks over the future of the see of Canterbury, as well as disputes concerning the scholars at Oxford and Cambridge, and the prices they were being forced to pay for their accommodation both proved unwanted distractions to the king at the end of a year that had already thrown up many troubles. A final footnote from that year concerned the granting of the earldom of Leicester to Simon de Montfort – about whom little more will be said in this book, only that his future influence on Henry III would be of great concern to the second half of his reign.[31]

Of more immediate significance to the king, the following year would throw up further troubles in Wales. Throughout the early part of the year, the prince of Gwynedd's forces continued to inflict much misery in the broader population: not least the lands of the Marcher lords. When the royal counsellors approached Henry directly, he pleaded that without financial aid, his hands were tied. When a council met at Westminster on 7 March 1232 to discuss the Welsh problem in greater detail, the majority of the barons refused to grant Henry further aid, citing previous funds had been squandered: not least on the Poitou expedition. With nowhere else to turn, Henry attempted instead to raise extra funds via payment of revenues, in particular from the various sheriffdoms. Achieving only limited success, the prospect of a further campaign with Wales was shelved.[32]

Problems with Rome also presented themselves that summer. On 7 June, Gregory wrote to Henry, angry that during the recent Eastertide two of his messengers had been the subject of violent assaults: leaving one dead and the other in critical condition. As usual, the violence stemmed from the collection of tithes. Building on accusations of recent years that the papal collections had been fraught with abuses from the collectors, a knight named Robert de Twenge rose in opposition to the dubious practices. Though any suggestion that the humble knight might be considered a candidate for the famous yeoman outlaw Robin Hood stretches a point, a mirroring of behaviour with the legendary outlaw – who the chronicler Walter Bower cited around 1440 as having lived during the mid-thirteenth century – is easily found in the fact that Twenge sought to relieve the Romans of their gains in order to replenish the recently impoverished. Of greater offence to Gregory, in the attack on his two messengers important letters they carried were destroyed, and the papal bulls trampled on. Incidentally, the pope specifically warned that such offences had been conducted against English messengers as well as Italian. On being challenged on the matter, Twenge left England for Rome, armed with letters of introduction from Henry, including a request that the pope hear his case personally.[33]

Further to Gregory's pleas for Henry to deal with such offenders, the pope wrote to Hubert on 9 June asking him to ensure that the rights of the Roman church remained unharmed. Somewhat bizarrely, the justiciar himself is alleged to have been partly responsible for the growth of a popular movement against the malpractices of the Roman visitors. Later that month, Hubert replaced his nephew Richard as justiciar of Ireland. Throughout his time in Ireland, Richard's possessions there had steadily risen, having inherited his father's – Hubert's brother's – castles at Tipperary and Limerick. In the previous year, Henry had also recognized his ancient claim to Connaught.[34]

Though appointment to the office of justiciar of Ireland for life may have offered an outward indication that all was well, behind the scenes, the tensions between king and justiciar were fast becoming untenable. Hubert's lack of affinity with the barons was starting to seriously affect their relations with the king, a fact not helped by the previous year's fallout with Richard le Grant, the disastrous Poitou and Welsh campaigns and the resumed influence of Peter des Roches. As Hubert's position became increasingly isolated, on 29 July, Henry gave in to the pressure and sacked him as justiciar as well as from all other offices.[35]

With this, the many complicated issues that Henry had long sought to keep closed would explode in dramatic fashion.

Chapter 17

1232
The Harrowing of Hubert de Burgh

The events that surrounded Hubert's dismissal must surely rank among the strangest to have ever occurred in the history of European government. For so long the central pillar of Henry's life and his administration, his removal would bring about not only dramatic changes in the way government business was conducted, but also Henry's attitude towards kingship.

When placed in the context of their previously close relationship, the charge sheet brought against Hubert is simply astounding. Building on the rumours concerning his poisoning of the late Longespée and younger William Marshal – as well as Falkes and Richard le Grant – the allegations ranged from moderate offences – such as theft, intimidation and bullying – to very serious – namely murder, extortion and treason. Among the strangest were claims that he had resorted to outright sorcery and dabbled in the dark arts. Particularly bizarre was the accusation that Hubert had stolen a precious stone from the treasury, which was now in the hands of Llywelyn. No accompanying description of the stone's pedigree has survived, other than an indication by the chroniclers that it was believed to have been a talisman in battle. Evidence that such stones were especially revered at that time is easily found. Earlier in his life, Henry had been gifted a stone by his father for use as protection against thunder, of which he had a mild phobia throughout his life. Similarly, in May 1205, Innocent III had sent John a set of four rings with precious stones.

More substantial were claims that Hubert's past policy had infringed the rights of the king himself. Prompted by his grievances, Henry ordered an investigation into the state of royal treasure and any other monies that had been paid into the exchequer going back to Hubert's appointment in 1215. This included any debts still owed to the king. A similar report was also demanded on all of Henry's demesnes (land belonging to a manor) in England and elsewhere. The same was true to the collection status of past scutages, carucages and anything else that fell under the justiciar's list of responsibilities. That such an inquiry was necessary seems incredible. Not only does it appear to illustrate just how much power Hubert had wielded prior to his dismissal, but it also casts significant doubt over Henry's effectiveness – or at least interest – in administrative duties up to that point. True, his lack of involvement in the years 1216–27 could be explained mainly by a combination of his youth and not owning the great seal; however, the same excuse cannot be offered as a defence of his activities post-January 1227.[1]

Taking Hubert's place at the heart of government was another of lowly birth, Stephen of Seagrave. Raised in Leicestershire, the son of a minor landowner, Stephen had thrived as a lawyer before enjoying an apprenticeship in the justiciar role in Hubert's absence during the Poitou expedition of 1230. Knighted around 1220, he had served as constable of the Tower of London 1220–24, high sheriff of Hertfordshire and Essex 1221–23, and Lincolnshire 1222–24. At the time of his appointment, he held the sheriffdoms of Bedfordshire and Buckinghamshire, Warwickshire, Leicestershire and Northamptonshire.[2]

Also promoted were the Poitevin duo, Robert Passelewe and Peter de Rivallis. Of similar upbringing to des Roches, Passelewe was, of course, already well experienced in legal matters, having served as a clerk for Falkes and des Roches. Prior to his mission to Rome in 1224 as Ranulf's agent during the Bedford fiasco, he had also served the legate Guala and regularly travelled to and from the papal court delivering cardinals' pension payments. After des Roches was deprived of the royal castles in 1223, Robert lost his property in England before regaining it in 1226.[3]

Of de Rivallis – also spelt in some sources des Riveaux – relatively little is known. A clerk of French upbringing, he was commonly referred to as the 'nephew' of Peter des Roches; however, according to Roger of Wendover, he was suspected of being the bishop's bastard. Clearly a kinsman of des Roches, de Rivallis was appointed as a chamberlain to the king around 1218 and served as Henry's keeper of the wardrobe from no later than 1221 until Hubert's chamberlain Luke – himself consecrated archbishop of Dublin in 1230 – replaced him in the role until around 1225. After an absence of at least three years, during which it is highly likely that he joined the bishop on crusade, de Rivallis reappeared on the scene in England around the time of des Roches's return under the title *capicerius Pictavis*, meaning treasurer of Poitou. Rather than having enjoyed a great office of state, his title here suggests he was attached to one or more of the region's churches. It is possible that de Rivallis was a native of that area or perhaps another of the Touraine region. Back in England, on 11 June 1232, possibly while the king was staying at Oddington in Oxfordshire, Henry formally reappointed de Rivallis keeper of the royal wardrobe, as well as granted lifetime custody of the royal chamber.[4]

Though once again the bishop of Winchester had been appointed to no official position in government, his renewed influence after this time is clear. Before the end of August, no less than nineteen of the thirty-five sheriffdoms had been bestowed on de Rivallis around which time he also practically stole the wardship of the earldom of Gloucester from Hubert. As previously recalled, Hubert had been somewhat contentiously awarded its care on behalf of the young Richard de Clare following the death of the earl of Gloucester in October 1230. Had Richard le Grant lived longer, that undoubtedly would have gone on to have significant ramifications; however, the see of Canterbury was then vacant.

Stripped of the de Clare wardship and absent from English government for the first time since the reign of John, Hubert's fall proved unnecessarily brutal. Like a death by a thousand cuts, deprivation of office occurred in stages. On 28 July, Hubert was forced to attest a humiliating charter that officially placed the financial administration of Ireland under de Rivallis. Within a day or so, he was either sent home or departed voluntarily from the king's ongoing tour en route to see Llywelyn. On 8 August, while at Shrewsbury and still officially titled justiciar, he was ordered to surrender to Seagrave eight of the royal castles in his custody, namely: the Tower of London, Dover, Hertford, Canterbury, Rochester, Windsor, Odiham and Colchester. Five days later, a second order was made regarding the other royal castles for which he had been appointed castellan. A separate writ dated 25 August demanding he leave the country was enrolled, but apparently never sent. Though this could indicate that Henry's anger had cooled slightly by that time, a combination of the requirement by Seagrave to take up judicial proceedings against the former justiciar and a general enthusiasm among the magnates to see justice served forced Hubert to prepare a thorough legal defence.[5]

Knowing that his best option was to hide out among the religious authorities, Hubert sought to make himself scarce. After initially taking temporary residence in south-west London with the canons of Merton, around which time he renewed his crusader vows, he was later seen heading north towards his ancestral homeland of East Anglia. Unable to make the trip in one go, he nevertheless appears to have achieved the impressive feat of making it from Merton to Brentwood in Essex in the space of one day. Reaching Brentwood before nightfall, he prepared to settle down for the night in a property owned by his nephew, Thomas Blundeville, the bishop of Norwich. Alarmed by word that the king had unleashed an armed mob to bring him in, he fled to the nearby Boisars Chapel.[6]

There, Hubert sensibly sought the ancient rite of sanctuary. Sanctuary was sacred in medieval England. Should one successfully obtain refuge within religious walls, it was then illegal for thirty-seven days for that person to be seized without papal permission. This included foreign soldiers and wanted murderers.[7]

It seems that Hubert's whereabouts were largely unknown to the king since leaving court. When word reached him of the former justiciar's alleged movements, Henry rallied the citizens of London to bring him into custody. That Henry's decision was made partly out of concern for Hubert's wellbeing cannot be ruled out. However, reports that Henry wanted him taken dead or alive perhaps indicated that his fickle temper was showing evidence of its poorer side. On learning of the former justiciar's arrival at the chapel, his initial reaction was to have him brought before him in chains. It took the sensible influence of Hubert's former chaplain, Archbishop Luke of Dublin, to calm the king's mood.[8]

A great council was called to meet in September at Lambeth. Among the matters of importance was an agreement among the laity that a grant of one-fortieth be allocated to fund the government's payments to the duke of Brittany. All of this was in connection with exploits on the Continent since the climax of the Poitou expedition of 1230.[9] This was a significant coup for des Roches's government as back in March Hubert's had failed to deliver the tax. Tournament licenses for Blyth, Dunstable, Stamford and Brackley were also granted for later that year. That the granting of permission to hold such events could be viewed as the beginning of a more liberal post-Hubert era and an insight into des Roches's military-like personality may contain a kernel of truth. Yet such conclusions possibly fail to take account of the gradual moves at local level to see their reinstatement. Without question, the fact that the holding of tournaments had been legalised illustrated a startling relaxation of the restrictions put in place the previous decade that any person found guilty of jousting or aiding a jouster would be punished with excommunication.[10]

Of far greater consequence to the king was the death, on or around 26 October, of the earl of Chester, Ranulf de Blondeville.[11] A candidate for the regency in his own right on John's death, Ranulf had enjoyed a significant career. A hero of the First Barons' War, he was subsequently a key contributor to the taking of Damietta during the mixed Fifth Crusade, prior to which he had advocated accepting the offer of the sultan of Damascus to gain Nazareth, Jerusalem, Bethlehem and parts of Galilee and Palestine peacefully in exchange for leaving Egypt alone. Ironically, such a policy would later prove a far more useful tool for Frederick II. In acknowledgement of his role in defeating Louis, Ranulf was also made earl of Lincoln before obtaining the wardship of Huntingdon on his return from Egypt.[12]

In his later years, Ranulf's contributions to English life appear more fragmented. Credited with the construction of Bolingbroke Castle in Lincolnshire, a building that would later be remembered as the birthplace of Henry IV, his relations with Hubert were often tepid. A snob of the lower classes, he also had more to lose than most in the surrender of the royal castles that finally occurred late 1223. An avoider of the carucage of 1220, the aid of 1225 and papal collections of 1229, he failed to avoid contributing to the latest fortieth. As an elder statesman, he had been a prominent witness of the reissue of the charters in 1225 and the debates of 1227. Small in stature, he was strong of heart. Nor would age prevent a final hurrah in the France campaign of 1230. Having remained on the Continent after Henry's return, he headed the efforts after the younger William Marshal's death and made a spirited attempt to reclaim Anjou, which at the time probably meant more to him than any other Englishman.

In the centuries since, Ranulf's achievements, both in history and legend, have been subject of debate: not least the curious mention by the fourteenth-century poet William Langland that the earl of Chester enjoyed similar fame to that of Robin Hood. Included in Langland's literary masterpiece *Piers Plowman*: an allegorical text written in Middle English is the tantalising passage in which a lazy priest laments his imperfections in reciting paternoster, but does know the rhymes of Robin Hood and Randolf, Earl of Chester. Sadly, whatever 'rymes' Langland wrote of have failed to survive – if indeed they ever appeared in print. Nor can it be ruled out that the passage referred to one of Ranulf's ancestors – not that they were necessarily possessed of better claim.

The truce with Louis would be among Ranulf's final acts. Aged 62, he died at Wallingford Castle, the location that would house his internal organs. That Ranulf's passing left a hole in the king's heart, as well as his government, can surely be illustrated by a personal visit Henry made to the great earl's deathbed before his generous offerings of gifts for his safe ascension. On learning of the earl's passing while still in sanctuary, Hubert is noted to have taken his psalter and read it through from start to finish for Ranulf's soul. After the great earl's heart was interred at his beloved Dieulacres Abbey in Cheshire, his body was buried at St Werburg's Church in Chester. Whereas Marshal was celebrated in his own time as the 'greatest knight', during the Victorian era, Bishop Stubbs composed a similarly appropriate description of Ranulf. Quite simply, he was 'almost the last relic of the great feudal aristocracy of the conquest'.[13]

Taking the childless Ranulf's place at the head of the baronage was none other than the man who had replaced the younger William as head of the Marshal clan. On ascending to the new realms of leadership, Richard Marshal wasted no time in warning the king that the presence of the 'Poitevins' at the heart of English government would cause his English subjects to withdraw from court. Though some of Richard's critics have a point to their argument that the long-time resident of Normandy was himself by no means the epitome of Englishness that the chroniclers made him out to be – it is unclear whether Richard was born in England or Normandy – as the inheritor of the Pembroke estates and the son of his great father, Richard was of the same mould and, therefore, another of the old school of Anglo-Norman magnates. More importantly still, the suggestion appears to have shaken Henry. Equally, and predictably, Richard's perceived interference was viewed with little enthusiasm by the recently re-empowered des Roches.

The situation with Hubert, meanwhile, was in danger of getting out of hand. Aiding Seagrave in his preparation to commence legal proceedings against the former justiciar was one Godfrey de Crowcombe, the steward of the royal household. Still sheltered within the cloistered walls of the chapel at Brentwood, Hubert was discovered by de Crowcombe before the high altar with a crucifix in one hand and the Eucharist in the other. Foolishly, de Crowcombe showed no regard for the rite of sanctuary and had the former justiciar dragged outside, fettered and hauled to the Tower of London. This treatment of Hubert caused a deep rift in the heart of government. Not only was he still to be found guilty of the charges made against him, but de Crowcombe had also deliberately ignored the privileges of sanctuary. Under increasing pressure from his prelates, especially the bishop of London, on 27 September Henry reluctantly approved Hubert's return to the chapel, on which he endeavoured to starve him out by cutting off all food supplies.[14]

Given the choice of starving or surrender, Hubert was left no option but to surrender. No sooner had he done so than he was back in the Tower with no guarantees of future release. News of Henry's actions would prove far from popular. Further to his having incurred the wrath of the bishop of London, a popular story that circulated around the time of Hubert's first imprisonment – seemingly courtesy of Hubert himself – was that a loyal blacksmith refused to chain the man widely celebrated as the protector of England following his success at Sandwich in 1217.[15]

On being ferried downriver from the Tower, Hubert appeared before the king for his trial on 10 November. Though he seems to have denounced the legality of the court that tried him, on the back of a constructive meeting in which he offered no formal legal defence, he was granted permission to keep his remaining lands. On receiving sureties from the four great earls: Richard, Earl of Cornwall, Richard Marshal, Earl of Pembroke, William de Warenne, Earl of Surrey and William de Ferrers, Earl of Derby – other sources name the fourth as John de Lacy, the earl of Lincoln – rather than return to the Tower, the former justiciar was instead granted permission to remain under the watch of four of their knights at Devizes Castle. The location was ironic for at least two reasons: not only had the castle assured the king's protection around the time of his father's death in 1216, but it had also been Hubert's property since John's reign. Perhaps guided by a deeply instilled gratitude, Hubert was sentenced to be held in captivity until he was either released with the consent of his keepers and the magnates or agreed to become a Templar. With the permission of the master of the Temple, the king also enriched himself of Hubert's treasures.[16]

Relations with his senior magnates still by no means on course, reforms into the financial areas were at least achieving more fruitful results for the king. The relinquishing of Hubert's treasures in addition to collection of the fortieth granted in September had worked wonders for the royal coffers. On 2 March the following year, this was supplemented further with a tallage on the Jews. In reality, the imposition was part of a broader strategy composed by des Roches during Easter at Canterbury that included the introduction of new legislation to curb the rates of interest. Though the combination of the tallage and reduced rates were harsh, it was also notable that such schemes had been implemented in France. In this, some have correctly discerned that Peter illustrated one of his clearest signs yet that he viewed the Capetian model of kingship as a far more relevant image for his Plantagenet protégé.[17]

Living in an age where crimes against ethnic minorities were no means considered worthy of incurring the wrath of the magnates, the reforms themselves had proved not unpleasing to the majority at court. Nevertheless, by setting out on a broader course that had the potential to wash away the reforms of his predecessors and endanger the constitution on which all progress had been made, it was little surprise that the waves on which the king then sailed were threatening to become ever more treacherous. To navigate the choppy waters safely, several obstacles needed to be avoided. As a witty clerk named Roger Bacon later analogised before the king, nothing in life did the sailors fear more than rocks and stones, and that only by steering a safe course between them could Henry himself avoid a fatal capsize.[18]

Chapter 18

1232–1233
Between a Rock and a Hard Place

Fifteen days of dreadful thunder, commencing on 12 November 1232, proved a foreboding portent of things to come. Around 4 December, a three-year truce was agreed with Llywelyn at Shrewsbury, a long-overdue culmination of a process that had seen conferences in April, August and October all end with matters still to be concluded.[1]

Relations with the prince of Gwynedd, seemingly, tied up, during the Christmas celebrations at Worcester the crafty Butterfly Bishop flexed his recently toned political muscles further by coordinating the removal of all the remaining English officials and replacing them with 'Poitevins'. To say des Roches's influence was a cause of concern among the barons would be an understatement. Though accusations from later commentator and chronicler alike that the bishop of Winchester had filled England with Poitevins and there was nowhere the king could move without their company is something of an exaggeration, the general antagonism towards the makeup of the new government offers a clear insight into the mood in England at the time. Once already in the thirteenth century, the influence of foreign royal officials, including the bishop of Winchester, had brought England to civil war. Now, history was threatening to repeat itself. Grumblings of dissent were being voiced from both England and Rome that many of the foreign appointees had only recently arrived in England and were far too inexperienced in English politics.[2]

There had been better news for Henry in recent papal correspondence. On 10 January 1233, Gregory had written to the king declaring null and void any oaths sworn out of fear at his coronation not to recall the grants made in prejudice of the rights of the crown. A prime example may have been the early issue of the charters. All of these had been made during his minority and had already provided the greatest curbs to absolute monarchy in the nation's history. The one possible exemption was the reissues of 1225, both of which the king had sealed personally.[3]

171

Throughout the early months of the year, Henry's court remained either in or around Westminster. Of particular concern, between October 1232 and May 1233, further to completing his deprivation of other estates held in the name of Hubert de Burgh, the king moved unjustly against at least seven far more innocent individuals. Among the principal people to suffer losses was Hubert's recent antagonist de Crowcombe who had earlier been granted the sheriffdom of Oxfordshire for life. Another such example was Walter Mauclerc, the bishop of Carlisle, who was not only removed from the treasury but also deprived of several hundred pounds of silver as well as the customs in Ireland earlier bestowed on him for life.[4]

Of key consequence to the events that would follow were the effects of Henry's deprivations on the new head of the baronage, Richard Marshal and two of his close allies: Richard Siward and Gilbert Basset. A capable fighter for the royalist cause at the Battle of Sandwich in 1217, Siward had sympathised with William of Aumale's rebellion of 1220. Throughout this time, he did much harm to the lands of Henry's counsellors, not least those owned by des Roches and Hubert, albeit operating within a strict code of conduct that no injury would be brought upon the undeserving. Pardoned for his misdemeanours along with Aumale himself, Siward later became a member of the king's royal council and had also served as a member of the household of the younger William Marshal, from which his friendship with Richard grew. Though little is known of his ancestry, in 1229 he was recorded as having married one Philippa Basset, who was related to Marshal's other key ally Gilbert Basset.

Basset's ancestral pedigree is less of a mystery. Son of the late baron Alan of Wycombe, Gilbert walked in the footsteps of one who had fought valiantly for the royalist cause throughout the First Barons' War. Alan had also served Henry bravely in the recent French expedition before succumbing to the same illness that had taken the late earl of Gloucester and convinced Henry of the need to return to England from Brittany. Since becoming a household knight in 1229, Basset had excelled as the principal negotiator of the truce with Llywelyn on Henry's behalf in 1231. Around this time, and perhaps in connection with his marriage to the daughter of the earl of Derby – also a niece of William Marshal II and great-niece of the former regent – Basset was made governor of St Briavels Castle in Gloucestershire as well as keeper of the Forest of Dean – both of which had been Marshal lands.

More directly connected to recent events, Basset had until recently served Henry as keeper of Devizes Castle. Partly as a consequence of the intrigue surrounding Hubert, Basset was stripped of his role as castellan around the time of the former justiciar's incarceration. Among the conditions of Hubert's sentencing, of course, had been for him to be kept there on the sureties of the four earls. Yet the castle's bailey and *banlieu* was actually granted to de Rivallis. To Basset's further detriment, de Rivallis also usurped him in his roles at St Briavels and the Forest of Dean, the latter of which was especially important through its connection with the great Marshal lands.[5]

Des Roches's strategy operated far beyond that of coincidence. Further to his recent deprivations, in early February Basset faced a further legal challenge that went on to have severe repercussions for the entire kingdom. At the behest of the bishop of Winchester, Henry made the controversial decision to strip Basset of the manor of Upavon in Wiltshire. Despite its relatively small size, Upavon was by no means unimportant. A charming site on which many key trade routes crossed, the manor was worth around £40 per year. In gratitude for the original grant, Basset willingly forewent two years of salary from the exchequer to the tune of £20 per year.[6]

The status of the manor was further complicated by a series of legal issues that had caused grievances on both sides. With Hubert de Burgh still directing matters and des Roches on crusade, Henry had decided to grant Upavon to Basset in 1229 at de Maulay's expense. This was not the first time de Maulay had been stripped of the manor. Accusations against him on the back of the fictitious Corfe Castle plot had already seen him deprived of it before being forced to vacate it a second time in 1229 as a consequence of des Roches's ousting. In Hubert's absence, de Maulay pushed his grievances that the threats of Hubert, who had apparently claimed refusal to comply would see him languish in the darkest of dungeons, had given him no choice but to relinquish what he had obtained back in 1204 by John on the loss of Normandy. By countering that his surrender of Upavon was in direct response to the threats of the now-imprisoned Hubert de Burgh, de Maulay played a trump card. On 4 February, Henry controversially reversed his decision. Two days later, the manor of Upavon was once again the property of Peter de Maulay.[7]

That the king feared a backlash from the earl of Pembroke at this time seems highly likely. Since his return, Marshal had become the most active of all the magnates at court. A startling insight into his influence comes in the knowledge that between July 1232 and the following April, Richard bore witness to twenty-eight royal charters compared to des Roches's eighteen. Well respected as his great father's son, Marshal had aligned himself closely with intermarried relations, namely the earls of Warenne, Derby, Norfolk and, more recently, Cornwall, two of which had taken on the mantle of offering sureties for Hubert at Devizes.

Predictably, Marshal took up Basset's cause. On paper, his case was a strong one. Unlike Basset, who had been granted the manor for life by royal charter, de Maulay possessed no such legal document. This may suggest that he had obtained the manor at the king's pleasure. In response to the disseisin, Gilbert claimed that after the First Barons' War the king's council had escheated the manor on him following its deprivation of the Normans in 1204.[8]

Further to having viewed the move as a provocative one in the sense that by depriving his key ally and returning the manor to de Maulay he had caused him great personal offence, Richard also complained vigorously of Henry's broader actions. Not only were a large number of aliens being promoted on des Roches's advice, but deprivation of the son of the loyal royalist Alan Basset in favour of the man alleged to have been responsible for the disappearance of Arthur of Brittany indicated particularly poor judgement. Besides his personal lack of loyalty, Henry was, he argued, now in danger of bringing about a major constitutional crisis by his blatant disregard for his own charter.[9]

Predictably talks did not go well. Marshal stormed from court on 9 February for reasons that remain unclear. The annals of Dunstable suggest Henry was angered by Marshal's protests and ordered him away. If the claims of Roger of Wendover are correct, des Roches was present at the talks, during which he argued that 'the king was surely allowed to summon as many foreigners as he chooses for the protection of his kingdom ... to reduce his haughty and rebellious subjects to their proper obedience'. Others have argued that Marshal was incensed that the de Clare wardship had gone to des Rivallis and not himself. As the boy's uncle, was he not better placed? A similar claim could have been made on behalf of the earl of Cornwall, himself now de Clare's stepfather since his marriage to Gloucester's widow.[10]

Richard's precise motives at that time are difficult to discern. On the one hand, Roger of Wendover had been only too lavish in his praise of the man: 'He fought for the cause of justice and the laws of the English people against the oppressions of the Poitevins', a strange thing, some have argued, to say of a man who had spent much of his life in Normandy and Brittany, albeit less so considering his father had been the same despite many years served on the Continent. On the other, back in November Richard himself had gained from the disseisin of the loyal German Waleran concerning a manor in Hampshire. Nor does he appear to have intervened concerning the losses experienced by the bishop of Carlisle, not that any of the other great magnates or prelates seemed to have either. On balance, Richard had gained little of material wealth during the previous six months. Deprivation of the many properties held by Hubert had done much to swell the Poitevin coffers, which would have sickened his father as much as himself and Hubert. Similarly, on the death of Ranulf, only two of the English manors he held of the Breton magnate William de Fougères – related to the wives of Chester and Marshal – were granted to Richard, whereas a third went to des Roches's old associate Engelard de Cigogné, himself without hereditary claim.[11]

That Marshal's grievances with the king and des Roches at this point were influenced by human nature undoubtedly accounts for at least one element of his ensuing fury. Further to his distrust of aliens, uncertainties about his marriage dower and that of his late brother also loomed large. Already on the back of a papal inquiry concerning his relations with wife Gervasia, William the Younger's death without issue had brought significant damages despite promoting himself to a higher point in the echelons of power. Not least of these was his deprival of family estates set aside as part of the dower of the king's sister. In the summer of 1231, Eleanor had been granted at least six of William Marshal II's manors as well as a dozen or so handed to her courtesy of being assigned life custody of her marriage portion. The consequences of this threatened to see Richard lose approximately a third of his English revenues with question marks remaining over the Irish and Welsh lands.[12]

On leaving court, Marshal rode for Wales. After joining with the king's brother, now his brother-in-law since Cornwall's marriage to Gloucester's widow, the pair sought to take on Llywelyn. Inevitably, the truce of December between the king and the prince of Gwynedd had not lasted long. By the following month, he had succeeded in driving Llywelyn back from the Marches, a primary factor of which had been Cornwall's 'illegal' rebuilding of Radnor Castle. Once this had been achieved, Marshal set sail for Ireland. Landing sometime before the end of March.[13]

The appearance of mock suns and beautiful halos in the skies over England was viewed with the usual feelings of hope and dread by the annalist of Worcester. First witnessed at sunrise on 8 April, a strange halo was recorded by Matthew Paris as having lasted till noon before disappearing without a trace. Around an hour later, in the borders of Herefordshire and Worcestershire, the annalist of Worcester was also treated to the sight of a semi-circle accompanying an identical halo on either side as well as four red suns and a fifth the colour of crystal. Known today as Parhelia – an atmospheric phenomenon, sometimes termed 'sundogs' – the appearance of the 'wonderful sight' had also happened to occur on Good Friday.[14]

A short time before this, Henry appears to have met with Basset at Stratford after spending Easter at Canterbury. Among those present were friars of Richard Marshal, who had recently made it to Ireland. Precisely what transpired there is unrecorded; however, Henry was clearly enraged by what was put to him. As punishment, the king ordered the removal of a knight named William de Rodune, who was Richard Marshal's deputy at the king's court. Not surprisingly, the news of the knight's removal without prior discussion did little to benefit Marshal's mood.[15]

Around Whitsuntide – the seventh Sunday after Easter – fears that Henry had been privately harbouring since his angry exchange with Marshal in early February began to darken. On 14 May, Gregory wrote to him again, this time concerning the soon to expire peace with France. Nine days later, Pentecost was celebrated at Gloucester, around which time reports followed of significant flooding throughout the country. Of potential harm to the king, a day earlier severe downpours had battered the buildings of nearby Worcester. Meanwhile, it was recorded in the annals of Waverley that bridges and houses had been swept away as the River Wey rose by up to eight feet in height.[16]

From there, the king embarked on a tour through the Vale of Evesham, reaching his manor at Feckenham in Worcestershire on 1 June. The manor was a personal favourite of Henry's, as it was esteemed for its magnificent fishponds. During his stay, instructions were made for the appointment of watchmen to implement a temporary curfew on every town and village, perhaps the surest sign yet that Henry privately feared all was not well. Heading north to Wenlock in Shropshire, during which he visited the priory, news reached him that Marshal was planning to hold a tournament in either Worcester or Northampton. Tournaments were of course forbidden without royal approval, leading to both summons for their arrests and a change in direction from the king. On 6 June this was done. On that same day, Henry acted against Richard for the first time by ordering immediate payment of the still outstanding first instalment of the £400 annual sum due in lieu of Eleanor's dowry from the late William Marshal II. To ensure payment, Henry ordered its collection through seizure of Marshal's property.[17]

Unsurprisingly this went down badly. Equally regrettable was the king's decision to encourage similar impositions on those he deemed rebellious, including Gilbert Basset, who was alleged to have spoken ill of the king at this latest gathering. Barely four months on from his loss of Upavon, Basset was deprived of a further two manors, including Sutton in Surrey, which had been in his possession since 1216. Once again, Basset was by no means alone in his grievances. Among those affected, on 7 June, was William Ferrers, the son of the earl of Derby, who lost a Norman escheat guaranteed by royal charter. The common link for all were family ties to Richard Marshal.[18]

In examining Henry's motivations here, two key factors must be considered. Already heavily under the influence of the bishop of Winchester, his arrival in Worcester on 9 June had failed to lead to either a meeting with or the seizing of the tournament gatherers personally. Their refusal to appear in court also raised important questions. That failure to attend a legal hearing should result in forfeiture was typical, yet, usually, this would have been only temporary. Around seven months previously, Hubert de Burgh had refused to acknowledge the legitimacy of the court that tried him. Similar doubts also existed in the minds of the recently disinherited.[19]

Insurrection by Llywelyn on 13 June posed a further complication. On that very day, the leading suspects gave hostages to Henry at Worcester, 'until there is a firm peace in the kingdom of England'. Among them appears to have been Richard Siward, Gilbert's nephew by marriage. New arrangements were also made for Hubert's keeping at Devizes. Among the decisions was the appointment of Walter de Godardville as keeper, an indication no doubt that the four earls, notably Marshal, could no longer be trusted to keep the former justiciar behind bars. Though de Rivallis kept the bailey, the dungeon remained off-limits.[20]

Two days later, summonses were put out for the arrest of Basset and one Walter of Clifford, a long time de Braose ally, whose forfeited lands would be granted to de Rivallis. On 20 June, confiscations were also suffered by Marshal in the form of two Norman escheats he had gained from Chester on the earl's death. A motivator for Henry in this case might well have been the rumour that Marshal himself had held some form of court in Worcester after Henry's departure. Instructions were also put out for the destruction of his property at Compton Basset in Wiltshire.[21]

Around the middle of the month, Henry arrived at his grandfather's magnificent palace at Woodstock from where a council was arranged to take place in nearby Oxford on 24 June. When the magnates refused to answer the summons, word reached the king through his envoys that baronial discontent was brewing. At least one such account had reached the king personally, courtesy of a Dominican friar named Robert – or Roger – Bacon. Of particular alarm was the suggestion that should Henry fail to right the recent wrongs he would be driven from his kingdom along with the interlopers. On asking the king what sailors feared most, the witty clerk went on to offer the amusing analogy of the need to steer carefully between rocks and stones – clearly a reference to Peter des Roches.[22]

A summer of heavy rains would provide a depressing backdrop for the stormy relations that were fast developing. As a consequence of the poor attendance at the Oxford council, the meeting was dissolved and rearranged for 5 July – other sources say 11 July – at Westminster. When the date arrived, the same thing happened again. Further to the developing resentment against the king and the butterfly bishop, the main reason on this occasion derived from stories that had reached the magnates' ears of armed gangs roaming the kingdom on horseback, allegedly at the king's prompting. Rather than attend, they bade the envoys return with the similar advice that if the foreign counsellors were not removed by way of common counsel, then they would be made to do so by means of force.[23]

Angered by the lack of respect for his authority, on des Roches's counsel a third date was circulated for 1 August. On this occasion, when summons were issued, attendance was deemed compulsory. Threats were also made that failure to attend would result in their being labelled a traitor. The latest plan proved effective; at least in terms of making the council achievable. It was the belief of many of the chroniclers at the time that the king had been forced to resort to bribery owing to fears that his orders were no longer being listened to.

Richard Marshal had deliberately made himself unavoidably absent from the Oxford and Westminster councils. While that was partially a rebuke against des Roches, fear of ill intent was also a key motivator. In truth, he had every right to be worried. After agreeing to abide by the summons to the third council – again after being faced either with threats or promised monetary reward – on reaching London on his way to Westminster, word reached him courtesy of his sister Isabel, now wife of the earl of Cornwall and with whom he had chosen to lodge, that the bishop of Winchester was planning to snare him into a trap. Knowing that his life was in danger, he changed his path and rode for the safety of Wales.[24]

What happened next was to be of profound consequence. On the way, perhaps while the council meeting at Westminster was underway, Marshal and his followers gathered heavily armed at the manor of Gilbert Basset at High Wycombe. Though the king clearly feared the meeting would prove the origin of insurrection, in the days that followed, as the king relocated to Windsor, it appears some form of agreement was reached. At the very least, word that Marshal and all close to him were prepared to throw themselves at the king's mercy appears to have been enough to persuade Henry to allow Marshal safe passage back to Wales.[25]

Any hopes of a successful resolution, however, were soon dissipated. Perturbed by the latest sign of perceived disobedience, the king reneged on his tournament licenses of the previous year and demanded all such gatherings be cancelled. Having used the mock battlegrounds of Stamford and Blyth so effectively in the First Barons' War, the risk that the barons would do so again was far too significant to be left to chance.[26]

Clearly worried that his realm was on the cusp of war, Henry made plans to strengthen his forces by sending for mercenaries from Flanders. Around the same time, des Roches ordered strict surveillance of the ports for messengers operating on Marshal's behalf. On 15 August, after arriving at Tewkesbury, Henry confiscated the lands of those known to have attended the meeting at Wycombe, including an order that Basset's manor at Wooton Basset be destroyed. Two days later, Henry gathered his charges at Gloucester in preparation to meet the new mercenaries and march on Hereford to reconnoitre the Usk Valley.[27]

As a consequence of his failure to attend the latest council at Gloucester – according to Wendover to be held on 14 August but according to the official rolls, 29 August – Henry followed through on his earlier threat and had Marshal officially declared a traitor and his lands subject to forfeiture. Another critical factor was Marshal's recent attack on the castle at Hay-on-Wye, which he had since fortified against Henry's forces. Shortly after followed that of Ewyas Harold, after which alliance was made with long time antagonist Morgan of Caerleon. Whether Marshal's recent movements were voluntary or inspired by the pleas of his supporters, namely Basset and Siward, is unclear. Only that there would be no going back.

Reaching Hereford on 19 August, Henry officially deprived the son of the great regent of his lands four days later. The same was true of the lands of Marshal's nephew, Roger Bigod, Earl of Norfolk, the only other magnate to have attended the gathering at High Wycombe. As a calculated move, Henry also devised means to split up the recent alliance between Marshal and the king's brother, the earl of Cornwall. Successful in liberating Radnor, Cornwall had since returned to court in June and become enriched with possessions of the earldom of Devon, which had on 3 August been obtained by des Roches. Inevitably, Cornwall's U-turn did little for his popularity among the Marshals. As Matthew Paris would later lament, 'Alas the cupidity.'[28]

As meadows remained unmown and hay destined to rot, the scene was set for civil war. Henry took Hay and Walter of Clifford's castle at Clifford on leaving Hereford on 30 August. From there followed Ewyas Harold. On intruding further into Wales and the town of Abergavenny, around which the Black Mountains cloaked the dreary skyline, he moved south to Marshal's castle at Usk. Henry began the siege on 4 September, around which time doubts were raised of the provisions and morale in the royal camp. Equally aware that the beautiful fortress would struggle to put up a strong enough defence in its own right, despite its hilly location, parley with the king ensured its temporary surrender on the promise it be returned within fifteen days. This was deemed sufficient time for Henry to correct 'whatever needed to be correct in the kingdom, with the counsel of the bishops'.[29]

On 8 September the omens were good that a compromise was within reach. Initially satisfied by the earl's explanation that he was by no means intent on conspiring, the alarm was raised when Marshal disappeared around Woodstock as he headed for another upcoming council at Westminster. By no means intent on commencing insurrection, Marshal suspected a trap on learning that agreement for Usk to be returned was yet to be honoured.

Furious that Marshal had failed to attend a further council, Henry unleashed his wrath. Marshal's moated manor – or small castle – at Inkberrow in Worcestershire was seized and dismantled, as were several of his other manors, most significantly those at Long Crendon and Hamsted Marshal. When the next council finally met at Westminster on 9 October, the barons and prelates urged Henry to make peace with the son of his great regent. Refusing to come to terms with a traitor, a compromise was suggested that Marshal be tried by his peers – a process typical in France and also permitted under clause 39 of Magna Carta.[30]

It was in the moments that followed that an irreconcilable, ill-thought-out, comment aroused the wrath of every Poitevin sceptic in attendance. Hero of the recent crusade in which the walls of Jerusalem had indeed rejoiced at their rebuilding, des Roches's conclusion that 'there are no peers in England as there are in France' threatened to tear apart the entire kingdom. What possessed the bishop to utter those words only he would know. In the inevitable aftermath, Peter's snobbery united the barons in a renewed outcry against the Poitevin faction, as well as inspiring threats of excommunication from the prelates.[31]

It was an act that would lead England once again to full-scale war.

Chapter 19

1233–1234
The Marshal War

Prior to this time, relations with the papacy had shown signs of deteriorating. On 3 May, eleven days before receiving correspondence from the pope concerning peace with France, Gregory had been forced to intercede in the developing rift between Henry and Hubert. Putting paid to any thoughts Henry might have had that there could be an element of truth in des Roches's later suggestion that there were no peers in England capable of trying his senior magnates, Gregory wrote to Henry confirming that English nobles were not to be tried abroad.[1]

That des Roches had contemplated as much seems highly likely. Since Hubert's confinement to Devizes, the bishop of Winchester had been keeping a particularly close eye on the ousted justiciar's situation. Having already succeeded in turning the tables on the man responsible for his downfall in 1227, des Roches attempted to twist the dagger further by asking for custody of Devizes Castle. Of Peter's exact motives here, conjecture has been rife. No stranger to the darker arts of national government, accusation that the bishop had busily plotted Hubert's murder is unsubstantiated. No saint himself, Hubert had, of course, been accused of murder on no less than two occasions; however, on neither had he faced legal justice.

Fortunately for Hubert, he received word of des Roches's scheming. After winning the trust of two sergeants responsible for his safekeeping, on 29 September these same men made their way into the dungeon and capitalised on the inattention of the guards. As Hubert was shackled, freeing him proved a particular challenge. Unable to remove the heavy irons, they carried him out of the imposing dungeons and through the dry moat. It was recorded by the chroniclers that so great had been the sergeant's loyalty that he only put Hubert down on reaching the high altar of the local church.

News of Hubert's second escape went down badly in all quarters. Fearing the combined wrath of the king and bishop, Hubert's keepers at Devizes ordered an immediate search of the nearby area. When news reached their ears that the former justiciar had been spotted in the local church, the officials swooped in numbers and found him praying before the altar.

For a second time in less than a year, history was repeated. A second violation of the rite of sanctuary saw Hubert returned to his prison and severely beaten, knowledge of which appalled the bishop of Salisbury, Robert de Bingham. When the guards at Devizes refused de Bingham's order to return Hubert to sanctuary, the bishop excommunicated them personally and, with the company of several other senior prelates, brought the matter before the king.[2]

Henry received the gathering at Oxford on 1 October – his twenty-sixth birthday – during which he received a stern lecture on the rights of sanctuary. Reluctantly agreeing after two and a half drawn-out weeks that sanctuary had indeed been violated, Hubert was returned to the church on 18 October. However, in another repeat of the Brentwood affair, Henry endeavoured to shut off the food supply and wrote to the local sheriff ordering him to besiege the church until his former chief advisor emerged.

Subsequent events must have shocked all concerned. On 29 October, market day in Devizes, a great mist swirled around the locality, greatly reducing visibility. Recently arrived in town were the newly disinherited Gilbert Basset and Richard Siward, who came with one clear intention. When the rebel pair reached the front of the church, they contacted Hubert and dressed him up as a knight. Successful in getting past the outsiders, during a nerve-racking few days the resourceful group made it across the River Severn and behind the safe walls of Chepstow Castle.[3]

For the king, learning of Hubert's inspiring escape was the start of an unhappy autumn and winter that proved not only disastrous in terms of unprecedented famine, but also returned England to the days of widespread violence. On hearing the news at Hereford, Henry's mood soured, a stark change from the recent progress that had been buoyed when he had gained the support of the earls of Cornwall, Chester, Derby, Hereford and Surrey, as well as many more minor players that included the recently won over Clifford and Norfolk. Contrastingly, Marshal's support was limited to the loyalty of his household and knightly tenants in Gwent.[4]

Prior to their role in the escape, still incensed by both des Roches's claims about the lack of peers in England compared to France and their own deprivations, Hubert's soon-to-be saviours Gilbert Basset and Richard Siward had already begun rebellion in earnest. Exactly how

Siward escaped being taken hostage is unclear, if indeed he was not released voluntarily. Before the end of September, Marshal retrieved Usk and entered a previously unthinkable alliance with his father's, and Henry's, archenemy Llywelyn.[5] Between them, the unlikely pairing of Marshal and Llywelyn wrought havoc in Glamorgan, which had grave ramifications for the earl of Cornwall as well as des Rivallis having recently been granted wardship over de Clare's Gloucester inheritance. Of particular consequence was the prince of Gwynedd's ravaging of Richard of Cornwall's lands in Brecon, including laying siege to the castle, and Basset's theft of, among other things, the bishop of Winchester's harness. Neither magnate able to put up a steady defence, the ongoing attacks saw several castles fall in a short period, most notably Cardiff and Abergavenny. A separate force laid siege to Carmarthen.[6]

Faced with the most significant domestic military crisis since the First Barons' War, Henry gathered his forces at Gloucester on 2 November and led them towards Chepstow, which Marshal had inherited as part of the Striguil estate. Expecting the royal troops to come upon him, Richard had earlier devastated the famine-ridden land so severely that little food remained to sustain them. While Henry remained in residence at Hereford, Marshal's fortress at Goodrich fell, and Llywelyn abandoned Brecon.[7]

Finding equally little joy throughout the Marshal lands of Gwent, Henry led his forces up the Wye Valley towards de Rivallis's three great castles of Skenfrith, Whitecastle and Grosmont, for so long under the guardianship of Hubert. On reaching Grosmont on 11 November, Henry's intention of spending the night recuperating was interrupted by a surprise night attack on his train in the valley below. Though the royals saw out the night with no casualties – other sources lament the death of one knight – the loss of several horses, possessions and a handful of deserters forced him to return to Hereford.[8]

Precisely two weeks after the Grosmont attacks, around which time the king was preparing to return to Gloucester, a strange confrontation took place close to Monmouth Castle. The date was 25 November: the feast of St Catherine. On this occasion, the victim had been Marshal, who had attempted to pass the royal fortress and surrounding town with a small band of men at arms. Though local lord John of Monmouth appears to have been absent, Marshal's movements were spotted by Baldwin III, Count of Guînes. When attacked by the royalist troops, Marshal was immediately isolated and left significantly outnumbered.

In a scene worthy of his gallant father, he somehow defended himself against a dozen men. Without support, the earl was overcome and then captured by Baldwin; however, fearing the end was near, providence then swung in his favour. In the chaos that followed, a crossbow bolt severely wounded Baldwin, prompting his men to flee. As Marshal prepared his escape, his men regrouped and launched a counter-attack.[9]

Almost unthinkably, Richard took possession of Monmouth Castle. During the month that followed, the area around the town was razed, and Siward laid waste to Cornwall's land at Beckley, Seagrave's home town in Leicestershire and des Roches's manor close to Winchester. In a sign of contempt for John of Monmouth, Richard's supporters also followed up the Welsh attack of the previous year on his family abbey of Grace Dieu and destroyed it barely seven years after construction had begun.[10]

Informed of the shock loss of his power base in Monmouthshire, Henry's Plantagenet temper was again unleashed. Not only had he lost a royal castle, but Marshal's control of Monmouth left the earl unopposed to join with the prince of Gwynedd and launch an assault on Shrewsbury. On 22 December, Henry reached out and offered terms, but the offer was rejected. A few days after keeping a humourless Christmas at Gloucester in the company of des Roches, further news reached the king of another group of royalist troops being severely beaten. Blighted by a combination of war, famine, and a hard winter frost, Roger of Wendover provided a shocking account of the state of Gloucestershire at this time. 'It was a wretched sight for travellers in that region to see on the highways innumerable dead bodies lying naked and unburied, to be devoured by birds of prey, and so polluting the air that they infected healthy men with mortal sickness.'[11]

A third military conflict in less than four years – the others being Poitou and Wales – had inevitably proven an unwelcome problem throughout the country. As usual in such circumstances, administration of the kingdom suffered, while the king's personal failure to tackle the carnage inflicted on the south-west by Siward and Basset severely threatened the royal finances. Worse still for Henry, he no longer had the self-assured Hubert alongside him to help deal with the problems. Despite his many talents as a lawyer, as justiciar Seagrave lacked the capabilities of his predecessor and was in practice little more than des Roches's puppet.

Of equally great importance was the vacant see of Canterbury. Proceedings for Henry by no means aided by his repeated violation of sanctuary and his poor treatment of the bishop of Carlisle, since le Grant died in 1231, a year after having taken his grievances with Hubert to Rome, Henry was still to approve a successor. Whereas John had been only too happy to profit from the empty see, Canterbury *sede vacante* at this time had serious implications for both church and state. That filling the vacant see could have prevented the war with Marshal is unlikely. It is far more evident that the abilities of Langton in curbing the past influence of des Roches would have been indispensable to the king.

In connection to the war and the imprisonment of Hubert, relations between Henry and Gregory threatened to fragment further. Of particular concern to the pope, Henry's treatment of the former justiciar seemed to mirror his attitude towards Agnellus of Pisa, the first English provincial of the Franciscans. Nor did Gregory's mood improve on hearing that Henry was at war with Richard Marshal, whose father was still fondly remembered. Conversely, shortly prior to Christmas, Agnellus had written to Marshal, building on previous correspondence from the future bishop of Lincoln, Robert Grosseteste, requesting he turn the other cheek and make peace with Henry. It appears to have been Agnellus who acted as Henry's envoy on 22 December. To this, Marshal responded that the present struggle went far beyond personal grievances and claimed if he submitted it would be of 'evil example'. In this, he pinned the blame fervently on the king's advisors and not Henry himself.[12]

When the question was put to Gregory about Grant's successor at Canterbury, Gregory rejected Henry's favourite, Ralph Neville, also chancellor and bishop of Chichester. No warmer was he about the king's fall back plan, the prior of Christ Church, due to concerns over his age and an alleged lack of knowledge. When Henry's third choice, John le Blund – an excellent scholar and expert on Aristotle – was also vetoed on the advice of the late Stephen Langton's brother, Simon, now archdeacon of Canterbury due to a combination le Blund's interest in a pagan subject and his good relations with des Roches, Gregory persuaded the monks of Canterbury to accept Edmund Rich, prior to his appointment, treasurer at Salisbury. Like the late Stephen Langton, Edmund came with a reputation as a fine scholar, having taught theology and arts at both Paris and Oxford. Despite lacking experience for his new role, the man later known as St Edmund of Abingdon possessed great strength of conviction that would leave a unique mark on the see of Canterbury.[13]

Away from England, Frederick II's success in taking Jerusalem had brought some much-needed stability to the Middle East. After obtaining

Christian control of Jerusalem, Bethlehem, Nazareth, Sidon and Jaffa, the Holy Roman Emperor also made peace with the Lombards.[14] Around that time the king of Jerusalem, John of Brienne, took the city of Durazzo. Located in modern-day Albania on the Adriatic Sea, Brienne's success culminated in his being elected emperor of the East.[15]

It was around this time that the order of Dominicans – commonly known as the Black Monks – began to set up home in an England that had already witnessed the formation of a Franciscan house at Reading, building on those already established at Canterbury, London and Oxford.[16] On a more disturbing note, the discovery of the mangled body of a young Franconian boy in January 1234 would send shockwaves throughout Bavaria. Suspicions as to the identity of the perpetrators saw the finger of suspicion pointed at the Jews of the nearby towns, leading to the torture and execution of eight. While events in Franconia marked the first occasion in the history of Germany when torture was used to expose guilt, such tales of cruelty and wrongful identity were by no means unprecedented. The annals of Winchester had carried a similar story dated 18 October 1231, regarding the crucifixion of a young child named Stephen, whose body was discovered close to St Swithun's. A near-identical account in the close rolls a year later tells of the shocking dismemberment of an unnamed child, apparently at the hands of his own mother. The two accounts appear to be related; while the mother absconded, initial blame was laid on one Abraham Pinche, a local Jew who was accused of ritualistic homicide. As a consequence, the sheriff was forced to imprison the entire local Jewry for their own protection. Though later released, charged on a crime of theft from two years earlier, Pinche was hung as a felon, most likely in retribution for his mother's local prominence as a usurer. Around this period, accusations of unlawful circumcision were laid against a Jew in Norwich.[17]

A hard frost that lasted until 19 January failed to prevent the unopposed march through Shropshire of the combined forces of Richard Marshal and Llywelyn. On reaching Shrewsbury the following month, the locals were unequipped and ill-prepared to prevent the enemy access to the town. Hearing of the razing of its pretty buildings, Henry initially vowed never to come to terms with Richard. This he would be forced to rethink in the light of the carnage undertaken by Siward on lands owned by des Roches and the king's younger brother.[18]

For the earl of Cornwall, the developing feud between his brother and brother-in-law was proving of cataclysmic consequence. Prior to the beginning of the war, Richard had been much occupied in Wales. Husband now of the wealthy heiress Isabel, widow of the earl of Gloucester yet a Marshal in her own right, Richard had been using his newfound wealth to acquire further property. Granted custody of Builth, which had been due to be lost by de Braose to Llywelyn prior to his execution, Richard had, of course, spent 1232–33 fighting in Wales alongside Richard Marshal and by March 1233 had succeeded in driving Llywelyn from Radnor. As Henry's feud with Marshal worsened, forced to pick a side, a combination of Richard's loyalty to his brother and being bought off with financial gifts saw Siward unleashed on his lands. Throughout the conflict, there was a sense that the earl of Cornwall's mind was often on other things. On 22 September 1232, Richard and his wife were saddened by the death of their son John, who had only entered the world in January. In September, the newly-weds had welcomed into the world a daughter, Isabel; however, she would sadly join John in being interred at Reading Abbey in October 1234.[19]

After leaving Gloucester, Henry summoned a council to meet at Westminster – sources vary as to whether it commenced on 2 or 4 February. Among the many prelates in attendance was Edmund Rich, who, along with the suffragans, was unequivocal in supporting the integrity of Marshal. As usual, dissent reined against the bishop of Winchester and his 'evil' counsellors, with many arguing for their expulsion. On this matter, Edmund shared their criticism and was stern in his warnings to the king over his past favouritism for the Poitevin faction.[20]

To appease his many critics, the king retired after promising to give the matter some thought. Give it some thought he certainly did. In need of spiritual enlightenment, he undertook a pilgrimage to Bromholm Priory in Norfolk. Ironically, two years earlier Henry had made a similar visit alongside Hubert at which point he bound himself in oath to his new counsellors. He also dined under Hubert's roof and made a similar sworn statement of fidelity to Hubert and Margaret.[21]

The story of this isolated site on the Norfolk Coast is a strange one. A small Cluniac priory, in 1223 it had obtained possession of an alleged piece of the true cross, which had found its way to St Albans after being located in Constantinople around 1204 after being taken from Jerusalem by the Saracens. That this double-cross-shaped piece of wood was the very item on which Christ was crucified was of course seen as a story too good not to be true by the monks of Bromholm, who began work a short time after its arrival on a new priory. As soon as 1225, the annals of Dunstable had recorded miracles taking place. A year later, and after Henry's first visit, permission was granted for an annual fayre to be held in mid-September for the feast of the Exaltation of the Holy Cross.[22]

On leaving the north coast, Henry's route passed Bury St Edmunds, Walsingham, Castle Acre, Ramsey and Peterborough. Apparently 'moved by piety' and perhaps a longing for recent memories, on arriving at Bury he came to make peace with Hubert's wife. During Hubert's captivity, Margaret is believed to have overseen the betrothal of Richard de Clare to their daughter, Meggotta; however, any sexual activity appears to have been later ignored.[23]

Regardless of any future political considerations, the path of the penitent had been the break the king needed. No longer concerned by reports that Marshal had crossed from Pembroke to Ireland in a bid to subdue any threats to his lands in Leinster, or that his justiciar Seagrave was perturbed by a raid on his villa at Alconbury close to Huntingdon by the ubiquitous Siward, Henry's heart continued to lighten. Wendover reported how, on watching the hapless justiciar flee in terror of Siward, the king and his attendants were 'excited to laughter at him'. By the end of February, Henry was at last ready to make peace. With the help of the bishops of Coventry and Rochester, a provisional agreement was in place, following which Marshal formally came to terms on 6 March. A council was organised for 9 April to make it law. As far as the history books would be concerned, the strange uprising recorded in the chronicles of the day as the Marshal War was officially over.[24]

For Henry, even at the time, there can have been no doubt in his mind that the end of the war would serve as a watershed moment. Peace with Marshal could never be achieved with words alone. Nor with so many wrongs that needed to be put right could things go back to the way they had been. To enforce this message, when the council came to Westminster on 9 April, the newly consecrated archbishop of Canterbury, Edmund Rich, unleashed a devastating discourse on Henry for his recent performance. There is little doubt from Henry's subsequent behaviour that Edmund's words tore at his very soul. In no doubt that the new primate of England would not hesitate to charge him with excommunication unless the king's counsellors were dismissed, Henry sacked des Roches and also removed de Rivallis from high office. The dates on which these occurred are no longer clear. De Rivallis's departure from his treasurer role is cited as having occurred no later than 15 April with deprivation of other offices following in May.[25]

Personal reconciliation with Marshal would have to wait as once again the earl was absent. Although peace had indeed been agreed, unbeknown to Henry, things had taken an unfortunate turn. Prior to the truce, Henry, still acting on the guidance of the bishop of Winchester, had attempted to stir up trouble for the Marshal lands in Ireland. In a joint plot, des Roches and Seagrave wrote to Hubert's replacement as justiciar of Ireland, Maurice Fitzgerald, as well as some of Richard's ill-wishers including Hugh and Walter de Lacy, regarding an alliance against the earl. By way of unscrupulous means, much damage was inflicted on Marshal's lands, prompting him to cross the Irish Sea to deal with the latest problems. On his arrival, he was met by Richard de Burgh's predecessor, Geoffrey le Marsh, who had served as justiciar of Ireland 1215–21 before retaking the job 1226–28 on the resignation of the younger William Marshal. Prior to his appointment in 1228, de Burgh had been keeper of Limerick Castle and seneschal of Munster. Though Marsh had resigned of his own accord in 1228, as a consequence of both terms, he was a man with whom the Marshals had a chequered past.[26]

Little did Richard know that the past would soon come back to haunt him. After a short siege, Limerick was recovered. In the days that followed, his enemies requested a truce. To consolidate an agreement, Marshal demanded his enemies' presence on the Curragh of Kildare on 1 April. Discussions through Templar intermediaries brought brief progress, yet the behaviour of Marsh in recommending Marshal reject any offer soon left the earl isolated. Leaving him on the excuse that taking up his sword for him would put him in conflict with his brother-in-law, on the breakdown of talks Richard was left with only fifteen knights against 140.

How exactly an occasion intended as a peace offering ended in full battle is still subject to much uncertainty. Whether contemporary accounts that Richard was tricked into fighting offers an accurate representation or whether the battle hardy charged all guns blazing into the abyss is a secret now known only to the open fields. Outnumbered by some nine to one, the Battle of Kildare saw a resolute Marshal slay at least six before being wounded. Captured, he was taken to Kilkenny, formerly his own fortress prior to it being confiscated by the justiciar. During his captivity, he was presented with a royal writ that revealed the conspiracy laid bare at the highest level, after which he was requested to open the gates of his castles. His health initially on the mend, even to the point that he was walking around and playing dice, medical treatment from a local surgeon saw his condition deteriorate. Whether foul play was involved or his poor health was a direct consequence of his earlier actions is unclear. After catching a fever, he died on 16 April and was buried at the nearby Franciscan church. As Wendover recalled painfully, 'Thus died the earl marshal, a noble knight, one skilled in learning and distinguished by his manners and virtue. He departed this life on Palm Sunday to receive from the Lord in heaven a palm for his reward; amongst the sons of men his person was so beautiful that nature seemed to have striven with the virtues in its composition'.[27]

Unaware of developments across the Irish Sea, talks between the newly installed archbishop of Canterbury and the king prompted Henry to request Edmund travel to Wales in a bid to broker a peace with Llywelyn and Marshal. Henry learned of Marshal's death while at Woodstock on 6 May. Accompanying the news was rumour of his hand in a plot. To this, a devastated Henry burst into tears. So wrote the annalist of Dunstable, 'he mourned for his friend as David had lamented Saul and Jonathan'. Roger of Wendover similarly praised the king's response, 'to the astonishment of all present', while noting Henry's declaration that the late earl 'had not left his equal in the kingdom'. Throughout the evening, mass was sung for Marshal's soul and alms delivered to the poor.[28] A tearful requiem noted in the annals of Waverley would later lament:

> Livor edax, morum subversio, fax vitiorum,
> Vitricus Anglorum, rapuit solamen eorum.
> Principis absque pare, gens livida mentis averæ
> Præsumpsit claræ decus indolis anticipare.
> Anglia, plange Marescallum, plangens lachrymare.
> Causa subest, quare; quia pro te planxit amare.
> Virtus militiæ, patriæ protectio, gentis
> Fraude ruit propriæ. Miserere Deus morientis.
>   Amen[29]

A translation of which could be:

> Voracious envy, that overthrows morality,
> That sets fire to faults, tore away their solace.

Without an equal of a leader,
A spiteful people of an averted mindset got ahead of the
glory of his brightness.
England, bewail thy Marshal,
Bewail him with tears!
The reason is, why?
Because on thy behalf England bewailed to love!
The virtue of the army,
The protection of the fatherland,
Through the fraud of its own people
It tumbled down.
God have mercy on the one who is dying!
    Amen!

Henry set out for Gloucester at some point within the next three weeks where he intended to await the archbishop on his return. On the way, news reached him that Siward had tracked him through Windsor Forest and attacked the royal train as it passed Woodstock. Greater success followed in the plundering of the possessions of the still in office Seagrave and one of Passelewe's manors.[30]

At the council that took place sometime between 16 May and the beginning of June, the remaining Poitevin counsellors were all dismissed, and a truce with Llywelyn discussed in detail. As a show of good faith, Siward was forgiven for his rebellion. Similarly, on learning that Richard Marshal was dead, the greatest knight's third son, Gilbert Marshal, was granted the offices and titles of his childless brother, and personally knighted by Henry.[31] Also present was the former justiciar, Hubert de Burgh, who had been officially pardoned for any past offences. As a token of good faith, and perhaps at the prompting of the peace brokers, Hubert formally resigned any future claim to his previous role. He was instead reinstated as a counsellor and granted ownership once again of the three castles of Gwent: Grosmont, Skenfrith and Whitecastle, thus depriving the already ousted de Rivallis. Fines and ransoms were imposed on those who fought for Marshal in Ireland; Henry also thanked Richard de Burgh for his support and permitted him to resume the government of Ireland. His treachery had been of particular importance in Marshal's demise.[32]

Edmund and his fellow bishops were back in Gloucester by the following month. Their talks with the prince of Gwynedd successful, including terms that would allow formal reconciliation between the king and the various noblemen with whom he had become estranged, a two-year truce was arranged and implemented on 21 June somewhere between Shrewsbury and Ellesmere. This would be the final disagreement between Henry and Llywelyn prior to Llywelyn's death in 1240.

All of the truces around this time were extremely pleasing to the pope. Earlier in the year he had also written to Louis in the hope of long-term peace. Arrangements were also made for des Roches, if necessary, to have been sent to discuss future relations with France. Besides sending some aid to the duke of Brittany in May, who thereafter had little choice but make amends with Louis, Henry's lack of finances and Louis's developing military might did little to whet the appetite for further action to reclaim the old lands. As usual, a difficulty arose with Lusignan, who refused to end his demand for the Isle of Oléron.[33]

With this, a year that could easily be regarded as the most tumultuous of Henry's adult life – if not his entire life – came to an end. If civil war and the continuous threat of conflict abroad was not enough, 1234 had marked the third year in a row of rampant famine and sickness. Undoubtedly a consequence of the war itself, of arguably even greater effect on the lives of the common people was a personal lack of affinity with their king. If trust was to be restored, the mistakes of the past needed to be put right. As a first step, Henry filled his government with low-ranking officials and appointed himself his own chief minister. Throughout his time on the throne, Henry had never ruled without a regent, a legate or a justiciar. As history would recall, the decision would put England on a twenty-four-year period of domestic peace before the ghost of Magna Carta would again cast its shadow. In so doing, the reforms of 1258 and the third baronial conflict that followed would forever define Henry's reign. Just like the first, it would change the way England thought about itself and its constitution, confining the events of 1233-34 to ignominy.

Epilogue

The Birth of a Nation

As I mentioned in the introduction, when I began writing this book, my initial intention had been to concentrate on the Marshal War alone. How was it possible, I had come to wonder, had such a brief yet highly contentious period in England's history unfolded the way it did, only to be so unknown eight centuries later. The severity of the violence that took place during the war, not least its impact on the mindset of the king and *ipso facto* the future of England, I realise now I significantly underestimated. Fortunately it also didn't take me long to pick up on an even greater fallacy. In no way should it be argued that the events of the Marshal War were isolated. Quite simply, no full appreciation of what happened can be achieved by concentrating on this one aspect alone. As with all things in history, what happened during this particular period was a direct response to what had gone before. The same is true of what transpired in the aftermath. In the case of this book, I decided to focus primarily on the former. The reasons for this, I believe, will become clear at the end.

Looking back in hindsight at the way this book unfolded, I realise now that the narrative could have evolved in a number of ways. Having already written a complete biography of Henry III – complete at least in the sense that it began with Henry's birth and ended with his death – returning to old ground was always going to be unavoidable. Similarly, it was never my intention to conduct an in-depth study into the implementation of the great charters, despite their unequivocal importance to both Henry's early reign and the war that followed. In this author's opinion, even now, nothing is ever likely to surpass the quality of Sir J.C. Holt's *The Northerners*, published in 1961. Starting on a new road is never easy and often takes great courage. That is not to say, of course, it is necessarily easy to follow in another's footsteps, especially when a mark has been made and made well.

Throughout my writing of this book, I have frequently held a sense that I was following in big footsteps. There is no doubt that any researcher of the thirteenth century is blessed by the teachings of many an outstanding historian and chronicler, be it Matthew Paris, Roger of Wendover, the anonymous annalists of Dunstable, Waverley et al. or the more recent Nicholas Vincent, David Carpenter and Sir Maurice Powicke. At the same time, focusing on those particular aspects has also allowed me to venture into less well-trodden areas. Prior to this book, only two works had been written on the minority of Henry III, penned by Kate Norgate and David Carpenter, respectively, the latter having been published in 1990. Similarly, the period 1232–34 has rarely been covered in detail; indeed, every attempt so far has been part of either a separate or broader study. I realise now that there were often good reasons for this. In producing his biography of Peter des Roches, published in 1996, Nicholas Vincent was wise to establish that a study of des Roches could best be presented by dividing the Butterfly Bishop's career into two parts: pre-1232 and post-1232. In the case of this book, such a challenge was to be avoided as the greater attention was on Henry III and his early reign. To obtain a thorough understanding of how the Marshal War came about, a similar knowledge of the circumstances that had brought Henry to the throne as a young boy was necessary. As I soon came to realise, particularly influential was John's loss of Normandy, or, as was so eloquently worded by the chroniclers, the separating of the sword from the sceptre. I hope to demonstrate that not only was the loss of Normandy and the wider Angevin Empire of clear importance to Henry III's reign – something that is widely accepted – but also one direct cause of the Marshal War itself.

In presenting my views, I do not claim that this endeavour, nor my personal conclusion, comes close to satisfactorily answering all questions. A greater hope is that it stimulates further study and discussion. By beginning with a presentation of the most serious troubles encountered by John, I believe that a far greater degree of clarity can be discerned of the problems that would define Henry's early reign, not least implementation of the charters. By following the course of Henry III's minority year-by-year, during which the personnel and objectives of Henry's government changed little, we can see his reign as a gradual and natural evolution that would ultimately culminate in the further change once the king declared himself of age. In this way, this otherwise continuous narrative can, for simplicities' sake, now be discussed not in two parts but several.

Following on from the reign of John and the country's drift towards civil war, we encountered Henry's reign under the regency of Marshal with the support of Hubert, des Roches and Guala. Following this we saw Henry's government operate in the form of a triumvirate comprising Pandulf, Hubert and Peter. On the legate's departure, Hubert took centre stage, culminating in Peter's gradual withdrawal from court. In 1232, on the bishop of Winchester's return, we witnessed Hubert's fall, which would ultimately lead to his imprisonment and rescue, both of which had some effect on the Marshal War. With that, Henry's reign took on a new form. As Sir Maurice Powicke rightly said, the des Roches regime could accurately be described as 'Henry III's Lesson In Kingship'.

Nor would he ever forget it.

Before reaching this point, the first logical step is to return to the beginning. Of the circumstances that would later bring about the First Barons' War, many accusations can justly be levelled at the personality and actions of John himself. Having knelt before the high altar at Westminster Abbey and sworn in the presence of the barons and clerics to observe peace with God and the church, to administer justice to those in his care and put an end to any evil laws or customs in his realm, John's apparent disbelief in God would prove itself a source of disbelief. The importance of this cannot be emphasised strongly enough, not least as the previous century had seen a significant growth in the cult of saints. From the Virgin Mary to the apostles and the first-century martyrs to the recently canonised, few stories of the miraculous could influence the faithful like those about whom such godly things had been written and sung. Intrigue of a greater power was by no means limited to saints. Living in an age where war and famine could wipe out a government in a single day, it is no great surprise that the multitude placed their faith in angels and saints as opposed to mere mortals. Not least those whose actions were consistently in conflict with that of scripture.

Beyond John's debatable atheism, his treatment of his subjects gave rise to a host of scandals. At times vulgar, cunning, cruel and lustful, John inherited many characteristics from his father Henry II, without enjoying similar success at government level. He was disloyal to his father and brother, not that Richard had necessarily earned his affection. The same was not true of the barons whose wives he is reputed to have seduced. Inherent acts of selfishness often undid his kindnesses.

Likewise, his occasional devotion and founding of religious orders does little to compare with his regular attempts to exhort money from them and his tendency to flout the rules. In an age where prisoners were treated with contempt, he starved innocents to death. It was probably his own hand that ended the life of his nephew. While some point the finger at the young duke's appalling treatment of Eleanor of Aquitaine, the only thing history agrees on is that his fate won John little favour among his supporters. In the centuries since, opinion has remained consistently against him. He was pelted not only by the barons but also the chroniclers. Likewise, many of the chroniclers correctly identified that many barons had justifiable personal grievances against John. Seldom in the context of English history has a king's sexual deviances proven so consequential.

True to later legend, his attempts to usurp Richard were notable, not that his treachery stopped there. Forever short of funds, and never slow to manipulate others for financial gain, John's lust for revenge proved particularly costly. His lack of mercy for his prisoners, including the knights of Anjou on liberating his mother from Mirebeau, lost him the respect of his important followers, not least William des Roches and Aimeri of Thouars, who defected to Philip. This mistake alone went a long way towards accounting for the losses in France. By early 1203 John had lost the key city of Angers in Anjou, and his withdrawal into Normandy left Philip unopposed to take Anjou, Touraine and Maine. With this, like the proverbial pack of cards, the ancestral lands fell.[1]

None of this is intended to suggest the challenges of maintaining order on the Continent were easy. In reality, some form of separation was inevitable, not least as John was operating against a formidable opponent in Philip II, and in lands so far from home. That is not to say he performed well either. In John's later reign in particular, failure abroad and domestic discord were closely aligned. If one lesson is surely true of Henry III's early reign, it is that John may have been the receiver of Magna Carta, but Henry would always be the man forced to deal with both its implementation and its restrictions.

Another lesson that can be discerned is that disloyalty against Henry early on was by no means a reflection on Henry himself. After all, as his father's son, was it not natural that the devil's brood required purging? Had it not been for John's final decision to entrust his realm into the capable hands of William Marshal, the loyalty of the royalists may well have been tested. Fortunately for Henry, his father's appointment of the 'greatest knight' may well have been the highlight of his kingship. With the aid of the loyal Guala, whose impressive red gowned and galeroed figure must have looked truly remarkable atop his magnificent white steed, as early as two weeks after Henry's makeshift coronation reform was already underway.[2] By implementing a reversion of the Charter of Liberties, Marshal offered the rebels an olive branch and the young king a safety net. In the years ahead, the legacy of events at Runnymede would extend far beyond the initial successes and subsequent failures.

Further reforms at the end of the war gave rise to Magna Carta and with it the Charter of the Forest. Had the latter not occurred, the likelihood that future conflict would be destined after Marshal's death seems high. That the 'greatest knight' feared this seems clear from his refusal to name a successor. Time would prove just how right he was.

Throughout the First Barons' War, Marshal worked well with Guala. The same was true of Pandulf, both of whom proved a calming influence on Peter des Roches. Though Pandulf's relations with Peter cooled somewhat after the return of Langton, a well-wisher of the king but never a friend of Peter, his role as the central pillar of the post-Marshal triumvirate ensured that Henry was always protected and his government on the right foot. While it may be generous to suggest that surrendering England to the papacy was also a masterstroke by John, not least as it destroyed his political credibility in the eyes of many of the prelates and magnates, he had at least ensured that no French invasion would occur while Philip was alive.

With Langton's return, Pandulf's time in England soon came to an end, after which the young king was presented with new challenges. That Langton had hoped to take Pandulf's place at the head of Henry's triumvirate seems probable, yet despite his many important contributions to court life, this would not come about. As a consequence of Pandulf's departure, what had earlier proved successful as a triumvirate was destined to fragment as a duumvirate. That Hubert and Peter were a match made in heaven is unlikely. Any suggestion that the pair were incapable of working together and achieving good progress, however, is also a simplification. That this says more about their personal aspirations and ability to work within the system as opposed to any lingering shows of affection for each other seems a fair assessment. A key obstacle to warmer relations was their respective backgrounds. Whereas Hubert was the English son of minor gentry, Peter was Touraine born and of material possession. That Peter maintained a great love for his homeland, and those of it, throughout his life, is easily demonstrated. One could argue the same of Hubert. That Peter bore Hubert a grudge due to Hubert's replacing him as justiciar seems likely, not that Hubert was responsible in any way for the clause in Magna Carta that led to Peter's dismissal. Likewise, many of the demands later made by Magna Carta predate des Roches's justiciarship, so any argument that his tyranny partially inspired the charter is made far stronger against John's manner of kingship, if not that of absolute royalty itself. A better argument is that following John's death des Roches became an outlet for frustration and symbolic of his poor decisions. The same can be said of Peter's 'alien' or 'Poitevin' entourage. Upholders of a legacy of duplicity and waste.

With Henry still young of age, and his key advisors very different men, it was little surprise that the personal, or professional differences, between his two most senior counsellors led to disagreements about the direction of royal policy. That Hubert initially took the ascendancy was also no great surprise. Neither back then nor in the days since have irritable students been renowned for showing unequivocal love for their teachers. In 1221, the king's boredom with the situation left him ready to strike out on his own. Whatever the truth of the Corfe Castle plot and the bishop's trip to Santiago de Compostela, it offered Henry the chance he needed to escape Peter's shadow and Hubert the opportunity to establish himself as the sole head of English government.

It is no coincidence that Hubert was keen for Henry to abide by the charters: a very English and somewhat radical way of government by comparison to the absolutist manner of the Capetians. Nor was it an accident on the justiciar's part that from November 1222 onwards, Henry and Hubert seem to have been inseparable.[3] That Hubert had personal motivations here should be suspected. The same may have been true of the deprivation of the senior magnates of their royal castles in 1223. That Hubert himself lost some ground at this point is true, but the argument that it was a gambit on his part is also a logical conclusion.

An Englishman to the core, his personal ambitions and political ones were closely intertwined. They were also aligned far more closely with the papacy than any other at court. Never an advocate of absolute monarchy, Hubert had less reason than Peter to advocate the regaining of the ancestral Plantagenet homelands. A far more careful man than most and arguably the shrewdest administrator Europe had ever seen, Hubert was far less prepared to gamble England's future than some of his alien rivals. The bishop, on the other hand, almost equally skilled in the management of the exchequer himself, would leave no stone unturned to make recovery of the lost lands a reality. That this important difference in policy set the two at odds is also a simplification. Nevertheless, when all of these issues are weighed in the balance, it is easy to see the different planes on which both men stood.

While the temptation to play blame games or attempt to establish which man was the more capable of the two has proven a temptation too great for some past commentators, even in their own times, neither Peter nor Hubert could be described as perfect. From humble beginnings, a rare talent for extraordinary patience and discipline, accompanied by an early ambition for property ownership, put Hubert on the path for great things. By 1215, he had already obtained many honours – something the reign of Henry would bring in greater quality. As Powicke was surely right to point out, there must have been traits in Hubert's character that peeved others. Sadly, we no longer know precisely what they were. Admirable characteristics such as determination, purpose and confidence in a new man could be a valuable asset to the government but also play at the insecurities of the old guard.[4]

That Hubert himself played on Henry's insecurities and affection is clear. No less true was this of Peter. Nor could it be said that either man was undeserving of reward. If Peter's magnificence at the Fair of Lincoln should be considered his crowning glory on English soil, Sandwich belongs to Hubert. Though a royal marriage and acquisition of an earldom put Hubert on a level almost unprecedented at the time – only the promotion of Marshal can compare – such rewards may also have been Hubert's greatest weakness. Putting the loud grumblings of jealousy aside, in reaching a zenith of power Hubert also had nowhere left to climb. If there is any truth in the old proverb the bigger they are, the harder they fall, Hubert's humbling from ownership of England's highest tower to the darkest depths of the Devizes dungeon offers its own foreboding analogy. With Hubert gone, the one surviving element of the post-William-Marshal triumvirate went with him. In so doing, the final unbroken link with the government of 1216 was finally severed.

As the turbulent events of 1234 would later demonstrate, Hubert's story was by no means over. Reacquainted with the court, and with the Poitevins gone, Hubert was reconciled with the king, just as Henry was with the other lords he had previously alienated. Though there would be no real return to power, reclaiming of his treasures from the Templars at least served as a sign all was forgiven. As Henry himself would later confess, 'above all our faithful men, he attended to our affairs most diligently and devotedly', a reference no doubt to Sandwich in particular.[5]

But no further. Hubert would never reclaim what he had once held: a sign, perhaps, that retirement was also overdue. In total, he occupied the post for seventeen years; more than fifteen of which was with Henry. Though accusations against him from the other magnates had been prevalent, his long period of authority should also be seen as a testament to the man's ability to survive as well as having marked a rare period of stability in an age where fortunes waxed and waned.

As for Peter, one might well argue there are many parallels. The broader considerations of his nationality and friendships aside, in Peter, Henry had another man with whom his life would be always intertwined. Any suggestion that Peter's contributions to the service of the king were universally negative would be a major disservice to his memory. The founder of great ecclesiastical buildings and religious orders, his love of hunting, luxury and occasional flamboyance should not detract from his fine intellect, skills of diplomacy and military talents. A friend of John, he was select in his cliques. No better illustrated is this by the knowledge that potential allies such as Aumale and Falkes never reached the same levels of trust as de Rivallis and de Maulay. Was their earldom status the reason? Undoubtedly true the canny cleric was never happier than in his own power. What should not be forgotten, however, is that unlike with his contemporaries at Canterbury, Peter enjoyed peace with his own monks. Despite becoming a figure of loathing during the First Barons' War, by the following year he was reconciled with all whom he had offended.[6] While Peter's most lasting reforms had occurred at the exchequer, it was in his see he won most hearts. Whereas Langton had used Becket's translation as an opportunity to highlight Becket's Englishness, Peter did the same for St Birinus. Ironic though it may seem, in this alien who promoted Poitevin to the deprivation of English, Peter espoused much that there was to be espoused of the developing national. The Butterfly Bishop, perhaps not, but no one during that time pushed the cult of the Anglo-Saxon saints more than Peter des Roches.[7]

Though by 1234 an old man, and a humbled one, one thing Peter had always done was survive. An ally and accompanier of great emperors and equal of popes at his height, he was an arrogant manipulator at his worst. Unlike Hubert, accusations of murder were never levelled at him, not that Hubert was ever found guilty of such either. If he had engineered such means to end Hubert's sorry lot during the latter's stay in the Devizes dungeons, that was a single act – driven by an intense rivalry that had been escalating since the reign of John. If one accusation can be laid at both, it can be the other old adage. Power corrupts; absolute power corrupts absolutely.

By 1235, there were signs that Henry had already learned his lesson. Among his claims of des Roches are that he made him 'deviate from the observation of justice, and that we were able to do injury to our faithful subjects at will', something the king attributed to 'the plenitude of royal power'.[8] At best, a combination of Hubert and Peter's similarities and differences bound them to a king whom they served for many years, the majority of which were peaceful. As such, it seems only fitting that in the end, as with Hubert, the king and des Roches were largely reconciled. Henry honoured the bishop's recent foundation at Selbourne with several liberties, yet this was merely a goodbye gift. The same would be less true of Seagrave and de Rivallis. Of the previous administration, only Neville remained in his job, retaining the role of chancellor and possession of the great seal. After ousting Seagrave as justiciar, Henry left the role unfilled, arguing that there should be no senior magnate, either church or lay. Only now, after eighteen years on the throne, did the full reign of Henry III finally begin.[9]

Thanks in large part to the misplaced direction of des Roches, the same king who had earlier been either too gentle in force or lacking in confidence of his own abilities to cast off the shackles of the great charters in asserting himself was ready to take on the challenge. By no means a ruler in the mould of Frederick II who had conquered the Holy Land by diplomacy and overcome his son's rebellion within a year of the Marshal War, at 27 he was ready to step into his prime.[10] Under Peter's guidance, Henry briefly envisaged a more absolute level of kingship. That he craved such power, even fleetingly, is unsurprising. King throughout his minority in name only, reports that he was dismissed as a mere boy when his father had wielded so much must have tugged deeply at his insecurities. As recently as 1232, the Margam chronicle had labelled Henry as 'boy king' at 25.[11] From 1234 onwards, it is perhaps more accurate to say not only had Henry received a great lesson but that many taught throughout the past eighteen years had provided the perfect apprenticeship. The outcome of the Marshal War had defeated the possibility of any return to the type of rule seen pre-Magna Carta. By this time, it is doubtful Henry even wished it.

As the years ahead demonstrated, the events of that strange period dubbed The Marshal War were of profound consequence, both short and long term. Past criticism of his officials had undoubtedly influenced Henry deeply, as perhaps had accusations of their lack of affinity with some of his subjects. The same may well have been true that des Roches's influence had retained at least one permanent mark. Throughout his time on the throne, Henry had never ruled without a regent, a legate or a justiciar. Not only was des Roches's dismissal the break from his past that Henry needed, but it also gave him the confidence to trust in his own decisions and become his own chief minister. From that time onwards, various clerks temporarily filled the role of treasurer, but Henry appointed no official replacement. One might argue, England was again ruled in a manner similar to that of his grandfather, Henry II: the subjects of the king became faithful but capable followers once more, rather than undermining his authority.

While the outcome of the Marshal War may have been of little benefit to the Poitevin faction, for those on the other side better fortune awaited. In the ensuing weeks, Gilbert Basset was restored to Upavon at de Maulay's expense and forgiven for any acts of dissent that may or may not have occurred during the war. Among others, Siward also came before the king at Gloucester to make peace. On 2 July the now diocese-bound Peter was attacked on his precincts by the hot-headed Siward, resulting in a fine. Fortunately for all concerned, that was a minor incursion, and the return to war was avoided.[12]

Another whose influence deserves praise at this time was the new archbishop of Canterbury. As Stephen Langton had known all too well, Edmund of Abingdon was similarly aware maintaining of the peace always required compromise. A great king was a loving one who lived in harmony with his subjects. For peace to be achieved, the state of the king needed always to be equal to the wellbeing of the realm. Just like

Marshal before him, forgiveness had been generous and expensive. It would be worth it.

What, one can only imagine, would the 'greatest knight' have said had he been alive to witness it all. A servant of five kings, in a career that spanned more than six decades, from Falkes's plundering of monasteries to the unhorsing of a would-be usurper, Marshal had seen it all. By no means a close friend of either Hubert or Peter, he worked hard to maintain good relations with both, clearly trusting Peter enough to ensure the young king's care when he was absent. However, this was less true about the regency on his death.

That the same diplomatic relations were shared by Marshal's sons is another matter. In some ways, one might see Peter's hatred of Richard Marshal as ironic. Having been brought up on the Continent, Marshal was far more accustomed to Capetian kingship than that of post-Magna Carta England. By 1227, much that had remained unanswered at the end of the First Barons' War appeared to have been settled. Henry accepted the charters and worked within them, albeit profiting whenever possible. For this, thanks could be laid partly at Hubert and Peter's doors, if not their predecessors of yonder years. Thanks to the effective practices of past administrators, administration in England was perhaps as well organised as anywhere in Europe, if not the wider world.

Yet whereas administration was built on solid foundations, the direction of Henry's kingship, as the years 1216–34 have demonstrated, was not. Indeed, it was mostly thanks to the calm head of Hubert that matters were kept in check. In his work on Henry's majority, David Carpenter concluded that the politics of the minority had created an instability that lasted until 1234. Should this be accepted, one could go on to argue that the politics of the minority was also at least partly responsible for bringing about the Marshal War. Does this serve to underplay Peter's role in courtly matters from 1232 onwards? Not in the least. As we have already discovered, the politics of the minority were inexplicably and inexorably linked with the dominant personalities of both Hubert and Peter.

That Henry himself was ever destined to be a military king is doubtful. An impressive, handsome lad of stocky features, his performance both in France in 1230 and the Wales campaigns 1223–34 confirm his limitations. Having adorned his first suit of armour in 1223, surrounded by the vibrant sights of the colourful banners in the breeze and the sound of trumpets on the air, there is a feeling Henry instantly fell in love with the sights of war, but not the process.[13] That this should be considered a surprise is unlikely considering his seeming indifference if not outright distrust of tournaments. Was it really not to be expected that a great warrior need learn his way first? Did the great Marshal not better some 500 knights in tournament prior to taking on the role of regent?

Among the many lessons to be discerned from Henry's early reign, two clear turning points stand out. As John of Earley had been only too shrewd to realise, acceptance of the regency for Marshal put him on a path to prominence. Had the regent faltered on his watch, England would have crumbled. Magnificent though Hubert's heroics at Dover were, without Marshal the realm could never have held out indefinitely. Nor could skilfully masterminded enterprises like that at Lincoln have won the war alone. With the Marshal's second son, we see a bizarre irony. Had William failed, England's history would have been very different. Had Richard succeeded, the same could also have been true. That Henry was ever in any threat of being dethroned throughout the Marshal War is unlikely. Undoubtedly threats were made; however, few of them were aimed at the king himself. Is this a sign of the king's perceived weakness? The strength of des Roches's hold? A combination of the two? In the end, perhaps it matters not. Only that the lesson was learned.

While much has been written of William Marshal's character, sources concerned with Richard are frustratingly scarce. By no means the epitome of Englishness that Roger of Wendover held him up to be, his lineage and upbringing alone places him in the same bracket as figures such as his father and Ranulf. A man of the world, Richard was quick of wit and highly intelligent. His father was dubbed the greatest knight, not only because of his valiant behaviour but also his honour. That the chroniclers longed for a return of that great character is unsurprising. Were they overly nostalgic in placing some of those values on Richard? Was he not a chip off the old block? While by no means his father's better, the great strength of character and tact displayed during his correspondence with Agnellus of Pisa makes it easy to understand why some felt he was of the same mould.

With hindsight, it is very easy to view figures such as Marshal who fought injustice as some form of freedom fighter; however, the reality is usually far more mundane than that presented by the movie theatre. Just as it was earlier true concerning the barons who had fought against

John, personal grudges against the person of the king were often as much to blame as the failures and personalities of those in authority. In the case of Richard Marshal, grievances for the war concerned both dower and household. By the time of his return to England, he was in a unique position, being one of the few magnates still possessed of land in England and on the Continent. In his own time, even the great Ranulf had lost much land there. That Marshal was incensed by the lack of personal gain from Ranulf's death, or Hubert's fall, is probable, especially in the context of enriching outsiders, yet that is not to say either Ranulf or his father would have behaved any differently. An uncle of Richard de Clare, Marshal was perhaps duly incensed that the de Clare wardship had gone to des Rivallis. Whether his backing of ally Basset while remaining silent about Mauclerc's disseising should be considered a sign of hypocrisy cannot be too readily dismissed. Nor did he object to gaining a manor of Waleran. Yet equally absent was the support of the other magnates. Why also were the clergy not more vociferous in their support for the disinherited treasurer?

If arguments can be made for occasional selfishness, greater evidence can be found for his military excellence and intellectual capabilities. His performance at Monmouth was particularly praiseworthy. Whether accounts that his horse was killed from under him only for him to jump on to that of one of his enemies and continue the fight twelve to one offers an accurate presentation or merely a romantic notion is sadly lost to history. One thing that continues to replay in Marshal's tale is that ever the underdog, he always punched above his weight. Victorious at Monmouth, he survived certain death at Kildare, at least for a while. The conqueror of the Marches, what is particularly notable is how he achieved so much without the support of the magnates. The losses inflicted by guerrilla warfare tactics on both his great and temporary enemies are itself testament to a character of excellent capability and cunning. His ability to turn long term feuds, i.e. with Llywelyn, into effective partnerships is also noteworthy. Richard was indisputably his father's son – far more so than any of his brothers! That he was prepared to continue the war until Henry buckled is testament to his resilience, regardless of his original motives. In circumstances such as those, while acknowledgement of his motivation for personal gain is vital, to also offer the benefit of the doubt that his argument to Agnellus of Pisa that bowing to injustice was a form of evil seems a fair testament to the man's character. How England would have fared had the great warrior survived is a story that will never be told. A far more satisfying conclusion is that the cause of the war was realised. Henry's lesson was learned. The Poitevins' departure from the government was made final.

In the introduction, I posed the question, was this conflict a civil war? Providing an answer to this question again depends partially on one's definition. Unlike in the First Barons' War – or the second 1263–67 – there were no famous battles in England that took place out in the field. Nor were the garrisons of the royal castles brought into play or the walls put under siege. The only battles fought were in Wales and Ireland, Monmouth and Kildare respectively. This itself confirms the war was not limited to England.

That civil disturbance occurred on a domestic front is indisputable. In most cases, it was limited to guerrilla warfare, not least the work of Basset and Siward on the manors of Richard, Earl of Cornwall, des Roches and Seagrave. Success by way of siege by Basset and Llywelyn took place mostly in Wales; Marshal's own great success was Limerick. The manors aside, the only major settlement laid to waste was Shrewsbury, for so long used as a middle ground to make or extend truce or peace between the two nations.

That this should, therefore, be considered a war with Wales is not wrong, yet it fails to capture its full importance. Unlike previous Welsh conflicts, the war itself was not with Llywelyn but an alliance of him and Marshal, a man typically his enemy. The Marshal War was not an epic war in the sense that the king was subject to invasion or lost control of his capital. Relatively speaking, it was also brief. As Nicholas Vincent was right to point out its extent should not be overstated. The opposite, however, is equally valid. There is no doubt that during the period August-September 1233 and October-April 1234 on the back of a failed truce, war waged in the Welsh Marches. While all six of the royal castles briefly seized occurred there, significant havoc was wrought on England. The king found himself at war with his greatest magnate. It cost him men, money and lands. Perhaps above all, it cost him his dignity.

Though in the grander scheme of things, the war was short and localised, it was not without importance. One might even argue, in its own way, the Marshal War was as significant as either of the barons' wars. As the actions of Simon de Montfort would later demonstrate, personal grievances, a highly capable warrior and a constitution open to abuse were often a deadly combination. In such ways, one might argue Richard Marshal was the Simon of his day: a force to be reckoned with, motivated by both altruism and personal gain. It could be strongly argued Richard was not only the better warrior but also a far better man. Both in their own way would leave their mark on Henry and England. Did Simon in Marshal have a ready-made role model if not a prototype plan for battle? It is strange in certain ways that both men grew up and made their mark in France only to become celebrated in certain quarters as true upholders of Englishness.

Perhaps there are other reasons why the Marshal War has been so little mentioned. Had the repercussions been more dramatic, there is little doubt this would have been different. Marshal died while the king was seeking peace, though the evidence suggests he was also keen to do so. Despite making mistakes, Henry was never accused of having been involved in the conspiracy. As history would recall, this time on a far happier note, by 1237 many members of Richard's family had re-established contact with the butterfly bishop. No less than six months after Marshal's death, his widow wrote to the king and des Roches asking for confirmation that the manor and church of Ringwood be bestowed upon the Norman abbey of Foucarmont for her husband's salvation. Though this never materialised, the letter could be seen as a sign that things were at least partially forgiven, if not totally forgotten.[14]

Throughout England in the years that followed, the memory of Marshal would be awarded high regard, not least among the chroniclers, themselves often the king's harshest critics. Just as Langton had dubbed William the 'greatest knight', his successor Edmund of Abingdon vouched for Richard's own honour. As a contemporary poet lamented: 'England weep for the Marshal'. Weep indeed they would. Prior to Richard being laid to rest in Ireland, the bones of the younger William had already been interred alongside those of his father in the Templar church in London. The third brother Gilbert fared little better, succumbing to death in a tournament in 1241 – ironically, an event Henry had explicitly forbidden due to fears he might lose a prime warrior. Having also died childless, the fifth earl Walter followed in similar footsteps, dying suddenly at Goodrich Castle in November 1245. With this, the earldom passed to the late regent's youngest son, Anselm. In what still to this day has the power to shock, within a month, the fifth son of the 'greatest knight' also died. The regent's bloodline survived through his magnificent daughters, but the earldom of Pembroke left Marshal hands. Marshal lands would fall to those of lesser status. The male line had died out. The Marshal Curse, it would seem, had been fulfilled.

With the death of all of William Marshal's sons without issue, it is hard to escape the feeling that in Henry we had a king forever destined to be plagued by a state of déjà vu. While a third civil war in England also occurred in 1263–67, especially repetitive were his experiences on the Continent. Thanks to the endeavours of younger brother, Richard, Earl of Cornwall, in 1225, success in Gascony had been a notable boon. As the next two centuries would clearly show, English control of Gascony would survive not only the remainder of Henry's reign but also the Hundred Years' War before falling in the reign of Henry VI, precisely 225 years after Richard's success.[15]

For Henry, Gascony proved to be the pinnacle of his achievements in France. Though another campaign to Poitou was repeated in 1242, the result was much the same as that of 1230. Throughout Henry's reign, the prospect of reclaiming the ancestral lands became more remote. The longer they remained in French hands, the more distrust of the Poitevins became inevitable. While French remained the language at court, throughout the general population pre-Chaucer English was widely adopted. If one lesson can be discerned, it is that the importance of the ancestral lands, at least in the hearts and minds of the population at large, had diminished considerably. No less true was this of the barons. From 1204 there is no doubt that a feeling of national identity arose from the loss: something that would go on to change the personality of the English elite. Even at the height of the Angevin Empire, the Norman lands were little more than a hotchpotch made up of various manors as opposed to a united area of land. Similarly, with the disinheritance of the Normans who pledged fealty to Philip Augustus, there was an opportunity to unite England.[16]

For John, a lack of affinity with those who could so easily have offered devoted loyalty saw him pass over the responsibility. In Henry, helped more than a little by a patriotic Hubert de Burgh, a far greater effort saw him win over the love of his people in a way John had never known. A generous giver of alms, an upholder of faith and a disciple of the Saxon Edward the Confessor, the Winchester-born king separated himself from his Norman predecessors. A hawker as opposed to a huntsman, Henry's personality had many differences to that of his lionhearted uncle and Scots hammering son. Not that this should be regarded as a criticism. An appetite for construction over destruction would in time lead to grand buildings. Where in the rules does it say that to be a great king, one must only excel in war? Only in 1234 was the final link with Henry's minority finally lost forever. As the next twenty-four years would demonstrate, England prospered.

That the scars of the Marshal War continued to haunt him is certain. Rarely again did he adorn his armour in battle. As such, his enthusiasm for the arts and flourishing of religious orders and new architecture would have a marked effect on England's construction. In later years a cult of Henry would surround his tomb at Westminster Abbey. Had he followed the example of his uncle, or contemporary Louis IX, and fulfilled his crusader vow there is little doubt history would have bestowed far more praise upon him. Not Henry the meek. But the confessor.

Perhaps even St Henry.

By the time of the Marshal War, there is little doubt that the magnates of England had little to gain by a conquest in Normandy. Within a generation, personalities like William Marshal would be lost forever. If Ranulf had been almost the last relic of the great feudal aristocracy of the conquest, it seems strangely fitting that Richard Marshal was indeed the last. With this, a dream that began in 1204 to unite the sword and sceptre was forever ended.

The healing of the deeper wounds would take far longer.

Bibliography

Primary Sources

Calendar of Charter Rolls, Henry III, (1903)

Calendar of the Patent Rolls, Henry, (1913), Public Records Office

Close Rolls of the Reign of Henry III, (1932), Public Records Office

Giles, J.A. (1849), *Roger of Wendover's Flowers of History, Comprising the History of England from the Descent of the Saxons to AD 1235,* Vols 1–2, Henry. G. Bohn

— (1852–4), *Matthew Paris's English History from the Year 1235 to 1273,* Vols 1–3, Henry. G. Bohn

Hallam, Elizabeth (2002a), *Chronicles of the Age of Chivalry: The Plantagenet Dynasty from 1216 to 1377*, Salamander

— (2002b), *The Plantagenet Chronicles: Medieval Europe's Most Tempestuous Family,* Salamander

Halliwell, James Orchard (1846), *Letters of the Kings of England,* Vols 1–2, Henry Colburn

— (1860), *The Chronicle of William de Rishanger, of the Barons' War: The Miracles of Simon de Montfort*, The Camden Society

Hardy, Thomas Duffus, *Syllabus (in English) of the Documents Relating to England and Other Kingdoms Contained in the Collection Known as 'Rymer's Fœdera'*

Hearne, Thomas (1810), *Robert of Gloucester's Chronicle*, Mercier & Chervet

Joinville, John de (1903), *Crusade of St Louis*, London

Luard, Henry Richards (1866–73), *Annales Monastici,* Vols I-V, Longmans, Green, Reader & Dyer

— (1877), *On The Relations Between England and Rome During the Earlier Portion of the Reign of Henry III*, Longmans, Green, Reader & Dyer

Shirley, Walter Waddington (1862–6), *Royal and Other Historical Letters Illustrative of the Reign of Henry III,* Vols 1–2, Longmans, Green, Reader and Dyer

Stubbs, William (1870), *Select Charters and Other Illustrations of English Constitutional History*, Oxford: Clarendon Press

Secondary Sources

Anonymous (1865), *History and Antiquities of Lincoln: Lincoln Cathedral, Brookes & Vibert*

Ashbridge, Thomas (2015), *The Greatest Knight: The Remarkable Life of William Marshal, The Power Behind Five English Thrones London: Simon & Schuster*

Bartlett, Robert (1993) *The Making of Europe: Conquest, Colonization and Cultural Change, 950–1350,* Harmondsworth: Allen Lane

— (2000), *England Under the Angevin Kings 1075–1225,* Oxford: Oxford University Press

Bennett, James (1830), *The History of Tewkesbury*, Tewkesbury: Longman, Rees, Orme, Brown & Green

Besant, Walter (1906), *Medieval London: Volume 1 – Historical and Social*, London: Adam & Charles Black

Blaauw, William Henry (1871), *The Barons' War Including the Battles of Lewes and Evesham*, Bell & Daldy

Bradbury, Jim (1998), *Philip Augustus, King of France, 1180–1223,* Longman

Britton, John, and Brayley, Edward Wedlake (1830), *Memoirs of the Tower of London*, Hurst, Chance & Co.

Brown, R. Allen (1977), *Allen Brown's English Castles*, B.T. Batsford London

Bumpus, T. Francis (1921), *The Cathedrals of England and Wales*, T. Wener Laurie

Carpenter, D.A. (1990), *The Minority of Henry III*, Los Angeles, CA: University of California Press

— (1996) *The Reign of Henry III*, Hambleton Press, London

— (2003) *The Struggle for Mastery: Britain 1066–1284*, Oxford: Oxford University Press

— Henry III (2020) New Haven, CT: Yale University Press

Carter, John (1824), *Specimens of Gothic Architecture and Ancient Buildings in England,* Vols 1–4, Edward Jeffrey & Son

Church, S.D. (ed.) (1999) *King John: New Interpretations,* Woodbridge: Boyd & Brewer

— *The Household Knights of King John*, Cambridge: Cambridge University Press, 2008

Clancy, Michael, *England and Its Rulers, 1066–1307* (2012). Oxford: Wiley-Blackwell

Cook, George Henry (1957), *The English Cathedral Through the Centuries*, Phoenix House

Costain, Thomas B. (1973), *The Pageant of England 1216–1272: The Magnificent Century*, Tandem, London

Crouch, David, *William Marshal: Knighthood, War and Chivalry, 1147-1219*, London: Routledge, 2016

Danziger, Danny, and Gillingham, John (2003), *1215: The Year of Magna Carta*, Hodder & Stoughton, London

Davis, John Paul (2020), *A Hidden History of the Tower of London*, Barnsley: Pen&Sword History,

— (2013), *The Gothic King: A Biography of Henry III*, Peter Owen, London

— (2009) *Robin Hood: The Unknown Templar,* Peter Owen, London

De Ros, Lord (1866), *Memorials of the Tower of London*, John Murray

Denholm-Young, N., *Richard of Cornwall*, Oxford: Basil Blackwell, 1947

Ditchfield, Peter Hampton (1907), *History of the County of Berkshire,* Vol. 3, Constable

Ellis, Alexander J. (1868), *The Only English Proclamation of Henry III, 18 October 1258,* Asher & Co.

Gascoigne, Christina, and Bamber Gascoigne (1976), *Castles of Britain*, Book Club Associates, London

Gasquet, Francis Aidan (1908), *The Greater Abbeys of England,* Chatto & Windus

— (1910), *Henry the Third and the Church: A Study of Ecclesiastical Policy and of the Relations between England and Rome*, G. Bell & Sons

Giles, J.A. (1848), *The Life and Times of Alfred the Great,* George Bell

Gillingham, John (1999), *Richard I,* New Haven, CT: Yale University Press

Hamilton, J.S. (2010), *The Plantagenets: History of a Dynasty*, Continuum, London

Harwood, Brian, *Fixer and Fighter: The Life of Hubert de Burgh, Earl of Kent, 1170–1243*, Barnsley: Pen&Sword Military, 2016

Harvey, John (1956), *The English Cathedrals,* B.T. Batsford, London

Hawkins, John Sidney (1813), *An History of the Origin and Establishment of Gothic Architecture*, S. Gothell

Hennings, Margaret (1924), *England Under Henry III*, New York, NY: Longmans, Green

Henisch, Bridget Ann (1999), *The Medieval Calendar Year*, Philadelphia, PA: Pennsylvania University Press

Henry, David (1753), *An Historical Description of the Tower of London and Its Curiousities*, J. Newberry

Henry, John, and Parker, James (1856), *Annals of England: An Epitome of English History,* Vols 1–2, Oxford and London: John Henry and James Parker

Holt, J.C. (1961), *The Northerners: A Study in the Reign of King John*, Oxford: Clarendon Press

— (1965), *Magna Carta*, Cambridge: Cambridge University Press

Hopkins, John Henry (1836), *Essay on Gothic Architecture*, Burlington, VT: Simoth & Harrington, 1836

Howell, Margaret (2001), *Eleanor of Provence: Queenship in Thirteenth-Century England*, Oxford: Blackwell

Hume, David (1858), *History of England from the Invasion of Julius Caesar to the Abdication of James the Second,* Vol. III, Boston, MA: Phillips, Sampson & Co.

Hunt, William (1888), *The English Church in the Middle Ages*, Longmans, Green & Co.

— (1900a), *King Edward the Confessor: A Short Biography*, Oxford: Oxford University Press

— (1900b), *Eleanor of Castile, Queen of Edward I: A Short Biography,* Oxford: Oxford University Press

(1900c), *King Henry I of England: A Short Biography*, Oxford: Oxford University Press

(1900d), *King Henry III of England: A Short Biography*, Oxford: Oxford University Press

(1900e) *King John of England: A Short Biography*, Oxford: Oxford University Press

Jeake, Samuel (1728), *Charters of the Cinque Ports: Two Ancient Towns and Their Members,* Bernard Lintot

Jones, Dan, *Magna Carta – The Making and Legacy of the Great Charter* (2014). London: Head of Zeus

Keen, Maurice (ed.) (1999), *Medieval Warfare: A History,* Oxford: Oxford University Press

Knight, Stephen, and Ohlgren, Thomas (1997), *Robin Hood and Other Outlaw Tales*, Kalamazoo, MI: Medieval Institute Publications

Lapper, Ivan, and Parnell, Geoffrey (2000), *Landmarks in History: The Tower of London*, Osprey Publishing

Lewis, Matthew, *Henry III: The Son of Magna Carta* Stroud: Amberley, 2016

Lewis, Suzanne (1987), *The Art of Matthew Paris in the Chronica Majora,* Berkeley, CA: University of California Press

Lockwood, Henry Francis, and Cates, Adolphus H. (1834), *The History and Antiquities of the Fortifications to the City of York*, J. Weale, Charles White, J. Lee, J. Noble, J. & G. Todd

Maddicott, J.R. (1994), *Simon de Montfort*, Cambridge: Cambridge University Press

McBrien, Richard (1995), *The HarperCollins Encyclopaedia of Catholicism*, San Francisco, CA: HarperCollins

McLynn, Frank (2006), *Lionheart and Lackland: King Richard, King John and the Wars of Conquest*, Vintage, London

Milman, Henry Hart (1868), *Annals of St Paul's Cathedral*, John Murray

Mitchell, Sydney Knox (1914), *Studies in Taxation under John and Henry III*, Yale University Press

Morris, Marc (2009), *A Great and Terrible King: Edward I and the Forging of Britain*, Windmill Books, London

— *King John: Treachery, Tyranny and the Road to Magna Carta* (2015) London: Windmill

Mortimer, Ian (2009), *The Time Traveller's Guide to Medieval England*, Vintage, London

Mortimer, Richard (1994), *Angevin England 1154–1258,* Oxford: Blackwell

Moule, Thomas (1860), *Descriptive Account of the Cathedral Church of York,* David Borgue

Nicolle, David (2002), *Medieval Siege Weapons: Western Europe AD 585–1385*, Oxford: Osprey Publishing

Noake, John (1866), *The Monastery and Cathedral at Worcester*, Longman & Co

Norgate, Kate, *The Minority of Henry III,* London: MacMillan and Co, 1912

Ohlgren, Thomas (1998), *Medieval Outlaws*, Stroud: Sutton Publishing

Parker, John Henry (1859), *An Introduction to the Study of Gothic Architecture*, John Henry Parker

Pettifer, Adam (1995), *English Castles: A Guide by Counties,* Woodbridge: Boydell Press

Polluck, Frederick, and Maitland, F.W. (2007), *The History of English Law before the Time of Edward I*, Clark, NJ: Lawbook Exchange

Powicke, Maurice (1947), *King Henry III and the Lord Edward*, Vols 1–2, Oxford: Clarendon Press

— (1962) *The Oxford History of England: The Thirteenth Century 1216–1377*, Oxford: Clarendon Press

Prestwich, Michael (1997), *Edward I*, New Haven, CT: Yale University Press

Prestwich, Michael, Britnell, Richard, and Frame, Robin (2005), *Thirteenth Century England X*, Woodbridge: Boydell Press

Prothero, George Walter (1877), *The Life of Simon de Montfort Earl of Leicester with Special Reference to the Parliamentary History of His Time*, Longmans

Pugin, A. (1838), *Ancient Edifices in England,* Vols 1–2, Henry G. Bohn

Reeve, Matthew M. (2008), *Thirteenth-Century Wall Painting of Salisbury Cathedral*, Woodbridge: Boydell Press

Ruskin, John (1854), *On the Nature of Gothic Architecture*, Smith, Elder & Co.

Soden, Iain, *Ranulf de Blondeville: The First English Hero,* Stroud: Amberley, 2013

Steane, John (1993), *The Archeology of the Medieval English Monarchy*, New York, NY: B.T. Batsford

Stone, John Benjamin (1870), *A History of Lichfield Cathedral with a Description of Its Architecture and Monuments,* Longmans, Green, Reader and Dyer

Stoughton, John (1862), *Windsor: A History and Description of the Castle and the Town*, Ward & Co.

Tout, Thomas Frederick (1900), *Richard, Earl of Cornwall: A Short Biography*, Oxford: Oxford University Press

— (1906) *The History of England: From the Accession of Henry III to the Death of Edward III (1216–1377),* Longman's, Green & Co

— (1933), *Chapters in the Administrative History of Medieval England,* Manchester: Manchester University Press

Vincent, Nicholas, *A Brief History of Britain 1066–1485: The Birth of a Nation*, London: Constable and Robinson, 2011

— *Peter des Roches: An Alien in English Politics, 1205–1238,* Cambridge: Cambridge University Press, 1996

Warton, T., *et al.* (1808), *Essays on Gothic Architecture*, J. Taylor

Whatley, Paul Rapin de Thoyras (1726), *Acta Regia, or an Account of the Treaties, Letters, and Instruments ...* J. Darby *et al.*

Wheeler, J. (1842), *A Short History of the Tower of London with a List of the Interesting Curiousities Contained in the Armories and Regalia*, T. Hodgson

Winkles, Benjamin, and Moule, Thomas (1838), *Winkles's Architectural amd Picturesque Illustrations of the Cathedral Churches of England and Wales*, Vols 1–2, Effingham Wilson

Woolgar, C.M. (2006), *The Senses in Late Medieval England*, New Haven, CT: Yale University Press

Notes and References

In certain cases, the sources used were eBooks. Due to their layouts, it has not always been possible to include exact page references.

Chapter 1 – 940–1204: The Devil's Brood

1. Giles, *Wendover*, pp. 377-80; Morris, *King John*, pp. 282-84.
2. Hallam, *Plantagenet*, p. 252; Stubbs, *Coventry*, pp. 141-42.
3. Carpenter, *Mastery*, p. 191; Hallam, *Plantagenet*, p. 49.
4. Vincent, *Britain*, p. 175.
5. Hallam, *Plantagenet*, pp. 19-30.
6. Hallam, *Plantagenet*, pp. 19-28.
7. Hallam, *Plantagenet*, pp. 38-47.
8. Vincent, *Britain*, pp. 175-79; Hallam, *Plantagenet*, pp. 19-30, 43-47.
9. Hallam, *Plantagenet*, pp. 43-88.
10. Vincent, *Britain*, p. 216.
11. Hallam, *Plantagenet*, pp. 91-97.
12. Hallam, *Plantagenet*, p. 22.
13. Hallam, *Plantagenet*, p. 125.
14. Hallam, *Plantagenet*, p. 125.
15. Gillingham, *Richard*, p. 118.
16. Luard, 'Burton', p. 198; Giles, *Wendover*, pp. 179-81; Morris, *King John*, pp. 105-25.
17. Luard, 'Dunstable', pp. 24-25.
18. Luard, 'Dunstable', p. 27; Luard, 'Margam', p. 24; Luard, 'Burton', p. 198; Luard, 'Wintonia', p. 72; Carpenter, *Mastery*, p. 263; Stubbs, *Coventry*, pp. 143-46; Giles, *Wendover*, pp. 180-81; Asbridge, *The Greatest Knight*, pp. 233-36.
19. Hallam, *Plantagenet*, pp. 238-39.
20. Hallam, *Plantagenet*, p. 262; Luard, 'Burton', pp. 202-03; Giles, *Wendover*, p. 200.

21. Luard, 'Dunstable', p. 27; Luard, 'Burton', pp. 199-200, 203-06; Luard, 'Wintonia', p. 74; Luard, 'Waverley', p. 252; Giles, *Wendover*, p. 184; Carpenter, *Mastery*, pp. 263-64.
22. Hallam, *Plantagenet*, pp. 259-62; Morris, pp. 112-16.
23. Luard, 'Burton', p. 201.
24. Luard, 'Burton', p. 202; Hallam, *Plantagenet*, pp. 259-62.
25. Luard, 'Dunstable', p. 28; Luard, 'Margam', p. 25; Luard, 'Waverley', p. 251; Hallam, *Plantagenet*, p. 259.
26. Luard, 'Burton', p. 206; Luard, 'Wintonia', p. 74; Giles, *Wendover*, p. 193.
27. Luard, 'Burton', p. 207; Carpenter, *Mastery*, p. 264.
28. Luard, 'Burton', p. 208; Giles, *Wendover*, p. 202.
29. Luard, 'Margam', p. 27; Hallam, *Plantagenet*, pp. 272-74.
30. Carpenter, *Mastery*, p. 264; Hallam, *Plantagenet*, pp. 272-74.
31. Luard, 'Margam', pp. 26-27; Luard, 'Burton', p. 209; Luard, 'Wintonia', p. 78; Luard, 'Waverley', p. 254; Giles, *Wendover*, pp. 204-05; Carpenter, *Mastery*, p. 275; Hallam, *Plantagenet*, pp. 274-75.
32. Giles, *Wendover*, pp. 204-07; Asbridge, *The Greatest Knight*, pp. 276-77; Harwood, pp. 22-27.
33. Giles, *Wendover*, pp. 205-06; Hallam, *Plantagenet*, p. 274.
34. Carpenter, *Mastery*, pp. 264-65; Hallam, *Plantagenet*, p. 274.
35. Hallam, *Plantagenet*, pp. 274-80; Luard, 'Waverley', pp. 255-56; Giles, *Wendover*, pp. 206-08, 214.
36. Hallam, *Plantagenet*, p. 280; Luard, 'Tewkesbury', p. 57.

Chapter 2 – 1204–1213: In God We Trust

1. Giles, *Wendover*, pp. 207-13.
2. Vincent, *des Roches*, pp. 28-29.
3. Luard, 'Margam', p. 27; Giles, *Wendover*, pp. 214-15; Morris, pp. 96-99.
4. Luard, 'Tewkesbury', p. 57; Luard, 'Waverley', pp. 257-58; Giles, *Wendover*, pp. 218-19; Morris, pp. 96-99.
5. Luard, 'Waverley', p. 256; Hallam, *Plantagenet*, pp. 266-67, Morris, pp. 117, 121.
6. Luard, 'Margam', p. 28; Luard, 'Wintonia', p. 79; Luard, 'Waverley', p. 257; Giles, *Wendover*, pp. 215-16.

7. Luard, 'Dunstable', p. 30; Luard, 'Bermondsey', p. 450; Luard, 'Margam', p. 28; Luard, 'Tewkesbury', p. 58; Luard, 'Burton', pp. 209-11; Luard, 'Wintonia', pp. 79-80; Luard, 'Waverley', p. 258-59; Luard, 'Wigornia', p. 395; Giles, *Wendover*, pp. 217-18, 238-44.
8. Giles, *Wendover*, pp. 244-45.
9. Luard, 'Dunstable', p. 30; Luard, 'Margam', p. 29; Luard, 'Tewkesbury', p. 58; Luard, 'Burton', pp. 209-11; Luard, 'Wintonia', p. 80; Luard, 'Waverley', p. 260; Luard, 'Wigornia', p. 396; Giles, *Wendover*, pp. 245-48; Hallam, *Plantagenet*, p. 290.
10. Luard, 'Wintonia', p. 73, 77; Giles, *Wendover*, p. 184.
11. Giles, *Wendover*, p. 246; McLynn, pp. 374-78.
12. Luard, 'Dunstable', p. 30.
13. Luard, 'Dunstable', p. 31; Luard, 'Waverley', p. 265; Vincent, *des Roches*, p. 83; Hallam, *Plantagenet*, pp. 288-90.
14. Luard, 'Dunstable', p. 32.
15. Giles, *Wendover*, pp. 249-51; Hallam, *Plantagenet*, p. 290.
16. Stubbs, *Coventry*, p. 204; Giles, *Wendover*, pp. 293-94.
17. Luard, 'Dunstable', p. 34.
18. Luard, 'Dunstable', p. 35; Stubbs, *Coventry*, p. 205; Hallam, *Plantagenet*, p. 294; Morris, pp. 214-15.
19. Luard, 'Tewkesbury', p. 60; Luard, 'Wintonia', p. 82; Luard, 'Waverley', p. 268; Luard, 'Wigornia', p. 400; Stubbs, *Coventry*, pp. 205-06.
20. Luard, 'Waverley', p. 268; Giles, *Wendover*, pp. 255-56; Morris, pp. 202-05
21. Hallam, *Plantagenet*, p. 293; Giles, *Wendover*, pp. 255-56; Luard, Margam, pp. 30, 32; Luard, 'Tewkesbury', pp. 59-60.
22. Luard, 'Waverley', p. 268; Carpenter, *Mastery*, p. 285; Morris, p. 205, 220.
23. Davis, Tower, p. 9.
24. Luard, 'Waverley', p. 268.
25. Stubbs, *Coventry*, p. 207; Vincent, *Britain*, p. 240; Hallam, *Plantagenet*, p. 296.
26. Hallam, *Plantagenet*, p. 289, 300; Stubbs, *Coventry*, pp. 207-08.
27. Luard, 'Dunstable', p. 36; Luard, 'Bermondsey', p. 453; Luard, 'Tewkesbury', pp. 60-61; Luard, 'Burton', pp. 217-23; Luard, 'Wintonia', p. 82; Luard, 'Waverley', p. 275; Luard, 'Osney', p. 56; Luard, 'Wigornia', p. 402; Stubbs, *Coventry*, p. 210; Hardy, *Rymer's Fœdera,* p. 17; Giles, *Wendover*, pp. 261-70.

28. Luard, 'Wintonia', p. 81; Luard, 'Osney', p. 56; Luard, 'Wigornia', pp. 399-400; Vincent, *des Roches*, pp. 80-81.
29. Luard, 'Dunstable', p. 37.
30. Luard, 'Dunstable', p. 37; Luard, 'Bermondsey', p. 453; Luard, 'Wintonia', p. 82; Luard, 'Waverley', p. 276; Luard, 'Waverley', p. 281; Luard, 'Wigornia', p. 402; Giles, *Wendover*, p. 273-75; Carpenter, *Mastery*, p. 286; Vincent, *des Roches*, pp. 88-93; Stubbs, *Coventry*, p. 213; Hardy, *Rymer's Fœdera*, p. 18.
31. Luard, 'Dunstable', p. 36; Giles, *Wendover*, pp. 293-95.
32. Luard, 'Wintonia', pp. 80-81; Luard, 'Waverley', p. 264, 266; Giles, *Wendover*, p. 253-54.
33. Luard, 'Dunstable', p. 41; Luard, 'Tewkesbury', p. 61; Luard, 'Burton', p. 224; Luard, 'Waverley', pp. 280-81; Luard, 'Osney', p. 58; Luard, 'Wigornia', p. 403; Giles, *Wendover*, pp. 293-303; Vincent, *des Roches*, pp. 102-04.
34. Luard, 'Dunstable', p. 42; Vincent, *des Roches*, pp. 102-04; Hardy, *Rymer's Fœdera*, p. 19.

Chapter 3 – 1214–1215: From Runnymede to the Wash

1. Vincent, *Britain*, p. 233.
2. Giles, *Wendover*, pp. 303-06; Holt, *Magna Carta*, pp. 135-38; Danziger and Gillingham, pp. 255-56; Davis, *The Gothic King*, p. 22.
3. Hardy, *Rymer's Fœdera*, p. 11, 15; Carpenter, *Mastery*, p. 135, 159; Holt, *Magna Carta*, pp. 22, 135-38; Holt, *Northerners*, p. 102.
4. Giles, *Wendover*, p. 276-78; Carpenter, *Mastery*, p. 287; Vincent, *des Roches*, p. 105.
5. Luard, 'Osney', p. 58; Hardy, *Rymer's Fœdera*, p. 20; Giles, *Wendover*, pp. 304-05; Holt, *Magna Carta*, p. 139.
6. Giles, *Wendover*, pp. 306-08; Carpenter, *Mastery*, p. 287; Hardy, *Rymer's Fœdera*, p. 20; Danziger and Gillingham, *1215*, pp. 255-60; Holt, *Magna Carta*, p. 153; Holt, *Northerners*, p. 107; Hallam, *Plantagenet*, p. 308.
7. Carpenter, Reign, pp. 1-16.
8. Luard, 'Dunstable', p. 43; Hardy, *Rymer's Fœdera*, p. 20; Carpenter, Reign, pp. 1-16.
9. Hardy, *Rymer's Fœdera*, p. 21; Vincent, *des Roches*, p. 122.

10. Hardy, *Rymer's Fœdera,* p. 21; Giles, *Wendover*, pp. 320-34; Holt, *Magna Carta*, p. 266.
11. Hardy, *Rymer's Fœdera,* p. 21.
12. Luard, 'Dunstable', p. 43; Giles, *Wendover*, pp. 340-3, 346-8; Vincent, *des Roches*, pp. 125-26.
13. Luard, 'Dunstable', p. 44; Luard, 'Tewkesbury', p. 62; Luard, 'Wigornia', p. 405; Giles, *Wendover*, pp. 334-40; Danziger and Gillingham, *1215*, p. 266.
14. Giles, *Wendover*, pp. 350-53.
15. Luard, 'Waverley', p. 281.
16. Giles, *Wendover*, p. 257.
17. Giles, *Wendover*, pp. 348-50; Danziger and Gilligham, *1215*, pp. 266-68.
18. Luard, 'Waverley', p. 284; Powicke, *Thirteenth Century*, p. 1; Giles, *Wendover*, pp. 340-41; Holt, *Northerners*, p. 1; Hardy, *Rymer's Fœdera,* p. 21.
19. Luard, 'Dunstable', p. 38; Vincent, *des Roches*, pp. 91, 115.
20. Giles, *Wendover*, pp. 361-64.
21. Luard, 'Burton', p. 224; Luard, 'Waverley', p. 283; Giles, *Wendover*, pp. 357-59, 362-64.
22. Luard, 'Dunstable', p. 45; Luard, 'Wigornia', p. 406; Vincent, *des Roches*, p. 126; Giles, *Wendover*, pp. 364-67.
23. Luard, 'Dunstable', p. 45; Luard, 'Waverley', p. 285; Stubbs, *Coventry*, p. 228; Carpenter, *Mastery*, p. 299; Carpenter, *Minority*, p. 30; Vincent, *des Roches*, pp. 126-27.
24. Luard, 'Wigornia', p. 406; Vincent, *des Roches*, p. 126.
25. Powicke, *Henry III*, p. 2; Vincent, *des Roches*, pp. 126-27; Luard, 'Waverley', p. 285; Luard, 'Wintonia', pp. 82-83.
26. Vincent, *des Roches*, pp. 126-27; Luard, 'Waverley', p. 285; Luard, 'Wintonia', pp. 82-83.
27. Luard, 'Dunstable', p. 47; Giles, *Wendover*, pp. 374-77.
28. Holt, *Northerners*, pp. 132-33.
29. Carpenter, *Mastery*, p. 299; Holt, *Northerners*, p. 138.
30. Giles, *Wendover*, pp. 377-78; Hallam, *Plantagenet*, pp. 317-20.
31. Luard, 'Dunstable', p. 48; Luard, 'Tewkesbury', p. 62; Luard, 'Burton', p. 224; Luard, 'Wintonia', p. 83; Luard, 'Waverley', p. 286; Luard, 'Wigornia', p. 407; Stubbs, *Coventry*, p. 231; Hallam, *Plantagenet*, p. 320.

32. Hallam, *Plantagenet*, p. 320.
33. Giles, *Wendover*, p. 379.
34. Luard, 'Waverley', p. 282; Carpenter, *Minority*, pp. 5-6.
35. Giles, *Wendover*, p. 379.
36. Hallam, *Plantagenet*, p. 22.

Chapter 4 – 1146–1216: The 'Greatest Knight'

1. Stubbs, *Coventry*, p. 232; Giles, *Wendover*, pp. 378-79.
2. Giles, *Wendover*, pp. 378-79; Powicke, *Henry III*, p. 1; Powicke, *Thirteenth Century*, p. 1.
3. Hallam, *Plantagenet*, p. 104.
4. Luard, 'Tewkesbury', p. 27; Powicke, *Henry III*, p. 1.
5. Luard, 'Waverley', p. 253.
6. Luard, 'Burton', pp. 211-13; Luard, 'Wigornia', p. 394, 401; Giles, *Wendover*, pp. 378-79; Powicke, *Henry III*, p. 1.
7. Powicke, *Henry III*, p. 1.
8. Luard, 'Burton', p. 224; Luard, 'Wintonia', pp. 82-83; Luard, 'Waverley', pp. 251, 284, 286; Luard, 'Wigornia', p. 407; Giles, *Wendover*, pp. 343-46, 398.
9. Luard, 'Wigornia', p. 406; Luard, *England and Rome*, p. 11.
10. Giles, *Wendover*, p. 378; Hallam, *Plantagenet*, p. 323.
11. Carpenter, *Minority*, p. 14; Asbridge, *The Greatest Knight*, pp. 4-5, 31-33, 389.
12. Asbridge, *The Greatest Knight*, pp. 26-29.
13. Asbridge, *The Greatest Knight*, pp. 31-85.
14. Asbridge, *The Greatest Knight*, pp. 61-72; Hallam, *Plantagenet*, p. 235.
15. Asbridge, *The Greatest Knight*, pp. 58, 72-87.
16. Asbridge, *The Greatest Knight*, pp. 85-104.
17. Asbridge, *The Greatest Knight*, pp. 115-39.
18. Asbridge, *The Greatest Knight*, pp. 139-71.
19. Asbridge, *The Greatest Knight*, pp. 175-204, 207-09.
20. Asbridge, *The Greatest Knight*, pp. 205-211.
21. Asbridge, *The Greatest Knight*, pp. 213-16.
22. Asbridge, *The Greatest Knight*, pp. 216-18.
23. Asbridge, *The Greatest Knight*, pp. 222-29.

24. Asbridge, *The Greatest Knight*, pp. 230-56.
25. Carpenter, *Mastery*, p. 263.
26. Asbridge, *The Greatest Knight*, pp. 254-61.
27. Carpenter, *Mastery*, p. 263.
28. Asbridge, *The Greatest Knight*, pp. 258-60.
29. Luard, 'Burton', p. 199; Luard, 'Wintonia', p. 72; Stubbs, *Coventry*, p. 146; Asbridge, *The Greatest Knight*, pp. 260-61.
30. Luard, 'Margam', p. 27; Luard, 'Tewkesbury', p. 57; Luard, 'Wintonia', p. 79; Luard, 'Waverley', p. 256; Asbridge, *The Greatest Knight*, pp. 280.
31. Asbridge, *The Greatest Knight*, pp. 280-84.
32. Asbridge, *The Greatest Knight*, pp. 280-86.
33. Luard, 'Wigornia', p. 394; Carpenter, *Mastery*, p. 283; Asbridge, *The Greatest Knight*, pp. 297-99.
34. Asbridge, *The Greatest Knight*, pp. 299-311.
35. Carpenter, *Mastery*, p. 278.
36. Luard, 'Margam', p. 29; Luard, 'Wintonia', p. 81; Luard, 'Waverley', pp. 261-62, 265; Luard, 'Osney', p. 54; Luard, 'Wigornia', p. 396; Asbridge, *The Greatest Knight*, pp. 311-14.
37. Asbridge, *The Greatest Knight*, pp. 314-16.
38. Asbridge, *The Greatest Knight*, pp. 319-321.
39. Asbridge, *The Greatest Knight*, pp. 319-325.
40. Norgate, *Minority*, chap 1.
41. Asbridge, *The Greatest Knight*, pp. 337-339.

Chapter 5 – 1216: The Hollow Chaplet

1. Luard, 'Dunstable', p. 48; Luard, 'Osney', p. 60; Luard, 'Wigornia', p. 407.
2. Powicke, *Thirteenth Century*, p. 1.
3. Carpenter, *Minority*, p. 19; Carpenter, *Mastery*, p. 300; Davis, *The Gothic King*, p. 15; Hunt, *Henry III*.
4. Carpenter, *Minority*, p. 20.
5. Luard, 'Dunstable', p. 29; Luard, 'Bermondsey', p. 451; Luard, 'Margam', p. 29; Luard, 'Tewkesbury', p. 58; Luard, 'Burton', p. 209; Luard, 'Wintonia', p. 80; Luard, 'Wigornia', p. 395.
6. Giles, *Wendover*, pp. 206-08; Danziger and Gillingham, *1215*, p. 161.

7. Davis, *The Gothic King*, p. 45.

8. Davis, *The Gothic King*, p. 45.

9. Carpenter, *Henry III*, chap 1.

10. Luard, 'Dunstable', p. 31; Luard, 'Bermondsey', p. 451; Luard, 'Margam', p. 29; Luard, 'Tewkesbury', p. 59; Giles, *Wendover*, p. 244; Carpenter, *Henry III*, chap 1.

11. Luard, 'Osney', p. 54.

12. Giles, *Wendover*, pp. 378-79; Carpenter, *Henry III*, chap 1.

13. Powicke, *Henry III*, p. 2; Powicke, *Thirteenth Century*, p. 1.

14. Hallam, *Chivalry*, p. 23.

15. Hallam, *Chivalry*, p. 23; Norgate, *Minority*, chap 1.

16. Hallam, *Chivalry*, p. 26; Norgate, *Minority*, chap 1; Carpenter, *Minority*, pp. 13-14; Carpenter, *Henry III*, chap 1.

17. Luard, 'Tewkesbury', p. 62; Hallam, *Chivalry*, p. 26.

18. Luard, 'Burton', p. 224; Giles, *Wendover*, pp. 379-81; Hallam, *Chivalry*, p. 26; Powicke, *Thirteenth Century*, pp. 1-2; Holt, *Magna Carta*, pp. 100-01.

19. Vincent, *des Roches*, p. 134; Hennings, *England Under Henry III*, p. 1.

20. Luard, 'Tewkesbury', p. 62; Luard, 'Wintonia', p. 83; Luard, 'Waverley', p. 286; Hallam, *Chivalry*, p. 26; Powicke, *Henry III*, pp. 1-2; Tout, *Richard, Earl of Cornwall*, p. 20; Norgate, *Minority*, chap 1.

21. Hallam, *Chivalry*, p. 26 .

22. Norgate, *Minority*, chap 1; Powicke, *Thirteenth Century*, pp. 3-4; Hennings, *England Under Henry III*, pp. 1-2.

23. Giles, *Wendover*, pp. 374-77; Hardy, *Rymer's Fœdera,* p. 22; Tout, *Richard, Earl of Cornwall*, p. 22; Powicke, *Henry III*, pp. 1-6; Powicke, *Thirteenth Century*, pp. 3-4; Carpenter, *Minority*, pp. 19-23.

24. Giles, *Wendover*, p. 381.

25. Luard, *England and Rome*, p. 12.

26. Giles, *Wendover*, pp. 378-79.

27. Hallam, *Chivalry*, pp. 26-29.

Chapter 6 – 1216–1217: The Long Winter

1. Luard, 'Wigornia', p. 405; Carpenter, *Minority*, p. 20.

2. Hallam, *Chivalry*, p. 26; Carpenter, *Minority*, p. 20.

3. Carpenter, *Minority*, p. 22.

4. Hallam, *Chivalry*, p. 26; Carpenter, *Minority*, p. 20; Norgate, *Minority*, chap 1.
5. Carpenter, *Minority*, p. 16; *L'Histoire*, lines 15500-04.
6. Stubbs, *Consitutional*, p. 47; Eales, *DNB*.
7. Hallam, *Chivalry*, p. 28; Carpenter, *Minority*, p. 19; Norgate, *Minority*, chap 1.
8. Carpenter, *Minority*, p. 13.
9. Luard, 'Waverley', p. 288; Stubbs, *Coventry*, p. 234; Luard, *England and Rome*, p. 16; Powicke, *Henry III*, p. 2; Tout, *Richard, Earl of Cornwall*, p. 21; Norgate, *Minority*, chap 1.
10. Carpenter, *Minority*, pp. 21-23; Norgate, *Minority*, chap 1 .
11. Powicke, *Thirteenth Century*, p. 2; Carpenter, *Minority*, p. 22.
12. Powicke, *Thirteenth Century*, pp. 2-3; Vincent, *des Roches*, pp. 134-35.
13. Norgate, *Minority*, chap 1; Powicke, *Henry III*, p. 5.
14. Luard, 'Wigornia', p. 399; Hardy, *Rymer's Fœdera,* pp. 22-23; Carpenter, *Minority*, p. 22.
15. Powicke, *Thirteenth Century*, p. 8; Powicke, *Thirteenth Century*, p. 15
16. Powicke, *Henry III*, p. 19; Powicke, *Thirteenth Century*, p. 8.
17. Luard, 'Waverley', p. 286.
18. Luard, 'Dunstable', p. 47; Stubbs, *Coventry*, p. 234; Giles, *Wendover*, pp. 381-82; Carpenter, p. 25; Hennings, *England Under Henry III*, pp. 4-5.
19. Luard, *England and Rome*, p. 12; Carpenter, *Minority*, p. 22.
20. Luard, *England and Rome*, p. 12; Carpenter, *Minority*, p. 25.
21. Stubbs, *Coventry*, p. 235; Carpenter, p. 25.
22. Vincent, *des Roches*, p. 135; Powicke, *Henry III*, p. 9.
23. Carpenter, *Minority*, pp. 25-27; Powicke, *Henry III*, pp. 7-9; Hennings, *England Under Henry III*, pp. 4-5.
24. Luard, 'Dunstable', p. 47; Luard, 'Waverley', p. 287; Carpenter, *Minority*, p. 29; Vincent, *des Roches*, pp. 120-21; Tout, *Richard, Earl of Cornwall*, pp. 22-23.
25. Shirley, Royal Letters, p. 529; Luard, *England and Rome*, pp. 12-13; Powicke, pp. 5-6.
26. Luard, *England and Rome*, p. 13.
27. Giles, *Wendover*, p. 382.
28. Norgate, *Minority*, chap 1; Carpenter, *Minority*, p. 27; Powicke, *Henry III*, pp. 9-11.
29. Luard, 'Dunstable', pp. 48-49; Powicke, *Henry III*, p. 10.

30. Knight and Ohlgren, Robin Hood, pp. 668-88.
31. Powicke, *Henry III*, p. 28.
32. Hallam, *Plantagenet*, p. 245, 289.
33. Carpenter, *Minority*, pp. 27-28; Norgate, *Minority*, chap 1.
34. Stubbs, *Coventry*, p. 236; Powicke, *Henry III*, pp. 10-11; Hennings, *England Under Henry III*, p. 5; Carpenter, *Minority*, pp. 27-28; Vincent, *des Roches*, p. 136; Tout, *Richard, Earl of Cornwall*, pp. 23-24; Norgate, *Minority*, chap 1.
35. Hardy, *Rymer's Fœdera,* p. 23.
36. Shirley, Royal Letters, pp. 529-32.
37. Norgate, *Minority*, chap 1; Powicke, pp. 11-12.

Chapter 7 – 1217: God Helps the Marshal

1. Luard, 'Wigornia', p. 408; Stubbs, *Coventry*, p. 236; Hallam, *Chivalry*, pp. 28-29; Tout, *Richard, Earl of Cornwall*, pp. 21-24; Powicke, p. 11.
2. Luard, 'Dunstable', p. 49; Luard, 'Wigornia', p. 408; Stubbs, *Coventry*, p. 237; Hardy, *Rymer's Fœdera,* p. 23; Giles, *Wendover*, p. 389-98; Powicke, *Henry III*, pp. 10-11.
3. Giles, *Wendover*, pp. 389-92; Carpenter, *Minority*, pp. 35-36.
4. Luard, 'Dunstable', p. 50; Luard, 'Burton', p. 224; Luard, 'Wintonia', p. 83; Luard, 'Waverley', p. 287; Luard, 'Osney', pp. 60-61; Luard, 'Wigornia', p. 408; Giles, *Wendover*, pp. 389-98; Carpenter, *Minority*, pp. 35-42; Norgate, *Minority*, chap 1; Powicke, pp. 11-13; Vincent, *des Roches*, pp. 138-39.
5. Luard, 'Dunstable', p. 50; Giles, *Wendover*, pp. 397-98; Tout, *Richard, Earl of Cornwall*, pp. 24-25; Norgate, *Minority*, chap 1; Carpenter, *Minority*, p. 41
6. Luard, 'Dunstable', p. 50.
7. Luard, 'Dunstable', p. 50; Hardy, *Rymer's Fœdera,* p. 22; Carpenter, *Minority*, pp. 40-41; L' Histoire, lines 17031-68.
8. Luard, 'Dunstable', p. 50; Powicke, p. 14; Carpenter, *Minority*, p. 41
9. Vincent, *des Roches*, pp. 174-75; Norgate, *Minority*, chap 1; Hardy, *Rymer's Fœdera,* p. 23; Powicke, pp. 13-14.
10. Shirley, Royal Letters, p. 532.
11. Hardy, *Rymer's Fœdera,* p. 23; Luard, *England and Rome*, pp. 14-15.

12. Carpenter, *Minority*, p. 43.
13. Carpenter, *Minority*, p. 35.
14. Luard, *England and Rome*, pp. 11-12.
15. Luard, 'Dunstable', p. 50; Luard, 'Waverley', pp. 287-88; Luard, 'Wigornia', p. 408; Stubbs, *Coventry*, p. 238; Carpenter, *Minority*, pp. 43-44; Norgate, *Minority*, chap 2; Powicke, *Thirteenth Century*, pp. 13-14.
16. Powicke, *Henry III*, pp. 16-29; Powicke, *Thirteenth Century*, pp. 13-14; Carpenter, *Minority*, p. 44; Hardy, *Rymer's Fœdera*, p. 23; Tout, *Richard, Earl of Cornwall*, p. 26.
17. Hardy, *Rymer's Fœdera*, p. 23.
18. Luard, 'Dunstable', pp. 50-51; Luard, 'Burton', p. 224; Luard, 'Wintonia', p. 83; Luard, 'Waverley', pp. 287-88; Luard, 'Osney', p. 61; Giles, *Wendover*, pp. 401-04; Vincent, *des Roches*, p. 141.

Chapter 8 – 1217–1219: Tearful Farewells

1. Luard, 'Dunstable', p. 53.
2. Giles, *Wendover*, pp. 388, 404.
3. Luard, 'Dunstable', p. 51; Powicke, *Henry III*, p. 20, 23; Carpenter, *Minority*, p. 50.
4. Luard, 'Waverley', p. 289; Tout, *Richard, Earl of Cornwall*, p. 27.
5. Norgate, *Minority*, chap 2.
6. Danziger and Gillingham, *1215*, pp. 123-35; Harwood, p. 81; Carpenter, *Minority*, p. 91; Carpenter, *Henry III*, chap 1.
7. Luard, *England and Rome*, p. 15.
8. Hardy, *Rymer's Fœdera*, p. 23; Luard, *England and Rome*, p. 15.
9. Hennings, *England Under Henry III*, pp. 10-11.
10. Powicke, *Thirteenth Century*, p. 16.
11. Giles, *Wendover*, p. 404; Carpenter, *Henry III*, chap 1.
12. Powicke, *Thirteenth Century*, p. 16; Carpenter, *Minority*, pp. 70, 74-78; Tout, *Richard, Earl of Cornwall*, p. 28.
13. Hardy, *Rymer's Fœdera*, pp. 23-24.
14. Carpenter, *Minority*, pp. 1, 81-82; Hardy, *Rymer's Fœdera*, p. 23.
15. Carpenter, *Minority*, pp. 57-58, 71-73, 85-88, 147, 229.
16. Giles, *Wendover*, pp. 404-05; Carpenter, *Minority*, pp. 74-78, 84-85.

17. Carpenter, *Minority*, pp. 92-93; Hardy, *Rymer's Fœdera*, p. 24.
18. Powicke, *Thirteenth Century*, p. 16; Hardy, *Rymer's Fœdera*, p. 24; Hunt, *Henry III*.
19. Luard, 'Waverley', p. 291; Powicke, *Thirteenth Century*, p. 16.
20. Luard, 'Waverley', p. 291; Luard, 'Wigornia', pp. 410-11; Shirley, *Royal Letters*, pp. 533-34; Luard, *England and Rome*, p. 17; Luard, 'Waverley', p. 291; Carpenter, *Minority*, pp. 93-103.
21. Luard, 'Dunstable', p. 53.
22. Powicke, *Thirteenth Century*, pp. 16-17; Tout, *Richard, Earl of Cornwall*, pp. 30-31; Carpenter, *Minority*, p. 133
23. Luard, 'Tewkesbury', p. 63; Luard, 'Waverley', p. 289; Luard, 'Wigornia', pp. 405-06; Luard, 'Wigornia', pp. 409-10; Stubbs, *Coventry*, p. 240; Powicke, *Henry III*, p. 1; Luard, *England and Rome*, p. 17.
24. Hardy, *Rymer's Fœdera*, p. 24; Luard, *England and Rome*, p. 17.
25. Carpenter, *Minority*, pp. 169-70.
26. Carpenter, *Minority*, pp. 103-04.
27. Carpenter, *Minority*, p. 104.
28. Carpenter, *Minority*, p. 106.
29. Carpenter, *Minority*, pp. 104-08, 135; Norgate, *Minority*, chap 2; Carpenter, *Henry III*, chap 1.
30. Luard, 'Osney', p. 61; Giles, *Wendover*, pp. 413-14; *L'Histoire*, lined 18979-82; Carpenter, *Minority*, pp. 104-08; Norgate, *Minority*, chap 2.
31. Carpenter, *Mastery*, pp. 300-01.
32. Norgate, *Minority*, chap 2.

Chapter 9 – 1195–1219: The Three Wise Men

1. Carpenter, *Minority*, pp. 128-35; Vincent, *des Roches*, p. 183; Norgate, *Minority*, chap 2.
2. Carpenter, *Mastery*, p. 301; Luard, *England and Rome*, p. 19.
3. Norgate, *Minority*, Notes.
4. Vincent, *des Roches*, pp. 3-4; Carpenter, *Henry III*, chap 1.
5. Carpenter, *Mastery*, p. 264.
6. Vincent, *des Roches*, pp. 15-21, 28.
7. Vincent, *des Roches*, pp. 15-25, 28-29, 39-40.
8. Vincent, *des Roches*, pp. 15-25, 42-50.
9. Vincent, *des Roches*, pp. 45-50.

10. Luard, 'Wintonia', pp. 72-79; Giles, *Wendover*, p. 214; Vincent, *des Roches*, pp. 47-53.
11. Vincent, *des Roches*, pp. 77-78.
12. Vincent, *des Roches*, pp. 56-71.
13. Carpenter, *Mastery*, pp. 286-87; Vincent, *des Roches*, p. 4.
14. Vincent, *des Roches*, pp. 3, 97-98.
15. Vincent, *des Roches*, p. 6, 70, 82.
16. Vincent, *des Roches*, pp. 3, 480.
17. Vincent, *des Roches*, pp. 2-6, 10; Carpenter, *Henry III*, chap 1.
18. Vincent, *des Roches*, pp. 31-33, 94-95.
19. Luard, 'Waverley', p. 274; Giles, *Wendover*, p. 282.
20. Vincent, *des Roches*, p. 92.
21. Vincent, *des Roches*, pp. 36-38, 105.
22. Harwood, pp, 1-10.
23. Carpenter, *Minority*, p. 138; Harwood, pp, 16-18.
24. Harwood, pp, 18-19.
25. Carpenter, *Minority*, p. 139; Harwood, pp, 21-30.
26. Carpenter, *Minority*, pp. 12, 21; Harwood, pp, 30-57, 66-67; Norgate, *Minority*, chap 1.

Chapter 10 – 1219–1220: Rocking the Castles

1. Carpenter, *Minority*, pp. 1, 162, 187; Vincent, *des Roches*, p. 141
2. Carpenter, *Minority*, pp. 116-31.
3. Hardy, *Rymer's Fœdera,* pp. 24-25; Carpenter, *Minority*, p. 104.
4. Luard, 'Dunstable', p. 56; Hardy, *Rymer's Fœdera,* p. 25; Luard, *England and Rome*, p. 18, 20; Carpenter, *Minority*, pp. 176-77.
5. Carpenter, *Minority*, pp. 154, 167.
6. Luard, 'Waverley', p. 290.
7. Stubbs, *Coventry*, p. 242.
8. Luard, 'Dunstable', pp. 54-55; Luard, 'Tewkesbury', p. 64, 66; Luard, 'Burton', p. 225; Luard, 'Wintonia', p. 83; Luard, 'Waverley', p. 292, 295; Luard, 'Wigornia', p. 410-11, 414; Giles, *Wendover*, pp. 405-26, 435-36 .
9. Carpenter, *Minority*, pp. 169-70.
10. Luard, 'Dunstable', p. 57; Luard, 'Tewkesbury', p. 65; Luard, 'Wintonia', p. 83; Luard, 'Waverley', p. 293; Luard, 'Wigornia', p. 412; Giles, *Wendover*, pp. 426-27.

11. Luard, 'Bermondsey', p. 455.
12. Vincent, *des Roches*, p. 154.
13. Luard, 'Dunstable', p. 57; Luard, 'Osney', p. 62.
14. Luard, 'Wigornia', p. 412; Harwood, p. 86; Carpenter, *Henry III*, chap 1
15. Hardy, *Rymer's Fœdera,* p. 25; Shirley, *Royal Letters*, pp. 535-36; Luard, *England and Rome*, p. 21.
16. Carpenter, *Mastery*, p. 270.
17. Luard, 'Dunstable', pp. 57-58; Luard, 'Waverley', p. 291; Carpenter, *Mastery*, p. 304; Luard, 'Wigornia', p. 412.
18. Shirley, *Royal Letters*, pp. 536-37; Luard, *England and Rome*, p. 23.
19. Carpenter, *Minority*, p. 193.
20. Hardy, *Rymer's Fœdera,* p. 25; Luard, *England and Rome*, p. 23; Danziger and Gillingham, *1215*, pp. 161-63.
21. Luard, 'Dunstable', p. 58; Carpenter, *Minority*, pp. 194-96; Hardy, *Rymer's Fœdera,* p. 25.
22. Vincent, *des Roches*, pp. 197-98; Carpenter, *Minority*, pp. 197-200.
23. Giles, *Wendover*, pp. 427-28; Carpenter, *Mastery*, p. 305; Carpenter, *Minority*, pp. 198-99.
24. Luard, 'Dunstable', p. 58; Luard, 'Tewkesbury', p. 65; Luard, 'Waverley', p. 293; Luard, 'Osney', p. 62; Luard, 'Wigornia', p. 412; Hardy, *Rymer's Fœdera,* p. 24; Giles, *Wendover*, p. 428; Luard, *England and Rome*, pp. 18, 24; Carpenter, *Minority*, pp. 195, 200.
25. Luard, 'Dunstable', p. 58; Carpenter, *Minority*, p. 200; Hardy, *Rymer's Fœdera,* p. 25.
26. Hardy, *Rymer's Fœdera,* p. 12, 14, 21-22; Luard, *England and Rome*, p. 15.
27. Hallam, *Plantagenet*, p. 213.
28. Hardy, *Rymer's Fœdera,* p. 25.
29. Luard, 'Dunstable', p. 60; Carpenter, *Minority*, pp. 214-15.
30. Hardy, *Rymer's Fœdera,* pp. 25-26.
31. Carpenter, *Minority*, pp. 229, 266; Hardy, *Rymer's Fœdera,* p. 26.
32. Carpenter, *Minority*, pp. 191-92; Messer, *Joan*, pp. 97-100.
33. Vincent, *des Roches*, p. 136.
34. Carpenter, *Minority*, p. 192.
35. Carpenter, *Minority*, pp. 203-05, 217-18; Hennings, *England Under Henry III*, pp. 16-17.
36. Luard, 'Dunstable', p. 61; Carpenter, *Minority*, pp. 219-200.

37. Hardy, *Rymer's Fœdera,* p. 26.
38. Luard, 'Dunstable', p. 63; Giles, *Wendover,* p. 428-29; Luard, *England and Rome,* p. 23; Carpenter, *Minority,* pp. 230-31.
39. Luard, 'Dunstable', pp. 63-64; Luard, 'Wigornia', p. 413; Stubbs, *Coventry,* p. 249; Powicke, *Thirteenth Century,* pp. 21-22; Tout, *Richard, Earl of Cornwall,* pp. 32-33; Giles, *Wendover,* pp. 428-29.
40. Luard, 'Dunstable', p. 62, 67, 75; Luard, 'Waverley', pp. 293-94, 296; Luard, *England and Rome,* p. 17, 21; Stubbs, *Coventry;* Carpenter, *Minority,* p. 266; Norgate, *Minority,* chap 3.

Chapter 11 – 1221–1223: War and Peace

1. Luard, 'Dunstable', p. 57; Luard, 'Burton', p. 202; Luard, 'Wintonia', p. 74; Luard, 'Waverley', p. 292; Giles, *Wendover,* pp. 197-200; Hardy, *Rymer's Fœdera,* p. 26; Giles, *Wendover,* p. 427; Luard, *England and Rome,* p. 20; Hallam, *Plantagenet,* pp. 264-66.
2. Luard, 'Wintonia', p. 83.
3. Luard, 'Dunstable', p. 62, 67, 75; Luard, 'Waverley', p. 294.
4. Luard, 'Dunstable', p. 66-67, 69.
5. Luard, 'Wintonia', p. 84; Carpenter, *Minority,* pp. 243-46.
6. Luard, 'Dunstable', p. 68; Carpenter, *Minority,* p. 239, 247.
7. Luard, 'Dunstable', p. 68; Stubbs, *Coventry,* p. 250; Vincent, *des Roches,* pp. 26-33.
8. Carpenter, *Minority,* p. 123.
9. Vincent, *des Roches,* pp. 201-04; Carpenter, *Minority,* pp. 249-51, 274-76.
10. Luard, 'Dunstable', p. 75; Stubbs, *Coventry,* p. 260; Carpenter, *Minority,* pp. 256-57, 270; Vincent, *des Roches,* pp. 204-07; Carpenter, *Henry III,* chap 1.
11. Carpenter, *Minority,* pp. 256-62.
12. Carpenter, *Minority,* p. 185, 241; Vincent, *des Roches,* pp. 154-55.
13. Giles, *Wendover,* p. 435; Carpenter, *Minority,* p. 253; Vincent, *des Roches,* p. 200; Carpenter, *Henry III,* chap 1 .
14. Luard, 'Waverley', p. 295; Vincent, *des Roches,* p. 207; Carpenter, *Minority,* p. 254.
15. Vincent, *des Roches,* pp. 105, 125; Vincent, *Britain,* pp. 230-31; Powicke, *Thirteenth Century,* p. 18.

16. Luard, *England and Rome*, p. 24.
17. Luard, 'Dunstable', pp. 68-69; Luard, 'Tewkesbury', p. 65; Luard, 'Wintonia', p. 84; Luard, 'Waverley', p. 294-95; Carpenter, *Minority*, pp. 252-54; Hardy, *Rymer's Fœdera*, p. 26.
18. Carpenter, *Minority*, pp. 270-71; Norgate, *Minority*, chap 3.
19. Luard, 'Dunstable', p. 76; Luard, 'Wintonia', p. 84; Luard, 'Waverley', p. 296; Luard, 'Osney', p. 62.
20. Carpenter, *Minority*, pp. 266, 276-77, 290, 295; Norgate, *Minority*, chap 4.
21. Hallam, *Plantagenet*, p. 297.
22. Luard, 'Dunstable', pp. 78-79; Luard, 'Waverley', p. 297; Giles, *Wendover*, p. 439; Carpenter, *Minority*, pp. 290-91.
23. Giles, *Wendover*, pp. 439-41; Carpenter, *Minority*, pp. 290-91.
24. Giles, *Wendover*, pp. 441-42.
25. Luard, 'Waverley', p. 296.
26. Luard, 'Waverley', p. 297; Luard, 'Wigornia', p. 415; Luard, 'Margam', p. 33; Luard, 'Bermondsey', p. 455; Giles, *Wendover*, pp. 441-42.
27. Luard, 'Dunstable', p. 80; Luard, 'Margam', p. 33; Luard, 'Tewkesbury', p. 66
28. Hardy, *Rymer's Fœdera*, p. 27; Carpenter, *Minority*, pp. 295-96.
29. Luard, *England and Rome*, p. 26; Giles, *Wendover*, p. 443; Hennings, *England Under Henry III*, pp. 147-48.
30. Shirley, *Royal Letters*, p. 538-39; Luard, *England and Rome*, p. 26.
31. Tout, *Richard, Earl of Cornwall*, pp. 34-35.
32. Giles, *Wendover*, pp. 443-44; Tout, *Richard, Earl of Cornwall*, pp. 34-35; Carpenter, pp. 306-08.
33. Giles, *Wendover*, pp. 432-33; Carpenter, *Minority*, pp. 308-13; Powicke, p. 58.
34. Powicke, *Henry III*, p. 58; Hennings, *England Under Henry III*, pp. 17-18.

Chapter 12 – 1223–1224: An Englishman's Home is His Castle

1. Luard, 'Dunstable', p. 81, 85; Luard, 'Tewkesbury', p. 67; Luard, 'Wintonia', p. 84; Luard, 'Waverley', p. 299; Luard, 'Bermondsey', p. 455; Vincent, *des Roches*, p. 234; Norgate, *Minority*, chap 4.

2. Shirley, *Royal Letters*, p. 539; Luard, *England and Rome*, p. 26.
3. Carpenter, *Minority*, pp. 316-20.
4. Powicke, *Henry III*, pp. 58-59; Luard, 'Osney', p. 65; Powicke, *Thirteenth Century*, p. 24.
5. Luard, 'Dunstable', p. 84; Stubbs, *Coventry*, pp. 261-62; Carpenter, *Minority*, pp. 320-22.
6. Luard, 'Dunstable', pp. 83-84; Powicke, *Henry III*, p. 59; Powicke, *Thirteenth Century*, p. 25; Carpenter, *Minority*, pp. 322-23; Norgate, *Minority*, chap 4.
7. Luard, *England and Rome*, p. 27; Luard, 'Dunstable', p. 84; Carpenter, *Minority*, pp. 323-27.
8. Luard, 'Dunstable', p. 84; Carpenter, *Minority*, pp. 323-27.
9. Shirley, *Royal Letters*, p. 548; Luard, *England and Rome*, p. 37; Carpenter, *Minority*, pp. 326-28, 340-41; Norgate, *Minority*, chap 3.
10. Carpenter, *Mastery*, p. 305; Carpenter, *Minority*, pp. 322-23, 326-327.
11. Vincent, *des Roches*, pp. 213-15.
12. Luard, 'Dunstable', p. 81; Luard, 'Tewkesbury', p. 66; Luard, 'Wintonia', p. 84; Luard, 'Osney', p. 63; Giles, *Wendover*, pp. 444-45.
13. Luard, 'Waverley', pp. 298-9; Shirley, *Royal Letters*, pp. 539-40; Powicke, *Thirteenth Century*, p. 15.
14. Hardy, *Rymer's Fœdera,* p. 27; Carpenter, *Minority*, pp. 7, 309-11.
15. Luard, 'Dunstable', pp. 81-82; Carpenter, *Minority*, pp. 309-11; Powicke, *Henry III*, pp. 170-71.
16. Hardy, *Rymer's Fœdera,* p. 26; Luard, pp. 25-27; Tout, *Richard, Earl of Cornwall*, p. 38.
17. Hardy, *Rymer's Fœdera,* p. 26; Luard, *England and Rome*, p. 26; Carpenter, *Minority*, pp. 345, 355-56.
18. Powicke, pp. 170-71; Luard, Luard, *England and Rome*, p. 28; Hardy, *Rymer's Fœdera,* pp. 27-28.
19. Luard, 'Dunstable', p. 86; Shirley, *Royal Letters*, pp. 541-43; Luard, *England and Rome*, p. 29.
20. Carpenter, *Minority*, pp. 355-59.
21. Powicke, *Henry III*, p. 3; Carpenter, *Minority*, pp. 266-67, 370-71.
22. Luard, 'Dunstable', p. 86; Giles, *Wendover*, p. 450.
23. Giles, *Wendover*, p. 450; Tout, *Richard, Earl of Cornwall*, pp. 38-41.

Chapter 13 – 1224: The Baying of Bedford

1. Stubbs, *Coventry*, pp. 268-69; Carpenter, *Minority*, p. 262; Giles, *Wendover*, pp. 450-51.
2. Carpenter, *Minority*, pp. 20-21; Vincent, *des Roches*, pp. 37-38; Stubbs, *Constitutional*, pp. 34-38; Power, *DNB*.
3. Church, *Household*, p. 9; Carpenter, *Mastery*, p. 306.
4. Giles, *Wendover*, p. 384; Powicke, *Henry III*, p. 26; Vincent, *des Roches*, pp. 145-46; Norgate, *Minority*, chap 5.
5. Carpenter, *Minority*, pp. 164-5, 175; Norgate, *Minority*, chap 5.
6. Luard, 'Dunstable', p. 84; Carpenter, *Minority*, pp. 323-27; Norgate, *Minority*, chap 5.
7. Carpenter, *Minority*, pp. 347-48; Norgate, *Minority*, chap 5.
8. Carpenter, *Minority*, pp. 78-79; Luard, *England and Rome*, p. 21.
9. Carpenter, *Minority*, pp. 347-48; Norgate, *Minority*, chap 5.
10. Carpenter, *Minority*, pp. 346-47, 355-56, 360-61; Norgate, *Minority*, chap 5.
11. Luard, 'Dunstable', pp. 86-90; Carpenter, *Minority*, pp. 357-61; Norgate, *Minority*, chap 5.
12. Luard, 'Dunstable', pp. 86-90; Giles, *Wendover*, pp. 450-52; Norgate, *Minority*, chap 5.
13. Luard, 'Dunstable', pp. 86-90; Brown, *Castles*, pp. 181, 190-94; Carpenter, *Minority*, pp. 364-65; Norgate, *Minority*, chap 5.
14. Luard, 'Dunstable', pp. 86-90; Luard, 'Tewkesbury', p. 67; Luard, 'Burton', p. 225; Luard, 'Wintonia', p. 84; Luard, 'Waverley', p. 299-300; Luard, 'Osney', p. 63; Luard, 'Wigornia', p. 416; Giles, *Wendover*, pp. 450-54; Luard, 'Bermondsey', p. 456 ; Norgate, *Minority*, chap 5.
15. Luard, 'Dunstable', pp. 86-90; Brown, *Castles*, pp. 190-94; Norgate, *Minority*, chap 5.
16. Giles, *Wendover*, pp. 453-54; Hennings, *England Under Henry III*, pp. 25-26; Hardy, *Rymer's Fœdera,* p. 28; Norgate, *Minority*, chap 5.
17. Giles, *Wendover*, pp. 454-55; Luard, 'Wigornia', p. 416; Hardy, *Rymer's Fœdera,* p. 28; Tout, *Richard, Earl of Cornwall*, pp. 35-36; Norgate, *Minority*, chap 5.
18. Shirley, *Royal Letters*, pp. 540-41, 543-45; Luard, *England and Rome*, p. 29

19. Hallam, *Chivalry*, p. 27; Carpenter, *Minority*, pp. 366-69.
20. Luard, 'Osney', p. 65; Giles, *Wendover*, p. 458.

Chapter 14 – 1224–1227: The Poitevin Potential

1. Luard, *England and Rome*, p. 28.
2. Luard, 'Dunstable', pp. 91-92; Luard, 'Wintonia', p. 84; Luard, 'Waverley', p. 299; Luard, 'Osney', p. 65; Luard, 'Wigornia', p. 415.
3. Hardy, *Rymer's Fœdera*, p. 28.
4. Luard, 'Dunstable', p. 93; Luard, 'Tewkesbury', p. 68; Luard, 'Burton', pp. 225-36; Luard, 'Waverley', p. 300; Luard, 'Osney', pp. 66-67; Luard, 'Wigornia', p. 417; Hardy, *Rymer's Fœdera*, p. 28; Giles, *Wendover*, pp. 455-56, 458; Carpenter, *Minority*, pp. 376, 379-88; Luard, *England and Rome*, p. 29.
5. Powicke, *Henry III*, pp. 33-34; Vincent, *des Roches*, pp. 196-97; Carpenter, *Minority*, p. 380.
6. Hardy, *Rymer's Fœdera*, p. 28; Luard, *England and Rome*, pp. 29-30.
7. Luard, 'Wintonia', p. 84; Hardy, *Rymer's Fœdera*, p. 28; Carpenter, *Minority*, p. 376; Vincent, *des Roches*, p. 265; Tout, *Richard, Earl of Cornwall*; Denholm-Young, pp. 1-3.
8. Luard, 'Dunstable', p. 94; Vincent, *des Roches*, p. 200, 250; Tout, *Richard, Earl of Cornwall*.
9. Hardy, *Rymer's Fœdera*, p. 28; Giles, *Wendover*, pp. 456-58; Carpenter, *Minority*, pp. 376-78.
10. Luard, 'Dunstable', pp. 98-99; Giles, *Wendover*, pp. 456-58; Carpenter, *Minority*, pp. 376-78
11. Luard, 'Dunstable', pp. 99-100; Giles, *Wendover*, pp. 468-69; Carpenter, *Minority*, p. 378.
12. Harwood, p. 101; Giles, *Wendover*, pp. 460-61, 465-66, 468-69.
13. Luard, 'Dunstable', p. 102; Luard, 'Waverley', p. 280; Tout, *Richard, Earl of Cornwall*, p. 40.
14. Powicke, *Henry III*, p. 159.
15. Luard, 'Waverley', p. 280; Luard, 'Dunstable', p. 89.
16. Luard, 'Dunstable', p. 100; Giles, *Wendover*, pp. 461-62, 469-70; Luard, *England and Rome*, p. 29.
17. Luard, 'Osney', p. 67; Giles, *Wendover*, p. 484; Luard, *England and Rome*, pp. 30-31.

18. Luard, 'Dunstable', p. 99; Giles, *Wendover*, pp. 461-62, 466-68, 472-74; Luard, *England and Rome*, p. 29.
19. Luard, *England and Rome*, pp. 30-31.
20. Shirley, *Royal Letters*, p. 545-47; Luard, *England and Rome*, pp. 33-34.
21. Luard, 'Osney', p. 66; Hardy, *Rymer's Fœdera,* p. 29; Giles, *Wendover*, pp. 475-76; Luard, *England and Rome*, pp. 31-33; Powicke, *Henry III*, pp. 346-47.
22. Luard, 'Osney', pp. 66-67; Hardy, *Rymer's Fœdera,* p. 29; Shirley, *Royal Letters*, p. 548; Luard, *England and Rome*, pp. 31-33.
23. Luard, 'Margam', p. 35; Messer, *Joan*, pp. 120-23.
24. Luard, 'Wintonia', p. 84.
25. Luard, 'Dunstable', p. 101; Luard, 'Tewkesbury', p. 69; Luard, 'Waverley', p. 302; Luard, 'Osney', p. 68; Luard, 'Wigornia', p. 418; Giles, *Wendover*, pp. 478-82.
26. Luard, 'Waverley', p. 302
27. Luard, 'Dunstable', p. 102; Luard, 'Burton', p. 239; Luard, 'Wintonia', p. 84; Luard, 'Waverley', p. 302; Luard, 'Osney', p. 67; Giles, *Wendover*, pp. 478-82
28. Luard, 'Dunstable', p. 102
29. Giles, *Wendover*, pp. 483-85; Tout, *Richard, Earl of Cornwall*, pp. 40-41; Hardy, *Rymer's Fœdera,* p. 29
30. Giles, *Wendover*, p. 485
31. Giles, *Wendover*, pp. 485-87; Carpenter, *Minority*, p. 389; Powicke, *Henry III*, pp. 43-45; Carpenter, *Henry III*, chap 1.
32. Giles, *Wendover*, pp. 485-86.

Chapter 15 – 1227–1230: A Steep Learning Curve

1. Carpenter, *Minority*, p. 109.
2. Giles, *Wendover*, pp. 485-86; Carpenter, *Minority*, pp. 389-90.
3. Luard, 'Dunstable', pp. 102-03; Luard, 'Waverley', p. 303; Harwood, p. 103.
4. *Luard, 'Waverley', p. 303; Vincent, des Roches, p. 225.*
5. *Luard, 'Dunstable', p. 102; Luard, 'Wintonia', p. 85.*
6. *Luard, 'Waverley', p. 303.*
7. *Luard, England and Rome, p. 37.*

8. *Hardy, Rymer's Fœdera, p. 29;* Hunt, *Henry III.*

9. Luard, 'Dunstable', pp. 103-04; Powicke, *Henry III*, pp. 176-77; Powicke, *Thirteenth Century*, pp. 92-94.

10. Luard, 'Dunstable', pp. 103-04; Giles, *Wendover*, pp. 487-88; Carpenter, *Reign of Henry III*, p. 59; Powicke, *Henry III*, pp. 71-72; Powicke, *Thirteenth Century*, pp. 40-42; Carpenter, *Henry III*, chap 2.

11. Luard, 'Wigornia', pp. 420-22; Vincent, *des Roches*, pp. 265-66; Carpenter, *Henry III*, chap 2.

12. Giles, *Wendover*, pp. 487-89; Hunt, *Henry III.*

13. Luard, *England and Rome*, p. 37.

14. Luard, *England and Rome*, p. 38; Giles, *Wendover*, pp. 509-11.

15. Luard, 'Osney', p. 70; Giles, *Wendover*, pp. 509-11; Carpenter, *Mastery*, pp. 311-12; Hunt, *Henry III*; Carpenter, *Henry III*, chap 2.

16. Hardy, *Rymer's Fœdera,* p. 32.

17. Luard, 'Dunstable', p. 117; Giles, *Wendover*, pp. 510-11; Hunt, *Henry III.*

18. Powicke, pp. 175-76.

19. Gasquet, p. 117.

20. Luard, 'Dunstable', p. 107, 109; Luard, 'Margam', p. 36; Luard, 'Tewkesbury', p. 70; Luard, 'Wintonia', p. 85; Luard, 'Waverley', p. 304; Harwood, p. 105; Giles, *Wendover*, pp. 508-09.

21. Luard, 'Dunstable', p. 112; Luard, 'Tewkesbury', p. 71; Giles, *Wendover*, pp. 519-21; Luard, *England and Rome*, p. 39.

22. Luard, 'Dunstable', pp. 107, 111, 116; Luard, 'Tewkesbury', pp. 72-73; Luard, 'Waverley', pp. 303, 307; Luard, 'Osney', p. 69; Luard, 'Wigornia', pp. 419-20; Giles, *Wendover*, pp. 499-531; Luard, *England and Rome*, pp. 39-41.

23. Luard, 'Dunstable', p. 109; Giles, *Wendover*, p. 498; Luard, *England and Rome*, p. 35; Carpenter, *Minority*, p. 390; Carpenter, *Henry III*, chap 1.

24. Luard, 'Tewkesbury', p. 84; Hardy, *Rymer's Fœdera,* p. 31; Giles, *Wendover*, pp. 530-31; Luard, *England and Rome*, p. 39; Vincent, *des Roches*, p. 291-92

25. Luard, 'Dunstable', p. 114; Luard, 'Burton', p. 245; Luard, 'Osney', p. 70; Giles, *Wendover*, pp. 528-31.

26. Luard, 'Dunstable', pp. 114-15; Luard, *England and Rome*, p. 4.

27. Luard, 'Tewkesbury', p. 73; Luard, 'Waverley', p. 306; Giles, *Wendover*, pp. 511-14; Hallam, *Chivalry*, pp. 38-43.

28. Luard, 'Dunstable', p. 125.
29. Luard, 'Dunstable', p. 115; Luard, 'Waverley', p. 301, 304.
30. Hardy, *Rymer's Fœdera,* p. 32.
31. Luard, 'Dunstable', pp. 116-18, 125.
32. Luard, 'Dunstable', pp. 118-24.
33. Giles, *Wendover*, p. 514.
34. Luard, 'Dunstable', p. 115; Luard, 'Waverley', p. 307; Luard, *England and Rome*, p. 40; Powicke, *Henry III*, pp. 175-77; Tout, *Richard, Earl of Cornwall*, pp. 40-41.
35. Giles, *Wendover*, pp. 531-32; Harwood, p. 107; Hunt, *Henry III*; Tout, *Richard, Earl of Cornwall*, pp. 36-41; Giles, *Wendover*, pp. 531-32; Powicke, *Henry III*, p. 72; Powicke, *Thirteenth Century*, pp. 94-95.
36. Luard, 'Dunstable', p. 124; Giles, *Wendover*, p. 533.
37. Giles, *Wendover*, pp. 533-34.
38. Giles, *Wendover*, pp. 534-37; Powicke, *Henry III*, pp. 167-69; Powicke, *Thirteenth Century*, pp. 94-95; Hennings, *England Under Henry III*, pp. 157-58.
39. Luard, 'Dunstable', p. 125; Luard, 'Waverley', p. 308; Luard, 'Wigornia', p. 421; Giles, *Wendover*, pp. 534-35; Luard, 'Tewkesbury', p. 74.
40. Giles, *Wendover*, pp. 534-35; Tout, *Richard, Earl of Cornwall*, pp. 41-42; Powicke, *Henry III*, pp. 167-69; Powicke, *Thirteenth Century*, pp. 94-95.
41. Giles, *Wendover*, pp. 533-38; Luard, 'Margam', p. 38; Tout, *Richard, Earl of Cornwall*, pp. 41-42; Powicke, *Henry III*, pp. 167-69, 182-83; Powicke, *Thirteenth Century*, pp. 94-95; Hennings, *England Under Henry III*, pp. 33-34.

Chapter 16 – 1230–1231: The Awakened Dragon

1. Luard, 'Dunstable', p. 126.
2. Luard, 'Dunstable', p. 125; Giles, *Wendover*, p. 535; Hallam, *Chivalry*, p. 44.
3. Luard, 'Waverley', p. 308.
4. Giles, *Wendover*, pp. 538-39; Powicke, *Henry III*, pp. 167-68, 182-83.

5. Giles, *Wendover*, pp. 538-39; Luard, *England and Rome*, p. 41; Hunt, *Henry III*; Powicke, *Henry III*, pp. 88-89; Powicke, *Thirteenth Century*, pp. 18-19

6. Giles, *Wendover*, pp. 541-42; Luard, *England and Rome*, p. 42.

7. Luard, 'Dunstable', p. 125; Luard, 'Osney', p. 71.

8. Luard, 'Waverley', p. 308; Harwood, pp. 111-13; Carpenter, *Henry III*, chap 2

9. Luard, 'Dunstable', pp. 125-26; Luard, 'Margam', p. 39; Luard, 'Tewkesbury', p. 77; Luard, 'Waverley', p. 309; Luard, 'Osney', p. 71; Luard, 'Wigornia', p. 423; Giles, *Wendover*, pp. 539, 542-44, 552; Luard, *England and Rome*, p. 43.

10. Luard, 'Margam', pp. 37-38; Luard, 'Tewkesbury', p. 74; Luard, 'Wintonia', p. 85; Luard, 'Waverley', p. 309; Luard, 'Osney', p. 71; Luard, 'Wigornia', p. 421; Tout, *Richard, Earl of Cornwall*, pp. 42-43; Giles, *Wendover*, pp. 539-41.

11. Luard, 'Dunstable', p. 126; Luard, 'Margam', p. 38; Luard, 'Tewkesbury', p. 78; Luard, 'Waverley', p. 309; Luard, 'Osney', p. 72; Luard, 'Wigornia', p. 422; Giles, *Wendover*, pp. 539-40.

12. Luard, 'Waverley', p. 309; Carpenter, *Henry III*, chap 2.

13. Giles, *Wendover*, pp. 539-40; Luard, 'Dunstable', p. 126.

14. Luard, 'Osney', p. 70; Hallam, *Chivalry*, pp. 44-46; Giles, *Wendover*, pp. 539-40.

15. Luard, 'Tewkesbury', p. 70; Hallam, *Chivalry*, p. 46; Luard, 'Margam', p. 38; Carpenter, *Henry III*, chap 2.

16. Giles, *Wendover*, pp. 539-41; Hallam, *Chivalry*, p. 46.

17. Luard, 'Dunstable', pp. 126-27; Luard, 'Wintonia', p. 85; Luard, 'Osney', p. 72; Luard, 'Wigornia', p. 422; Giles, *Wendover*, pp. 542-43.

18. Hardy, *Rymer's Fœdera,* p. 32.

19. Luard, 'Dunstable', pp. 126-27; Luard, 'Wigornia', p. 422; Harwood, p. 117; Giles, *Wendover*, pp. 541-42.

20. Vincent, *des Roches*, p. 230.

21. Vincent, *des Roches*, p. 247.

22. Luard, 'Dunstable', pp. 112, 126; Vincent, *des Roches*, p. 248.

23. Vincent, *des Roches*, pp. 248-51.

24. Vincent, *des Roches*, pp. 251-52.

25. Vincent, *des Roches*, pp. 252-54; Giles, *Wendover*, pp. 490-96, 505-08, 511-14, 19, 521-28; Luard, 'Tewkesbury', p. 76; Luard, 'Dunstable', p. 126.

26. Luard, 'Wintonia', p. 86; Luard, 'Waverley', p. 310; Vincent, *des Roches*, p. 254, 257.
27. Luard, 'Wigornia', p. 422; Vincent, *des Roches*, pp. 36-38, 324-26.
28. Vincent, *des Roches*, p. 37.
29. Hardy, *Rymer's Fœdera,* p. 32; Vincent, *des Roches*, p. 273; Giles, *Wendover*, pp. 542-43.
30. Luard, 'Dunstable', p. 127; Giles, *Wendover*, pp. 543, 546-47.
31. Luard, 'Dunstable', p. 128; Hardy, *Rymer's Fœdera,* p. 33; Hennings, *England Under Henry III*, pp. 242-43.
32. Giles, *Wendover*, pp. 546-47; Hallam, *Chivalry*, pp. 46-48.
33. Luard, 'Burton', pp. 239-43; Luard, *England and Rome*, p. 44-46; Hennings, *England Under Henry III*, pp. 35-36; Vincent, *des Roches*, p. 307.
34. Powicke, *Henry III*, p. 79; Carpenter, *Reign of Henry III*, p. 52; Carpenter, *Henry III*, chap 1.
35. Luard, 'Tewkesbury', p. 86; Luard, 'Burton', p. 245; Luard, 'Waverley', p. 311; Luard, 'Osney', p. 73; Luard, 'Wigornia', p. 423; Luard, 'Margam', p. 39; Luard, 'Wigornia', p. 423; Hennings, *England Under Henry III*, pp. 36-39; Hallam, *Chivalry*, pp. 48-52.

Chapter 17 – 1232: The Harrowing of Hubert de Burgh

1. Vincent, *Britain*, p. 209; Giles, *Wendover*, pp. 553-56; Tout, *Richard, Earl of Cornwall*, pp. 40-41; Hallam, *Chivalry*, pp. 48-52; Powicke, *Henry III*, pp. 80-83; Powicke, *Thirteenth Century*, pp. 50-51; Hunt, *Henry III*.
2. Luard, 'Waverley', p. 311; Luard, 'Osney', p. 73; Carpenter, *Minority*, p. 319.
3. Carpenter, *Minority*, p. 117, 304, 325, 331, 350-51.
4. Vincent, *des Roches*, pp. 17, 18, 32, 235, 295; Giles, *Wendover*, p. 565; Carpenter, *Henry III*, chaps 1-2.
5. Powicke, *Henry III*, pp. 80-81; Harwood, pp. 120-23; Vincent, *des Roches*, pp. 313-15; Hallam, *Chivalry*, pp. 48-52; Carpenter, *Henry III*, chap 2.
6. Luard, 'Dunstable', p. 129; Luard, 'Burton', p. 245; Giles, *Wendover*, pp. 557-58; Hennings, *England Under Henry III*, pp. 37-38; Weiler,

Kingship, p. 13; Harwood, pp. 123-25; Vincent, *des Roches*, pp. 314-15; Carpenter, *Henry III*, chap 2.

7. Harwood, p. 121.
8. Giles, *Wendover*, pp. 556-58; Hennings, *England Under Henry III*, pp. 37-38.
9. Luard, 'Tewkesbury', p. 87; Luard, 'Waverley', p. 310; Luard, 'Osney', p. 74; Hardy, *Rymer's Fœdera,* p. 33; Giles, *Wendover*, pp. 555-57, 559-61; Powicke, *Henry III*, p. 35.
10. Luard, 'Dunstable', p. 130; Vincent, *des Roches*, p. 285; Giles, *Wendover*, pp. 555-56.
11. Luard, 'Tewkesbury', p. 87; Luard, 'Burton', p. 245; Luard, 'Osney', p. 73; Giles, *Wendover*, pp. 561-62.
12. Carpenter, *Minority*, p. 253; Giles, *Wendover*, p. 561.
13. Eales, *DNB*; Stubbs, *Constitutional*, p. 47.
14. Luard, 'Waverley', p. 311; Luard, 'Osney', p. 73; Giles, *Wendover*, pp. 557-59; Hennings, *England Under Henry III*, pp. 37-39; Vincent, *des Roches*, p. 201.
15. Giles, *Wendover*, p. 558.
16. Luard, 'Tewkesbury', p. 88; Hardy, *Rymer's Fœdera,* p. 34; Luard, 'Wigornia', p. 424; Hallam, *Chivalry*, pp. 48-52; Vincent, *des Roches*, p. 317; Giles, *Wendover*, p. 561-62; Powicke, *Henry III*, pp. 138-39; Carpenter, *Henry III*, chap 2.
17. Vincent, *des Roches*, p. 363.
18. Vincent, *des Roches*, pp. 3-4.

Chapter 18 – 1232–1233: Between a Rock and a Hard Place

1. Hallam, *Chivalry*, pp. 52-54; Carpenter, *Henry III*, chap 3.
2. Giles, *Wendover*, pp. 565-66; Hennings, *England Under Henry III*, pp. 39-40; Tout, *Richard, Earl of Cornwall*, p. 47; Hunt, *Henry III*.
3. Shirley, *Royal Letters*, p. 551; Luard, *England and Rome*, p. 46.
4. Giles, *Wendover*, pp. 565-66; Carpenter, *Henry III*, chap 3.
5. Vincent, *des Roches*, p. 318, 338, 380-81; Powicke, *Henry III*, p. 128.
6. Carpenter, *Henry III*, chap 3; Vincent, *des Roches*, pp. 334-37.
7. Luard, 'Dunstable', p. 136; Luard, 'Waverley', p. 313; Luard, 'Wigornia', p. 425; Carpenter, *Henry III*, chap 3.

8. Carpenter, *Henry III*, chap 3.
9. Luard, 'Dunstable', p. 136; Luard, 'Waverley', p. 313; Giles, *Wendover*, p. 566.
10. Giles, *Wendover*, p. 566; Luard, 'Dunstable', p. 137; Carpenter, *Henry III*, chap 3.
11. Carpenter, *Henry III*, chap 3; Vincent, *des Roches*, pp. 320-21.
12. Vincent, *des Roches*, pp. 327-28.
13. Carpenter, *Henry III*, chap 3; Vincent, *des Roches*, pp. 338-39.
14. Luard, 'Wigornia', p. 424; Giles, *Wendover*, pp. 566-67.
15. Carpenter, *Henry III*, chap 3.
16. Luard, 'Waverley', p. 312; Luard, 'Osney', pp. 74-76; Luard, 'Wigornia', p. 425; Luard, *England and Rome*, p. 47.
17. Vincent, *des Roches*, p. 377; Carpenter, *Henry III*, chap 3.
18. Vincent, *des Roches*, pp. 377-78; Carpenter, *Henry III*, chap 3.
19. Weiler, *Kingship,* p. 17; Vincent, *des Roches*, pp. 318, 378-79.
20. Carpenter, *Henry III*, chap 3; Vincent, *des Roches*, pp. 378-79.
21. Giles, *Wendover*, pp. 569-71; Vincent, *des Roches*, pp. 380-81.
22. Vincent, *des Roches*, pp. 3-4; Giles, *Wendover*, pp. 569-70; Hallam, *Chivalry*, pp. pp. 52-53; Carpenter, *Henry III*, chap 3.
23. Giles, *Wendover*, pp. 567-70.
24. Giles, *Wendover*, pp. 569-70; Hallam, *Chivalry*, pp. pp. 52-53.
25. Vincent, *des Roches*, pp. 386-87.
26. Vincent, *des Roches*, p. 285.
27. Powicke, *Henry III*, pp. 129-31; Tout, *Richard, Earl of Cornwall*, pp. 48-49; Giles, *Wendover*, pp. 569-71; Carpenter, *Henry III*, chap 3.
28. Carpenter, *Henry III*, chap 3; Vincent, *des Roches*, pp. 386-92; Giles, *Wendover*, pp. 568-71.
29. Giles, *Wendover*, pp. 570-73; Hunt, *Henry III*; Carpenter, *Henry III*, chap 3.
30. Giles, *Wendover*, pp. 572-73; Powicke, *Henry III*, p. 131; Powicke, *Thirteenth Century*, pp. 54-55.
31. Vincent, *des Roches*, p. 409; Giles, *Wendover*, pp. 572-73.

Chapter 19 – 1233–1234: The Marshal War

1. Luard, *England and Rome*, p. 47.

2. Giles, *Wendover*, pp. 571-72.
3. Luard, 'Tewkesbury', p. 91; Luard, 'Waverley', pp. 313-14; Luard, 'Osney', pp. 75-76; Luard, 'Wigornia', p. 425; Giles, *Wendover*, pp. 571-73; Hallam, *Chivalry*, pp. 52-53; Powicke, *Henry III*, pp. 138-40.
4. Carpenter, *Henry III*, chap 3.
5. Giles, *Wendover*, pp. 572-73.
6. Luard, 'Tewkesbury', p. 92; Carpenter, *Henry III*, chap 3; Vincent, *des Roches*, p. 380.
7. Carpenter, *Henry III*, chap 3.
8. Luard, 'Dunstable', p. 137; Luard, 'Tewkesbury', p. 91; Giles, *Wendover*, pp. 572-74.
9. Giles, *Wendover*, pp. 574-76.
10. Luard, 'Tewkesbury', p. 91; Luard, 'Waverley', p. 312; Vincent, *des Roches*, p. 419; Giles, *Wendover*, pp. 580-82; Carpenter, *Henry III*, chap 3.
11. Giles, *Wendover*, pp. 580-82.
12. Giles, *Wendover*, pp. 576-80; Carpenter, *Henry III*, chap 3.
13. Luard, 'Dunstable', p. 130-32, 135; Luard, 'Tewkesbury', p. 92; Luard, 'Burton', p. 246; Luard, 'Waverley', p. 312; Luard, 'Osney', p. 73-74; Luard, 'Wigornia', p. 423; Giles, *Wendover*, pp. 567-68.
14. Luard, 'Dunstable', p. 132.
15. Luard, 'Dunstable', p. 133; Luard, 'Wintonia', p. 85.
16. Luard, 'Dunstable', p. 134.
17. Luard, 'Wintonia', p. 86; Vincent, *des Roches*, pp. 288-90.
18. Luard, 'Wigornia', p. 425.
19. Luard, 'Tewkesbury', p. 89, 93; Denholm-Young, p. 18.
20. Giles, *Wendover*, pp. 580-82; Powicke, *Henry III*, pp. 134-35.
21. Harwood, pp. 120-211.
22. Luard, 'Dunstable', p. 97; Luard, 'Tewkesbury', p. 93; Luard, 'Wintonia', p. 86; Giles, *Wendover*, p. 446-48; Harwood, p. 120; Vincent, *des Roches*, p. 298.
23. Harwood, p. 122, 128-29; Powicke, *Henry III*, pp. 135-36.
24. Powicke, *Henry III*, p. 136; Giles, *Wendover*, pp. 585-88; Hunt, *Henry III*.
25. Carpenter, *Henry III*, chap 3.
26. Luard, 'Waverley', p. 314; Carpenter, *Minority*, p. 239; Giles, *Wendover*, pp. 585-88; Carpenter, *Henry III*, chap 3.

27. Luard, 'Dunstable', p. 136; Luard, 'Wigornia', p. 425; Giles, *Wendover*, pp. 585-92.
28. Luard, 'Dunstable', pp 136-37.
29. Luard, 'Waverley', p. 315.
30. Carpenter, *Henry III*, chap 3; Giles, *Wendover*, pp. 592-93.
31. Luard, 'Dunstable', p. 137; Carpenter, *Henry III*, chap 3.
32. Luard, 'Wigornia', p. 426.
33. Luard, *England and Rome*, pp. 47-48; Powicke, *Henry III*, pp. 136-37.

Epilogue: The Birth of a Nation

1. Carpenter, *Mastery*, p. 264; Danziger and Gillingham, *1215*, p. 159.
2. Carpenter, *Henry III*, chap 1.
3. Carpenter, *Minority*, p. 305.
4. Powicke, *Henry III*, p. 50.
5. Carpenter, *Henry III*, chap 3; Harwood, pp. 130-31.
6. Luard, 'Wintonia', p. 87.
7. Vincent, *des Roches*, pp. 6, 21, 39, 196, 243-47.
8. Carpenter, *Henry III*, chap 3.
9. Luard, 'Waverley', p. 315; Hardy, *Rymer's Fœdera,* p. 34.
10. Weiler, *Kingship,* p. 11.
11. Luard, 'Margam', p. 138.
12. Luard, 'Wintonia', p. 86; Vincent, *des Roches*, p. 466.
13. Carpenter, *Minority*, p. 315.
14. Vincent, *des Roches*, pp. 469-70.
15. Carpenter, *Minority*, pp. 2, 4, 376.
16. Vincent, *des Roches*, pp. 42-46.

Index